From Blood to Ink

PRINT CULTURE IN THE SOUTH

SERIES EDITORS

Sarah E. Gardner, Mercer University
Jonathan Daniel Wells, University of Michigan

Print Culture in the South addresses the region's literary and historical past from the colonial era to the near present. Rooted in archival research, series monographs embrace a wide range of analyses that, at their core, address engagement and interaction with print. Topics center on format/genre—novels, pamphlets, periodicals, broadsides, and illustrations; institutions such as libraries, literary societies, small presses, and the book industry; and/or habits and practices of readership and writing.

MATTHEW J. LARSON

From Blood to Ink

How the Press Covered the Gettysburg Campaign

The University of Georgia Press *Athens*

Athens, Georgia 30602
www.ugapress.org

Set in Arno Pro by Westchester Publishing Services

Printed digitally

EU Authorized Representative
Easy Access System Europe—Mustamäe tee 50, 10621 Tallinn, Estonia,
gpsr.requests@easproject.com

Library of Congress Cataloging-in-Publication Data

Names: Larson, Matthew J., 1988– author
Title: From blood to ink : how the press covered the Gettysburg Campaign / Matthew J. Larson.
Description: Athens : The University of Georgia Press, 2026. | Series: Print culture in the South | Includes bibliographical references and index.
Identifiers: LCCN 2026008548 | ISBN 9780820377537 hardback | ISBN 9780820377544 paperback | ISBN 9780820377551 epub | ISBN 9780820377568 pdf
Subjects: LCSH: Gettysburg Campaign, 1863—Press coverage | Press and politics—United States—History—19th century | Journalism—United States—History—19th century | Pennsylvania—History—Civil War, 1861–1865—Press coverage
Classification: LCC E475.51 .L795 2026
LC record available at https://lccn.loc.gov/2026008548

Contents

Illustrations

Preface

The men helming newspapers in mid-nineteenth century America wore multiple hats. They were publishers, partial or sole proprietors, editors, columnists, and often much more. Narrowing their job function to any single role feels needlessly reductive. Thus, I use the term "printer" liberally in the pages that follow. As a catchall, the term is meant to encompass any and all hats worn while referring to the person helming a newspaper. To avoid beating the reader down with the cudgel of an overused word, however, "newspaperman" and "printer" are used interchangeably. "Newsman" and "pressman" are also used interchangeably but in a different sense. Both are meant to embrace anyone, including correspondents and printers, involved in the news-making business.

I took care to spare the reader from a second cudgel. At first, citing the date of every quoted newspaper in the main text seemed like best practice. The reader ought to know, after all, precisely when things were said. Yet on further reflection it not only seemed unnecessary (since all dates are provided in the notes) but also excruciatingly repetitive. Rather than essential mile markers, the dates became an endless parade of unnecessary road signs—distracting the reader like they would a highway driver. Thus, where they were not needed, I removed dates from the main text.

To that same end I axed something else. It goes without saying that the English language has changed since the mid-nineteenth century. Many linguistic norms then have evolved into taboos today. Mid-nineteenth century newsmen were not "wrong" in the context of their time. Nor were they infallible. Different spellings, grammar, and punctuation—often done purposefully, sometimes mistakenly, according to standards at the time—abound in the quoted newspapers to follow. To avoid another unnecessary distraction, "[*sic*]" has been omitted from all quoted content, including newspapers. I believe that, as much as possible, the reader ought to see what people in history themselves said without the conceit of a present-day hand interposing.

I strove to draw on a wide array of sources. I consulted nineteenth-century journals and governmental documents and primary sources such as letters and diaries, as well as secondary sources, but newspapers form the core of this study. Although I attempted to cast a wide net and include newspapers small and large from both the North and South, my sample is anything but perfectly representative. My conclusions, therefore, are not scientific and should be taken as more indicative than definitive.

That said, newspapers were vital. In addition to proffering history's first rough draft, they functioned as the lifeblood of Americans both before and especially during the Civil War. What they said, particularly those cited herein, mattered enormously. I was taken aback by the story they tell about the Gettysburg campaign. At times that story aligned with the history I knew, the history I had been taught. No less often, however, that story diverged from the history I thought I knew and the history one might expect. I originally set out to tell something novel about the Civil War press using Gettysburg as a prism for investigation. But that pursuit also shed light on its reciprocal. This book is also about Gettysburg as seen through the lens of the Civil War press. While I attempted to keep focused on the former, I never eschewed the latter. Ultimately, I believe that approach made what follows here more worthwhile.

Acknowledgments

The seeds of this book were planted years ago when I was in graduate school. To William Garrett Piston, my thesis advisor at Missouri State, thank you for encouraging me to pursue the topic of the press and Gettysburg alongside the often-neglected influence of bias—an angle that stuck with me like ink to newsprint. Thanks also to Diane Mutti Burke, my dissertation advisor at the University of Missouri–Kansas City. By giving me the space and support needed to dive deeper into the topic, she—more than anyone else—helped water the seeds that grew into this book.

I also owe a debt of gratitude to those undergraduate professors who sparked in me a zeal for history, without which this would never have come to light. I consider myself fortunate. In the degree factory too often typical of undergraduate education, I thrice struck gold with professors who brought history to life and crystallized in me what I wanted to do with my own. Poet W. B. Yeats once said, "Education is not the filling of a pail, but the lighting of a fire." Robert Williams, Joel Benson, and Michael Steiner kindled that fire in me.

Thanks to the fine folks at the University of Georgia Press who helped make this book a reality. To Rebecca Norton, thank you for your help with the illustrations. To Mick Gusinde-Duffy, thank you for graciously shepherding this project through to publication, as well as hiring out some excellent anonymous reviewers. Their feedback proved invaluable.

This book stands in the shadows of giants. Thank you to historians past, such as J. Cutler Andrews and Louis M. Starr, and to historians present—such as James McPherson, Gary W. Gallagher, and Carol Reardon—whose scholarship provided the inspiration and foundation needed to write the ensuing chapters.

Lastly, thank you to my wife, Vincie, whose loving support made all that follows possible. This is for you and Rhone.

From Blood to Ink

Introduction

The mid-1950s saw the history of Civil War journalism boom with new scholarship. No subject generated new work like that of the North's reporters. As if in a sprint to beat their colleagues to print, several historians raced out new books. In 1953 Bernard A. Weisberger crossed the finish line first with *Reporters for the Union*; a year later Louis M. Starr charged forth with *Bohemian Brigade*; a year after that J. Cutler Andrews trotted out *The North Reports the Civil War*; and in 1956 Emmet Crozier brought up the rear with *Yankee Reporters*.[1] The photo finish created a sudden crowding that no doubt lessened each book's impact. But viewed as a whole, these works launched a new and sustained era of interest in Civil War journalism—one that grew to include much more than just the topic of the North's reporters and one that, to a great extent, laid the groundwork for the chapters to follow.[2]

No historian contributed more to the topic of the press and its Gettysburg coverage, the focus of those chapters, than Andrews. *The North Reports the Civil War* and its 1984 complement, *The South Reports the Civil War,* became mainstays in the history of Civil War reporting. In two respective chapters (one in each book), Andrews chronicled how Northern and Southern reporters saw the great Battle of Gettysburg unfold before them. By design, however, both primarily detailed how newspaper correspondents viewed events during the battle rather than focusing on the more manicured takes developed by printers in the days and weeks afterward.

The distinction matters. As much as the Civil War foregrounded the essential and often death-defying exploits of frontline reporters, it remained an age dominated by the newspaperman—printing giants like Northerners James Gordon Bennett and Horace Greeley and Southerners James Cowardin and John M. Daniel, whose long shadows extended over nearly every column of nearly every issue. If reporters were the Civil War's "knights of the quill," as one recent work styled them, then printers were its journalistic kings.[3] Indeed, it was the printer, far more often than the reporter, who directed the course of Civil War news. And printers on both sides of the Mason-Dixon Line purposefully packaged news of Gettysburg into biased narratives meant to sway how Northerners and Southerners viewed the battle's immediate and long-term importance.

While Andrews, due to his emphasis on correspondents, left that news unaddressed, more recent scholars have begun to address it. In a chapter of his 2001 book *Lee and His Army in Confederate History*, Gary W. Gallagher inspects several Southern papers published in the battle's aftermath, aiming to better understand its impact on the Confederate home front. Gallagher thrusts a saber into the idea that most Southerners saw Gettysburg as a defeat, arguing that "Confederate reaction to Gettysburg covered a wider spectrum than is commonly supposed."[4] But the broader extent of those reactions, especially among both Southern and Northern printers, remains largely unexplored.

Carol Reardon traverses some of that unexplored terrain in her 1997 work *Pickett's Charge in History and Memory*. Reardon draws from a deep pool of Southern and Northern Gettysburg press accounts immediately following the battle as she tracks the drift of Pickett's Charge away from the reliable moorings of history toward the hazy shores of mythology. By design, however, Reardon does not specifically home in on the press. And due to her focus on Pickett's Charge, she leaves the coverage of the many other aspects of the battle and broader campaign untouched.

Although other historians—notably Ford Risley, David W. Bulla, and Gregory A. Borchard—have recently helped advance the subject, scholarship on the press and Gettysburg remains a jigsaw puzzle pieced only at its edges.[5] This book aims to move that scholarship forward by picking up where historians like Andrews, Gallagher, and Reardon have left off. While centering the printer without sidelining the reporter, the following chapters trace the development of the American press through the Civil War, with a concentrated examination of how both the Northern and Southern presses covered most major aspects of the Gettysburg battle and broader campaign. It incorporates into that examination the increasingly adopted pro- and anti-administration framework for studying press partisanship.

Bias ran through the Civil War press like thread through cloth. To better reflect the intense partisanship that pervaded the press, literature on Civil War journalism—such as David B. Sachsman's 2014 volume, *A Press Divided*—has increasingly assessed newspaper coverage based on the bias of printers for or against their respective administration. The Civil War's outbreak in 1861 not only divided Americans into two sides but also divided printers on both sides into two rival camps. Southern printers either championed or thundered against Confederate president Jefferson Davis while Northern printers either supported or combated Union president Abraham Lincoln. To both forward this framework and gain new insights, the coverage assessed here is sorted accordingly for the first time in a press study on Gettysburg.

The book is split into two parts. Part 1 comprises the first three chapters and sets the foundation on which part 2 is built. After surveying the rise of the press in the antebellum period and overviewing the Northern and Southern presses during the Civil War, part 1 introduces the reader to the epic and fateful clash of arms at Gettysburg. While drawing on material presented in part 1, part 2 analyzes Southern and Northern Gettysburg campaign coverage, particularly in the days and weeks following the battle, through the pro- and anti-administration framework.

What follows, then, is first and foremost a study of the press. The Battle of Gettysburg functions as a case study to further deepen our historical understanding of the press during the Civil War. This approach is designed to shed light on such topics as news trustworthiness during wartime, the influence of political bias in Civil War coverage, and the nature and limitations of Civil War news gathering. But it is impossible to learn more about one without learning something about the other. While my primary objective is to enhance our understanding of the Civil War press through its Gettysburg coverage, a secondary benefit of that objective is that our understanding of Gettysburg might also be enriched in the process.

Perhaps this raises a question: if the primary focus is the Civil War press, why zero in on Gettysburg specifically? Setting aside the historiographical holes left to be filled, Gettysburg emerged as my point of contact for multiple reasons. Like a peerless sentinel, the battle ineluctably towers over Civil War history. Gettysburg proved by far the war's bloodiest battle, represented the deepest penetration north by a Confederate army, and starred the war's most recognizable armies and some of its most recognizable generals. The battle also acted like a journalistic magnet, pulling to it an inordinate number of Northern and Southern correspondents who yielded an unparalleled number of gripping, firsthand reports. The unique quantity, and in notable instances quality, of Gettysburg coverage magnified the battle's importance and partially influenced Lincoln's Gettysburg Address—a speech that went on to further magnify the battle's significance in America's collective consciousness.

Gettysburg became, rightly or wrongly, the iconic battle that defined the struggle to preserve the Union. Unlike most other military engagements in U.S. history, most Americans—irrespective of their historical training—know of it to some extent. It was seen then and in lay circles today is still seen as the turning point of the American Civil War. As a uniquely venerated touchstone in Civil War history and memory, Gettysburg functions fittingly as the touchpoint for this study of the Civil War press.

But something else, no less significant, put Gettysburg in my crosshairs. Just as the opposing armies disengaged in southern Pennsylvania, the campaign for Vicksburg, Mississippi, came to a decisive close. When diving into Gettysburg coverage, one inevitably wades into that of Vicksburg. And drawing on the latter's coverage informs how newsmen at the time judged the former's significance. This is especially interesting when one considers that despite the unique gravitational pull Gettysburg exerted then and still exerts today, historians tend to privilege Vicksburg as the more significant Union victory and a better overall candidate as the turning point of the war.[6] Assessing Gettysburg's coverage while considering that of Vicksburg, then, offers a unique glimpse into their comparative significance according to the press at the time and may help inform the ongoing debate among historians over the place of each in Civil War history.

While each chapter makes a distinct argument, one center seam binds them tightly together. As the press grew in importance before and during the Civil War, it also grew more partisan. By the summer of 1863 nearly all pretenses for objective, fact-based reporting had been supplanted by a bias-riddled, narrative-driven journalism. The Battle of Gettysburg, which wrought more casualties than any other Civil War engagement, became a casualty itself of the biases that reigned over the Northern and Southern presses. As the partisan vanguards of history, the Northern and Southern presses cast the first great account of Gettysburg in a miasma of misinformation—one that so strayed from the truth that it not only significantly misled the people of two warring nations but also helped obscure the battle's significance long after the war ended.

Part I

CHAPTER ONE

The Antebellum News Revolution

One score and twelve years before the Battle of Gettysburg, a French nobleman sailed to the New World to explore a new nation. For nine months, twenty-five-year-old Versailles magistrate Alexis de Tocqueville crisscrossed the United States by steam, mount, coach, and paddle—studying his hosts like an anthropologist might a newfound tribe. Few things impressed Tocqueville more than the young nation's fascination with newspapers. Everywhere he went, from the East Coast to the Michigan frontier, newspapers seemed embedded like limestone in the American landscape. "In America there is scarcely a hamlet which has not its own newspaper," he marveled.[1] "Its influence . . . is immense . . . the power of the periodical press is only second to that of the people."[2]

Tocqueville proved a quick study. Americans already produced and consumed newspapers like no other people in the world, and their appreciation for the press appeared as unshakable as the freedom of the press enshrined by their constitution. But had Tocqueville revisited the United States on the eve of the Civil War he would have noticed that Americans' obsession with newspapers in 1831, as remarkable as it seemed, remained cribbed in infancy.

Over the next thirty years the United States grew into the undisputed world capital of newsdom. The number of different papers in circulation more than tripled, while circulations soared higher than anywhere else on the planet.[3] Meanwhile, the newspaper went from an important information source made for an elite few to a vital democratic cornerstone made for and consumed by the masses. This expansion of and increasing admiration for the antebellum press did not occur in a vacuum. By the start of the Civil War, well before its great battles like Gettysburg, a series of revolutionary developments conspired to create a nation that bred, read, and respected newspapers like no other.

Population growth fueled the explosion in newspaper reading. In the three decades before the Civil War the U.S. population swelled two and one-third times over, outpacing every country on earth.[4] When the war erupted in April 1861, the United States overtook the twenty-nine million people of Britain, its former mother country, with a population of thirty-two million—14 percent of whom were enslaved. The population did not rise equally in all places. Only twelve million people, whether under the lash or their own volition, laid down roots in the overwhelmingly rural South. And while most Americans continued to live in rural areas, the urban population climbed fastest. In the fifty years before the war, urbanites jumped from 6 percent to 20 percent of the overall population, a trend that made possible the tremendous circulations of major urban papers in the latter half of the nineteenth century.[5]

High literacy rates stimulated the American appetite for newspapers. By the 1850s over 90 percent of white U.S. adults could read and write compared to only two-thirds in Britain and Northwestern Europe.[6] While literacy among white men and women stood virtually equal, regional rates varied. New England's 2 percent adult illiteracy rate marked the lowest in the country and matched Sweden for the lowest in the world.[7] From New England the light of literacy dimmed the farther west and especially south one went. Below the Mason-Dixon Line, where anti-literacy laws barred slaves from what Frederick Douglass called "the pathway . . . to freedom," only four in five white adults and one in ten black slaves could read and write.[8] Yet the nationwide picture, despite these regional and racial disparities, remained impressive. Literacy among all American adults, slaves included, shot to nearly 80 percent at mid-century, better than most of Europe and far better than the rest of the world.[9]

The Second Great Awakening raised the national tide of literacy as much as religiosity. An individual relationship with God required owning a Bible and knowing how to read it. Several evangelical organizations—such as the American Bible Society, which alone doled out twenty-one million Bibles between 1816 and 1866—worked tirelessly to put God's word into the hands of His people.[10] To read the Bible, Sunday schools provided weekly literacy instruction. Only after the establishment of public education did Sunday schools shift focus from basic literacy lessons to biblical ones. The rise of common schools, wrote one historian, relieved "Sunday school workers . . . of the burden of teaching reading and enable[d] them to concentrate on religious studies."[11]

The transition toward public schooling molded Americans into a reading people.[12] In the 1830s states began adopting taxpayer-funded common schools. With literacy foundational to any education, states that backed common schools saw illiteracy plummet. New England's six states made illiteracy nearly extinct by enrolling three quarters of their youth in school.[13] But in the South, where the Jeffersonian resistance to expanding government remained strong, support for public education was weak. North Carolina's illiteracy rate among white adults topped 28 percent in 1840, the highest in the Union. When the state allowed public schools into assenting counties, however, the figure sank faster than a millstone. By the Battle of Gettysburg in July 1863 white illiteracy among adult Tar Heels had plunged to 11 percent.[14]

Public education went well beyond literacy in facilitating newspaper reading. With common schools came a common curriculum, one intended to sear students with the cattle brand of civic responsibility and democratic participation.[15] This required an informed citizenry. Mid-century Americans, especially the publicly educated, turned to newspapers for the information they needed to play their part as citizens. It was widely thought and even taught that uninformed citizens were ignorant and incapable of safeguarding their freedom. In 1835 a newspaper warned, "The man who pretends that an ignorant and vicious people can long remain free, is a fool or a knave."[16] By stressing literacy and informed citizenship, public schools heaped fresh coal into the furnace of demand. As one historian pruned the point: "the more schooling was encouraged; the more literacy increased, [and] the more market there was for newspapers."[17]

Increasing political equality reinforced this culture of citizen news readers. By Andrew Jackson's 1828 presidential election most states had eliminated property requirements for voting. Rather than a right reserved for a select few, the right to vote broadened its arms to embrace most adult white men. The essential tools of democratic participation, newspapers, became more important than ever. As Tocqueville explained, newspapers "become more necessary in proportion as men become more equal."[18] In fact, increased egalitarianism equaled a healthier national press. By 1833 the U.S. touted more newspapers than England and France combined, where manhood suffrage remained far more restricted.[19] "What best explains . . . the enormous circulations . . . in the United States," inferred Tocqueville, "is that amongst the Americans I find the utmost national freedom combined with local freedom of every kind."[20] Ultimately, expanding political equality in the Jacksonian age encouraged more citizens to read the news.[21]

Advances in printing ensured that the public's mounting thirst for newspapers did not go unquenched. In 1450 the German printer Johannes Gutenberg invented a printing press with metal movable type. The Gutenberg press thrust printing so far forward that centuries would pass before anyone significantly improved it. Finally in 1811, Friedrich Koenig, another German, devised a cylinder press powered by a steam engine. Like Gutenberg, Koenig made copying information faster than ever before. In 1825 the New York *Daily Advertiser,* the first U.S. newspaper to acquire a Koenig-style steam press, could spew forth two thousand copies every hour.[22] Over the next several years, Englishman David Napier, followed by New Yorker Richard Hoe, improved Koenig's press. In 1832 Hoe's much larger, dual-cylinder press could fire off four thousand double impressions in an hour.[23]

Meanwhile, papermaking innovations guaranteed that these improved presses did not outproduce their chief input. For centuries papermaking, like printing, advanced not through great leaps and bounds but in small improvements and workarounds. Until the early 1800s, millworkers toiled in a miasma of vapor and lint, cleaning, fermenting, and hand-shredding linen rags—the raw material used to make paper—before pressing the pulped remains through a rectangular sieve to dry as separately sheeted paper. But in 1816 Philadelphian Thomas Gilpin designed a machine that spared workers of toil's worst while producing paper on continuous reels, which fed the voracious mouths of steam presses more efficiently than separately sheeted paper. By the 1830s mechanized paper production had largely replaced manual papermaking, greatly accelerating the production of all reading materials. Paper itself, however, continued to be milled from rags until after Gettysburg, when wood pulp paper production finally became feasible.[24]

Large-scale ink and press manufacturing accompanied that of paper. In the early nineteenth century most printers brewed their own ink. Like witches in a fable, they hunched over fire-heated caldrons, boiling oils with lampblack or turpentine, stirring regularly to achieve ideal consistency, in what amounted to a time-sapping diversion from their many other responsibilities. But in 1804 another Philadelphian, Jacob Johnson, established a company devoted entirely to developing inks commercially. By the 1830s the company Wrigley and Johnson supplied more printers with ink than any other American manufacturer.[25] At the same time, printing press manufacturers sprouted up across the North like an invasive weed. By the 1840s Richard Hoe's New York City–based R. Hoe and Company became the leading printing press manufacturer in not only the United States but also the world.

These technological leaps revolutionized the newspaper industry. Inadequate presses alongside paper and ink shortages had handicapped newspaper growth. But by the 1830s improved presses—complemented by advances in paper, ink, and press production—ensured that the newspaper supply could meet the growing demand. By boosting output, these innovations helped engineer a newspaper the masses could afford, which made possible the astronomic circulations of papers during the Civil War—circulations that crested in the wake of large battles like Gettysburg. Newspaper mass production, however, depended on a system capable of mass distribution. To get papers into readers' hands the antebellum press relied heavily on an extension of the federal government: the post office.

The U.S. Post Office's vast network made large-scale information dissemination possible. The post office proved the largest federal bureaucracy and the only federal government arm felt by the average antebellum American. In 1831 its eighty-seven hundred employees, most of whom worked part-time as rural postmasters, not only formed over three-fourths of all federal civilian employees but also outnumbered the sixty-three hundred men then serving in the armed forces. With seventy-four post offices for every one hundred thousand Americans (more in absolute and per capita terms than any other country), the omnipresence of the post office rivaled the Lord Himself and made mass press circulation possible. In 1830 the post office distributed over sixteen million newspapers. A decade later that number vaulted to thirty-nine million.[26]

The speed that newspapers were rifled through the mail increased alongside the volume. In 1810 sixteen days separated news in Philadelphia from Lexington, Kentucky, but by 1839, years before Americans saddled up the iron horse for widespread use, the post office slashed that time in half. Over the same period, delivery from Portland, Maine, to Savannah, Georgia, withered like an outworn vine from twenty-seven days to twelve.[27] Contemporaries marveled at the speeds and their implications. Supreme Court justice Joseph Story described it as the "wonders of magic."[28] U.S. senator John C. Calhoun roistered, "Let us conquer space. It is thus that a citizen of the West will read the news of Boston still moist from the press."[29]

Yet many craved even faster delivery. Nothing crystallized the need for timely news like the War of 1812. The Treaty of Ghent, signed in Europe by the United States and Britain on Christmas Eve 1814, formally ended the conflict. But word of the treaty took six weeks to drift like a log across the Atlantic, and in the interim, on January 8, American and British forces collided like mountain rams outside New Orleans. While the United States scored a decisive victory, one that earned then-General Jackson the nickname "Old Hickory" for holding firm and later helped win him the White House, hundreds needlessly died, and two weeks passed before word of the superfluous battle reached the major urban papers dotting the East Coast. Exasperated by belated reports, eastern printers hired private express riders to transmit dispatches faster than the mail.

Like Jackson at New Orleans, however, the post office refused to yield ground. In 1825 it launched the "express post," which cost three times the postage but halved delivery times using a simple yet highly efficient relay network. Express post riders swapped their bushed horses hourly for four fresh legs, and soon news galloped from New Orleans to New York in just one week, half what it took during the War of 1812.[30]

Postal policy spurred newspaper growth. To forge enlightened and engaged citizens beyond urban areas through broadly circulated news, Congress passed the Postal Act of 1792.[31] The act took a paring knife to newspaper postage and codified a Benjamin Franklin–inspired colonial custom wherein printers exchanged their papers with each other postage-free. While discounted delivery helped spawn a national market for newspapers, codification of the exchange steeped newspapermen nationwide in nonlocal news.[32] By the 1840s American printers, rural as well as urban, received on average forty-three hundred exchange papers each year for free.[33] Stunned by the impact, Tocqueville remarked, "The post, that great instrument of intellectual discourse, now reaches into the backwoods."[34]

Indeed, it did. In fact, codifying the exchange breathed fresh life into the emerging country press. Rural printers necessarily suffered from a lean purse and sparse access to information. While cheap postage helped them reach their subscribers, this crutch alone could not keep them upright. Enshrining the exchange in law, however, helped rural printers stand on two legs. By providing free access to the national news of large metropolitan papers, the exchange flooded rural newspapermen with the information they needed to publish their mostly weekly issues. Since the wholesale recycling of articles from exchanged papers proved a widely accepted practice in antebellum journalism, one printers paid lip service to by preceding the copied content with phrases like "From the *Richmond Dispatch*," rural Americans often enjoyed the exact same news as their urban countrymen. The exchange later ensured that the Gettysburg coverage of urban papers graced the front pages of rural publications North and South.

Historians understandably emphasize the role transportation technologies played in building America's modern communications systems. Canals, steamboats, and railroads did much to develop that system and, alongside better roads, greatly enhanced the post office's capabilities.[35] But the era's technological superstars need not and should not outshine its role. Decades before these technologies left their mark, the post office left its stamp on American history.[36] For all the mostly private technological innovation, the public post office proved no less fundamental to large-scale information distribution and the ascension of American newspapers before the Civil War. And, unsurprisingly, no delivery mechanism proved more instrumental in supplying readers with Gettysburg news than the Northern and Southern post offices. That said, canals, steamboats, and railroads transformed the nation and the nation's press. By mid-century this transportation revolution joined a communications revolution to alter the speed and manner in which news traveled, where newspapers sprang up, and the nature of news gathering itself.

Canals refashioned the nation economically and demographically, which helped construct a national news hub and reorient where new papers appeared. No canal occasioned this like the famed Erie. Opened in 1825, the Erie Canal stretched 363 miles from Albany to Buffalo, yoking New York City via the Hudson River to western New York and the Upper Midwest. Because the canal axed transportation costs, goods dove sharply in price (including paper and ink). This in turn ignited an economic boom in New York City, one so ripe with opportunity that it engendered a corresponding demographic surge. The 9 percent of U.S. exports that flowed through the city in 1800 grew to 62 percent by 1860, while the population ballooned from 123,700 in 1820 to 814,000 in 1860.[37]

New York City's new promise pushed its press through the forest canopy. In 1820, before the Erie's completion, only twelve different papers published in New York City for a time. In 1830, five years after the canal opened, that number nearly tripled.[38] New York circulations soon ruled the American roost. In the early 1830s the *Courier and Enquirer*, founded by New York native James Webb, tallied four thousand readers, more than any other American paper and on par with the London *Times* for the most in the world. Transatlantic news pumped first into New York, the American press's beating heart, before circulating across the country. Boston, a city closer to Europe, obtained European news secondhand from New York via shippers and express riders. Ultimately, the growth sparked by the Erie Canal cemented New York as not only the country's largest city and commercial center but also the epicenter of news in the New World.

The Erie Canal's success also expedited migration from the Northeast to the Upper Midwest, where important regional news hubs emerged. In the three decades before the Civil War, Chicago's population inflated like a zeppelin from less than one hundred to over one hundred thousand. In 1833 Chicago had only one obscure paper, the *Weekly Democrat*, but by the Civil War it had one of the most influential newspapers in the region. The *Chicago Tribune*—founded in 1847 and purchased in 1855 by native Canadian and early Abraham Lincoln backer Joseph Medill—became an outstanding regional paper before and during the Civil War, later leading the Midwest in Gettysburg campaign coverage.[39]

Other cities connected to the Erie, like seeds along an irrigation line, saw their populations and presses blossom. By mid-century, bourgeoning Buffalo, Cleveland, Detroit, and Milwaukee birthed several successful dailies of their own. In 1844 the *Milwaukee Sentinel* marked Wisconsin's first daily four years before the Badger State made its mark by entering the Union. But while canals influenced where national and regional press hubs developed, they did little to hasten the delivery of news published by those hubs. Instead, that credit belongs to a triumph of transportation, one that morphed America's natural and artificial waterways into a new national highway system: the steam engine.

The steamboat, unveiled in 1807 by Pennsylvanian Robert Fulton, enabled goods, people, and information to travel on water where it once proved impractical. Before the steamboat, rivers operated as stubborn one-way highways, permitting movement downstream while forbidding it upstream. Western farmers, for example, used flatboats to transport crops with ease down the Mississippi for sale in New Orleans. Rather than pole a craft back upriver or pull one rope-and-tie from along the shoreline, which took three times longer than going downriver and entailed enough torture to make a Spanish inquisitor blush, many just disassembled their flatboats to sell as lumber and then walked home. But the steamboat could overcome stubborn river currents, making two-way traffic practical. In 1828 a teenage Abraham Lincoln guided a flatboat to New Orleans. Rather than pole or pull his way against the Mississippi and Ohio Rivers 1,276 miles back to Rockport, Indiana, he hopped on a steamboat. The trip by steamer took less than two weeks, whereas the upriver peregrination otherwise, like something from a Mark Twain novel gone wrong, would have taken three months of spine-cracking labor.[40]

Steamboats not only opened rivers to two-way traffic, they also accelerated it. Clocking twenty miles an hour by 1863 and the Battle of Gettysburg, steamboats chugged news up the Hudson from New York City to Albany in less than eight hours and up the Mississippi and Ohio Rivers from New Orleans to Louisville in just four days.[41] Meanwhile, steamships trimmed news lags between New York City and other major ports. Whereas five days had separated sailing vessels from Boston, by 1817 steamships helped shear that to just two days.[42] Tocqueville could scarcely believe his eyes. "Steamboats have established daily means of communication between the different points of the coast," goggled the Frenchman. "[And] an inland navigation of unexampled rapidity conveys commodities up and down the rivers of the country."[43]

The steamship also hastened news distribution over oceans. Since sailing vessels harness wind as power, they are constrained by when and where it blows. But oceangoing steamships, like steamboats going upriver, could defy nature's mulish currents. Less constrained by wind's timing and pathways, steamships took more direct transoceanic routes than their sailing counterparts. Rather than six weeks in the War of 1812, by mid-century news steamed across the Atlantic in just ten days.[44] Steamships ensured that news of the Battle of Gettysburg—after reaching its gory end July 3, 1863—reached Britain by the week of July 13. Through unrivaled speeds, steamships moored the New and Old Worlds closer together. Not until the laying of transatlantic cables after the Civil War was a swifter form of communication hatched between Europe and the United States.[45]

With the steam locomotive, a new age in overland news delivery dawned. From Alexander the Great to Thomas Jefferson, the horse had proved the fastest means for transporting physical news overland. The Persians, whose empire Alexander conquered, understood this well. They established the first relay system in history to gallop urgent news across Persia's major roads. Using this ancient predecessor to the pony express, the Persians conveyed news from one end of their great Royal Road to the other, sixteen hundred miles, in just one week. The iron horse, however, outpaced the galloping horse. Peaking at thirty miles an hour by the Civil War, the train surpassed Persia's ancient riders and America's express riders as the swiftest means of delivering newspapers overland.

The steam locomotive also outperformed the steamboat in promptly delivering news internally. Canals and rivers, the inland highways on which steamboats traveled, often froze in winter, which slowed traffic or stalled it completely. And steamboats usually took longer, less direct routes than rail to reach their destinations, as their highways were meandering rivers. The distance from Pittsburgh to St. Louis, for example, totaled 1,164 miles by steamboat compared to just 612 miles by rail.[46] Shorter distances combined with swifter speeds and immunity to seasonal change made railroads the best option to move newspapers rapidly in the United States.

But the relationship between press and rail went well beyond swift news distribution. According to the emerging vision of national progress, the newspaper and the railroad represented the twin heralds of American civilization. Where they went, civilization followed. Adventurous printers hauled presses west of the Appalachian Mountains long before territories there became states. The Minnesota Territory contained printing offices in more than forty different settlements before becoming a state in 1858.[47] The press went west not only before many settlers but also before other traditional societal markers. "The printing press preceded all of the usual agencies of society," commented an editor at the time. "The spirit of adventure thrust it forward ahead of the calaboose, the post office, the school, the church, and made it a symbol of conquest."[48]

Tiny settlements anchored by a local paper burst into towns or cities with the railroad's arrival. Although the trend intensified after Gettysburg and the Civil War, the late antebellum period saw the iron horse begin shuttling new faces to western towns while tethering those towns to the benefits of a national marketplace. Settlers advertised products in local or regional papers and then shipped them to buyers by rail less expensively than ever before. It might seem trite today, but to many antebellum Americans the press and the railroad roped the frontier into the nation's fold, and together they began erasing the "wild" from "the wild West."[49]

The transportation revolution kickstarted a sectional realignment with national consequences. Most canals and railroad tracks spidered their many webs across the North, not the South, and most (including all but one railroad) ran east–west. This soldered the Midwest economically and demographically to Yankeedom far more than to Dixie.[50] By 1860 the Midwest's once large transplant population from the South saw itself outnumbered by transplants from New England and the Mid-Atlantic, who could ship products more cheaply and directly to markets back east using east–west railroads, rivers, and canals.[51] The once crucial New Orleans market to the south, the one Lincoln cashed in on as a young man, became less vital to the Midwest's economy. Then, just before the Civil War, Republican-leaning politics followed demographics and economics in fastening the Midwest to the North, which helped secure its loyalty to the Union cause. Ultimately, the transportation revolution weakened the Midwest's bonds with the South while strengthening its ties with the North, forming a new North-West union strong enough to preserve the Union itself.

This wrapped an albatross around the Southern press's neck. Transportation technologies helped circulate news more widely, swiftly, cheaply, and reliably. But the South's inchoate transportation network made it difficult for most Southern newspapers to circulate beyond their hometown, let alone state or section.[52] The South's dearth of railroads also raised transportation costs, which slapped Dixie printers with higher operational bills than their Yankee counterparts. As if this were not bad enough, fewer railroads vitiated print-related manufacturing, especially papermaking, in the South.[53] Before the Civil War, the South housed only 5 percent of the nation's paper mills, and these mills met only half of the section's paper demand.[54] Without enough Southern manufacturers to satisfy demand, Southern printers relied on Northern imports, which added shipping charges and compounded their higher operational costs. Lastly, firms that operated nationwide saw little reason to advertise in Southern papers reaching mostly local audiences. According to one historian, in 1856 the publishing company Harpers "spent more money advertising in the *New York Times*—$573.76 worth of space—than . . . in the entire South."[55]

Despite this sectional disparity, the transportation revolution reconstituted the nation's press. Canals, steamboats, and railroads reduced newspaper-related costs, produced regional and national news hubs, widened newspaper markets, and hastened news transmission both by land and by sea. During the Civil War, steam power, especially in the case of the iron horse, proved crucial to the expeditious and wide dissemination of national papers and their coverage of great battles like Gettysburg. Steam power, however, only temporarily held the trophy for technology enabling the swiftest news transmission. Instead, a revolutionary new invention snatched it from both the steamship and the steam locomotive by divorcing communication from transportation.

On May 24, 1844, Boston-born Samuel Morse demonstrated the effectiveness of his electromagnetic telegraph. Radiating aplomb, Morse sat arrow-straight at a desk in the U.S. Capitol, surrounded by eager lawmakers. Using his patented code, he carefully tapped four words: "What hath God wrought." From Washington, D.C., the message shot like lightning through thirty-eight miles of wire hung on poles parallel to the Baltimore and Ohio Railroad. Morse's assistant in Baltimore received the message and batted the same coded words back to Morse and his dumbfounded audience. That same day Morse darted off the first wired dispatch ever published in the papers.[56] Printed just a few days later in the *Baltimore Patriot*, Morse's message read, "There has just been made a motion in the House to go into committee of the whole on the Oregon question. Rejected—ayes, 79; nays, 86."[57] What that message represented for the press dwarfed the importance of the message itself. What God had wrought was the virtual elimination of space through nearly instant communication.

The telegraph severed communication's historical link with transportation. With few exceptions, such as signal fires, messages were physical objects, and spreading the news had required physically carrying it. This not only intertwined communication with transportation but also meant that the speed at which news spread hinged entirely on the speed of the carrier. "Messages," as historian George R. Taylor put it, "could travel no faster than the messenger."[58] The telegraph, however, allowed for nonphysical news transmission, which finally decoupled communication from its historical link with transportation. Freed from the speed of the transporter—whether a train, steamship, horse, or even pigeon—news could now travel at unbelievable and unbeatable speeds.

When war erupted with Mexico two years after Morse's demonstration, newspapermen leapt at the chance to exploit the telegraph. Printers paid correspondents to report on the fighting firsthand, transactions that became the genesis of modern war reporting. From Veracruz, reports steamed across the Gulf of Mexico to New Orleans, where express riders rushed them overland to telegraph operators in Richmond, Virginia. At war's start, the country's 146 cabled miles spanned no farther south than Richmond. But the appetite for war-related news fueled a construction frenzy.[59] By 1848 a concatenation of wires—measuring thousands of miles and resembling a nervous system in its capacity for head-to-toe, supercharged communication—connected New Orleans to the national press hub of New York City.

The line connecting the Crescent City to the nation's news mecca snaked its way across Mississippi, Alabama, Georgia, and the Carolinas before reaching Richmond and the wider telegraph network to its northeast. The two-plus weeks that news had crawled between these cities in the War of 1812 shrank to less than an hour by the end of the Mexican War. Belated news almost became a thing of the past. Thanks to the telegraph, Mexican War reportage proved more abundant and up to date than reportage in any war previous.[60] Covering the conflict taught printers the value of telegraphy and field correspondents, a lesson they remembered well during the Civil War—especially when it came to Gettysburg. That colossal three-day battle was immediately followed by an ultra-competitive telegraphic blitz and like a journalistic lodestone drew some forty-five Northern and Southern correspondents, more than covered the entire, nearly two-year-long Mexican War.

Telegraphy's use in the Mexican War also foaled the Associated Press. Wired news proved expensive. At mid-century, with mileage-based rates, a ten-word message between New Orleans and New York cost $2.40.[61] Additionally, early wires only permitted communication in one direction at a time. Telegraphic traffic jams sometimes stymied the transmission of urgent war news. In 1848 several New York printers established the Associated Press, pooling their resources in order to better manage telegraph messages and bargain for better telegraph rates.

Printers managed telegram costs in other ways as well. While Morse code functioned as telegraphy's primary language, brevity became its second tongue. Reporters typically wired a story's bare bones that printers expanded on themselves to avoid the high cost of a more detailed dispatch. Abbreviating words also helped lower the price tag. "Understand" became "un" and "through" simply "thro," while whole words that could be spared without muddying the message, such as the article "the," largely disappeared from wired messages entirely.[62] In the early twentieth century, Ernest Hemingway described the telegraph's language of brevity as a "great . . . new language" with "no fat, no adjectives, no adverbs—nothing but blood and bones and muscle."[63]

Telegraphy ultimately refashioned the nation's press. The phrase "by magnetic telegraph" became common press parlance and by merely preceding a story endowed it with a sense of modern wisdom. By 1861 express services tottered toward extinction as fifty thousand miles of wires were strewn across the nation like a giant net, and a transcontinental telegraph allowed its coasts to communicate in real time. But, like the railroad, which the telegraph supported and its wires often paralleled, the fruits of telegraphy spread unevenly across the country. Most lines were hung in the North, not the South, and the South lacked its own skilled telegraph operators—which disadvantaged Southern news gathering both before and during the Civil War.[64] Nonetheless, the telegraph—or "lightning" as Americans fittingly nicknamed it—empowered more printers to gather more news faster than ever before. By the Civil War most dailies and many weeklies regularly used telegraphy and its awe-inspiring, punctual power, which made possible news of battles like Gettysburg while those battles still raged. During the antebellum era, the telegraph excited an expansion in newspaper reading—one that accelerated with yet another revolutionary development: a newspaper for the masses.

The rise of the penny press put newspapers within reach of ordinary Americans. Up to the 1830s printers primarily sold their papers as annual subscriptions sent through the mail. While yearly subscriptions defrayed the per paper cost, at a subscription price of between eight and ten dollars, most Americans scoffed at their unaffordability. Non-subscription readers could still purchase one-off papers, but doing so proved inconvenient and pricey. Without street vendors in most cities they needed to trek to a printer's office, and without a subscription to defray the per-paper cost an individual issue cost anywhere from three to six cents. Starting in the 1830s, however, this all changed. The new rotary steam press alongside improvements in paper, ink, and press production made possible a newspaper priced at just one cent.

Ambitious printers hoped to profit on a paper marketed to the masses, while the phrase "penny paper" captured the public mind and kindled a hunger for newspapers like never before.[65]

But, like many new endeavors, failure littered the road to success. Philadelphian Christopher Columbus Conwell became the first casualty when his aptly titled daily *The Cent* collapsed in 1832 after a wobbly two-year run.[66] The following year, with the help of two partners, a determined twenty-one-year-old from the Granite State sought penny paper glory. Unfortunately for young Horace Greeley, the *New-York Morning Post* faded into the night faster than *The Cent*. While its price appealed to commoners, its stuffy content did not, and despite tinkering with a still-novel sales method—street vendors who sold news directly to readers—Greeley confronted something equally novel: a New York City blizzard. When his sales force hit the streets in January, New York looked less like a temperate New World metropolis and more like Moscow in 1812. Although Greeley later founded one of the era's most successful newspapers, the *New-York Tribune*, he and his partners abandoned the *Morning Post* in less than three weeks.

On September 3, 1833, a Bay Stater struck gold where Greeley hit rock bottom. With more obliging weather, Benjamin H. Day—founder of the New York *Sun*—actually got the chance to push his paper on the streets to passersby. The *Sun*'s price widened eyes and left mouths ajar. Not only could readers nab a single copy for just a penny, but they also could go the traditional route and buy an annual subscription for just three dollars—one-third the normal price. Day's first issue made his aim clear: "To lay before the public, at a price within the means of everyone, all the news of the day."[67] The *Sun* grew hot fast. The first issue sold out, and within six months the paper mounted a daily circulation of eight thousand, the largest in the world.[68]

The *Sun*'s rise set all newsdom aflame. Soon penny papers swept the nation—the *New York Transcript* arose in 1834, the Philadelphia *Public Ledger* in 1836, the Baltimore *Sun* and Boston *Daily Times* in 1837, and the *Boston Herald* in 1844—and triggered a circulation upswing.[69] The Boston *Daily Times* reached a circulation of eight thousand within a month, the Baltimore *Sun* counted ten thousand in less than a year, and the *Public Ledger* clawed in a circulation of twenty thousand in just a year and a half—ten times more than any other Philadelphia daily.[70] Yet the greatest impact on overall readership was seen not in the City of Brotherly Love, but rather in what one 1834 publication called, "The Empire City of the New World."[71] By the mid-1830s the total readership of all New York City dailies more than tripled, from 18,200 to 60,000.[72]

In addition to affordability, the penny press expanded readership through its innovative delivery model. Day sold bundles of one hundred copies of the *Sun* to vendors, who then sold them to passersby in hopes of pocketing a profit. Day charged sixty-seven cents a bundle to vendors who paid in cash and seventy-five cents to those who bought on credit.[73] While thin margins discouraged adults from vending the *Sun*, boys with few prospects pounced at the opportunity. The newsies, as these young hawkers became known, so brazenly peddled papers directly to the man on the street that it bordered on harassment. After Gettysburg the *Richmond Whig* griped, "The boys are rendering themselves a *news*ance by assembling at all hours . . . chattering like magpies to the annoyance of every person [and using] profanity as freely from their lips as . . . dicer's."[74] But thanks to newsies, readers no longer needed to buy expensive subscriptions or trudge like pilgrims to a newspaper's office for a single paper. Instead, affordable penny papers came conveniently to the urban reader for individual purchase.

Alongside novel distribution and affordability, Day and his imitators succeeded because they recognized the traditional American newspaper appealed little in content to most Americans. Before the mid-1830s printers designed their newspapers for the business elites who could afford them. They functioned, according to one historian, as "little more than bulletin boards for the business community."[75] Printers jammed their columns to the masthead with dense economic information: ship arrivals and departures, ship cargo reports, bond prices, and an eye-numbing number of advertisements. Before the mid-1830s, ads consumed well over half the content of most newspapers even though they accounted for less than half of most printers' revenue. "In France the space allotted to commercial advertisements is very limited," observed Tocqueville, "In America three-quarters of the enormous sheet . . . set before the reader are filled with advertisements."[76] Even newspaper titles—such as Baltimore's *American and Commercial Daily Advertiser* and New York City's *Mercantile Advertiser*—reflected the ad-obsessed focus. In fact, 50 percent of all dailies printed between 1810 and 1820 took the name *Advertiser*.[77] Simply put, in both content and name, ordinary Americans found newspapers unappetizing sources of mental indigestion.

This all changed in the 1830s with the penny paper revolution. Names like the *Sun, Herald,* and *Tribune* rose rapidly to prominence and implied a popular agency, an intent by newspapermen to do right by the people—to illuminate the world, to announce the peoples' concerns, to serve the common plebeians like the tribunes of the Roman Republic.[78] They also reflected the Jacksonian era's emphasis on political egalitarianism, albeit for white men only. The growth of the penny press, a press for the masses, not only paralleled but also reinforced the growth of mass democracy.

Changes in content by the penny press also reflected mass democracy's anti-elitism. Day designed the *Sun* for a large and diverse audience, not the business elite. To draw common readers into its orbit, the *Sun* featured short ads, digestible news stripped of elitist jargon, local human-interest stories, and reports featuring violence and sensationalism. Day's first issue recounted the story of a Vermont boy with a chronic whistling condition that tortured him to death's brink. The boy's cure came literally at the hands of another youngster, who struck the whistler on each outburst until the ailment magically abated. A second-page story reported a "shocking murder" in Ohio, while another described a New York newcomer who took his own life by overdosing on laudanum. An investigation determined that "an affair of the heart in which his happiness was deeply concerned" had precipitated the suicide.[79] The story no doubt resonated with New York's large migrant community.

With a style reminiscent of tabloids a hundred years or more later, these stories represented a dramatic deviation from the conventional news formula and called into question the very nature of what constituted news. The *Sun*'s first issue, for example, resembled the established press in only one aspect: a shipping news column on page three. Thus, the penny press threatened the era's journalistic standards at the same time journalism found its influence expanding through an enlarging audience. Demand snowballed, however, for a paper that combined the penny press's readability and affordability with the more newsworthy content of earlier newspapers.

By the 1840s several printers were meeting that demand and in the process jolting journalism into the modern age. No two newspapermen contributed more to that effort than Horace Greeley and the Scottish-born printer James Gordon Bennett. The *New York Herald*, which Bennett debuted in 1835, avoided the unreadable haughtiness of conventional papers as well as, at least usually, the blatant sensationalism of penny printers like Day. Fancying himself "the Napoleon of the American Press," the bombastic Bennett introduced readers to regular Wall Street, sports, and weather reports. He also pioneered the large-scale use of steam power, telegraphy, and field correspondents to create a news-gathering organization second to none.[80] Naturally, Bennett's penny paper found wide reception among commoners and elites alike. Within six months the *Herald*'s circulation eclipsed the *Sun* to lead the nation. By 1860 the paper's daily circulation climbed to 77,000.[81] And during the Civil War Bennett's world-leading daily readership surpassed six figures when covering important battles such as Fort Sumter, First Bull Run, Antietam, and, of course, Gettysburg.

Founded in 1841, the *New-York Tribune* redeemed Greeley's failed bid at a penny paper eight years earlier. The *Tribune* attracted readers not through sensationalism but instead through well-written and generally more measured news. As one historian explained, "Greeley proved that an appeal could be made to a mass audience without playing to their emotions."[82] But while Greeley avoided emotional coverage, he did not avoid taking political stances. Unlike Bennett, who feigned nonpartisanship but leaned Democratic, Greeley openly championed the Whigs and later the Republicans.[83] Crusading in ink, he hoped to show readers what they could be rather than, like Bennett, reflect what they were. This won him many critics, but it also landed him a sizeable readership. By the Civil War the *Tribune* raked in a daily circulation of 55,000, and its weekly edition, which reached a national audience through the mail, notched nearly 300,000 readers.[84] Unsurprisingly, Greeley—alongside Bennett—led the Northern and Southern presses in the circulation of Gettysburg news.

The penny paper revolution fundamentally reimagined the antebellum newspaper. In addition to redefining how newspapers could be sold, reconsidering their content, and revamping the names they bore, it made newspapers broadly affordable, sparking a circulation explosion nationwide. The ninety million newspaper copies sold by printers in 1835 catapulted to over nine hundred million in 1860.[85] Over that same time the number of newspapers in the United States, something Tocqueville thought in 1831 surpassed belief, mushroomed from twelve hundred to four thousand.[86] This sum not only doubled the number published in Britain, it also accounted for nearly one-third of all newspapers published worldwide.[87] Although the influx of inexpensive alternatives drove a stake deep into the established press's heart, the decline of traditional papers did not necessarily lead to a decline in news quality. Thanks to successes like the *Herald* and the *Tribune*, the growth in circulation ignited by inexpensive news did not sacrifice news quality itself.

While penny papers set newsdom ablaze, press politicization added fuel to the fire. American printers took political stances long before Greeley. Since the nation's founding most newspapers had acted not only as bulletins for businesses but also as party organs committed to ruthlessly lambasting the opposition.[88] Despite George Washington's farewell plea to lay aside the "baneful effects . . . of party," the early republic saw Federalist and Democratic-Republican printers maul their political party opponents. As historian Gordon Wood writes, "Except for the era of the Civil War, the last several years of the eighteenth century were the most politically contentious in United States history."[89] As the nineteenth century began and proceeded, Whig and Democratic newspapers carried the banner of press partisanship into the next generation. An 1852 report listed 815 Whig and 742 Democratic newspapers.[90] Just 5 percent of all papers identified as "neutral" or "independent" according to that same report.[91] "All the political journals of the United States are . . . arrayed on the side of the administration or against it," noted a surprised Tocqueville.[92] But antebellum Americans found nothing surprising about it. To question the partisanship of a newspaper before the Civil War was like questioning the wetness of water. As one paper reported, "Neutrality in this country and this age is an anomaly."[93]

Press partisanship did nothing to dampen newspaper demand. Circulations only scaled higher as the storm clouds of civil war drew nearer and the number of partisan papers grew. This occurred largely because the 1850s, which ushered in the Civil War era's hyper-contentiousness, witnessed a cascade of events for printers to politicize and politically concerned citizen-readers to consume. The Compromise of 1850, the Kansas-Nebraska Act of 1854, the *Dred Scott* ruling in 1857, and John Brown's 1859 raid on Harpers Ferry provided rich fodder for the party press to attack opponents and attract readers. Passage of the Kansas-Nebraska Act, which tolerated slavery's extension by popular sovereignty, damaged the slavery-equivocating Whig Party beyond repair. Like passengers abandoning a sinking ship, antislavery Northerners deserted the Whigs and rowed straight to the newly minted, antislavery Republican Party. Likewise, Whig papers either sank with their party or jumped ship (in the North many became Republican papers). Although some newspapers continued to bear "Whig" in their names, before the Civil War and well before Gettysburg the press divided along Democratic and Republican lines.[94]

The Southern press emerged as the exception, however. The antislavery Republican Party existed almost exclusively in the North, rendering Republican newspapers in the South even rarer than nonpartisan papers nationally. When the Whig Party capsized, few Whig newsmen in the South dared to lock arms with Republicans. Without a strong opposition press to temper their tone, Southern Democratic printers grew more extreme, as in the words of a Georgia printer: "[The Republican Party is] revolting, loathsome, a menace not only to the Union of these states, but to Society, to Liberty, and to Law. It has drawn to it the corrupt, the vile, the licentious . . . it decrees but the will of a wild mob." Radical rhetoric like this helped convince Southern leaders to secede following Lincoln's election as the nation's first Republican president. Whereas strong and vigorous competition raged on between Republican and Democratic printers in the North, a one-party press with no "institutionalized check on extremism," as one historian phrased it, gripped the South in a vise of dogmatism.[95]

Despite increasing politicization, the press grew more diverse as the Civil War approached, particularly in the North. Yankee readers could choose from a library of religious, labor, foreign language, ethnic, Native American, black, and abolitionist newspapers.[96] The nation's first great abolitionist tract, William Lloyd Garrison's Boston-based *Liberator,* founded in 1831, fought uncompromisingly for the immediate, uncompensated emancipation of slaves on moral and religious grounds. By mid-century several free black newspapermen joined Garrison and the abolitionist print movement to see their Southern brethren freed. No black paper shined brighter than Frederick Douglass's *North Star*. As a former Maryland slave, Douglass's words carried greater weight than those of white abolitionists like Garrison. Before Gettysburg and the Civil War, the *North Star*—later renamed *Frederick Douglass' Paper*—became the country's leading antislavery publication and a staunch Republican Party backer.

The South answered the Northern abolitionist with the Fire-Eater. Named for their inflammatory rhetoric, Fire-Eaters combated abolitionists, unionists, and the Republican Party with an extremist zeal that gave Garrison's brand of uncompromising abolitionism a run for its money. The Fire-Eater crown garlanded the brow of South Carolina's Robert Barnwell Rhett. Dubbed "the Father of Secession," Rhett channeled his influential *Charleston Mercury* to push incessantly for a national annulment. He railed against the Republican Party, warning Southern readers, "We cannot submit to the government of a sectional party. . . . We cannot submit to an irresponsible, limitless government by which our property may be [stolen] and this great country convulsed."[97] Fire-Eaters like Rhett seldom masked what property they dreaded losing to the North. In 1858 the *Mercury* crowed, "On the subject of slavery the North and South . . . are not only two Peoples, but they are rival, hostile Peoples."[98]

Eventually Rhett's rhetoric helped persuade the Palmetto State to sunder itself from the Union, which set off a secessionist domino effect that rolled like thunder across the Deep South. It can be safely said that while abolitionists energized Northerners against Southern slavery, Fire-Eaters animated Southerners against an antislavery Republican North. As the most extreme element of a Southern press with no check on extremism, Fire-Eaters helped push the war of words between North and South into the bloodiest shooting war in American history.

By 1860 support for the Union was weak while popular support for the press was stronger than ever. In the three decades before the Civil War the newspaper became central to the average American. A growing literate, educated, and politically engaged population increasingly turned to newspapers for the information they needed to meet their civic obligations. Meanwhile the press—assisted by the post office and propelled by revolutions in printing, transportation, and communication—supplied affordable newspapers targeted at a mass audience.

Press politicization and diversification accompanied these transformations. While the latter drew marginalized Americans into the news-reading mainstream, the former consigned most newspapers to a political party, which served to stoke the political passions of the reading public. Ultimately, the antebellum news revolution cultivated a nation that produced, consumed, and valued newspapers like no other. By the eve of the Civil War, years before Gettysburg, newspapers functioned as an essential part of American life. When the war finally broke out, Oliver Wendell Holmes wrote, "Only bread and the newspaper we must have, whatever else we do without."[99]

CHAPTER TWO

"Bread and the Newspaper"

One score and six months before the Gettysburg campaign—at precisely 4:30 a.m. on Friday, April 12, 1861—a *New York Herald* correspondent watched the city of Charleston, South Carolina, awaken to the eruption of cannon fire. "With the very first boom of the gun thousands rushed from their beds."[1] Like children on Christmas morning, Charlestonians abandoned modesty for zeal, running into the predawn dark half-dressed while clambering to slip on shoes and socks without sacrificing speed. As they stampeded down King, St. Philip, and Meeting Streets they took notice of one another's exhilarated faces and began whooping uncontrollably. As the *Herald* reporter explained, "they needed some such safety-valve for their enthusiasm or be suffocated."[2] Within minutes, wide- and wild-eyed Charlestonians crammed shoulder to shoulder along the city's waterfront, gazing with feral delight at the "spectacle" of light and sound engulfing their harbor.[3]

Whether worthy of revelry or not, the occasion was momentous. Confederate troops under General P. G. T. Beauregard, a personal friend of the *Herald* correspondent, unleashed a forty-three-gun bombardment against Fort Sumter's slenderly defended, eighty-five-man federal garrison. The *Herald* reporter did not celebrate the moment, unlike those around him, but he firmly grasped its meaning. As he beheld the bright artillery bursts "flash as if by magic from the windows of every house, and in the twinkling of an eye," the Boston-born Felix Gregory De Fontaine started his report with six sobering words: "Civil War has at last begun."[4]

After finishing his story, De Fontaine scrambled through Charleston's streets to the telegraph office. He hoped to wire his story straightaway, but the city lay under a news embargo. No word could be sent, as a distrust of Southern reporters, some of whom remained in the area, clenched the city in its paranoid fist. In fact, that same morning an armed gang arrested George Salter, a *New York Times* correspondent, and tossed him in the city jail on spying charges. Although the jailers released Salter after twenty-four hours, the arrest convinced the few Northern reporters still in Charleston to either flee or lie low. De Fontaine, however, did neither. His well-known Southern sympathies, friendship with Beauregard, and employment with the *New York*

Herald—the most widely read Yankee paper in Dixie—extended to De Fontaine the Southern hospitality denied to his peers.[5]

De Fontaine's status particularly benefited James Gordon Bennett, the man helming the *Herald*. As soon as the fist unclenched, De Fontaine rode several dispatches on the "lightning" to Bennett in New York. The first, sent April 12 at 3:00 p.m., announced the start of the Civil War. Bennett sprang like a fox into action. Not only was the news historic, it also gave him the chance to beat his competition to print. The next morning, Saturday, April 13, De Fontaine's account landed on the *Herald*'s front page alongside a sprawling map of Charleston Harbor. When De Fontaine wired news of Sumter's surrender later that day, Bennett again acted without delay. The story appeared on the *Herald*'s Sunday morning front page next to an impressive topographical sketch of Fort Sumter. Thanks to De Fontaine, the telegraph, and an impious Sunday issue, Bennett led the Northern press with news both of Sumter's bombardment and surrender.

Bennett's breaking coverage left New York City spellbound. All that weekend news-hungry New Yorkers packed the blocks outside the *Herald* office, forcing "the Metropolitan Police . . . to barricade the streets and reroute traffic." Like scraps thrown to animals between meals, *Herald* employees posted updates—based on news wired by De Fontaine—on an outside bulletin between issues. Meanwhile, inside the *Herald* building, Bennett worked his state-of-the-art printing press overtime. For the Sunday morning issue declaring Sumter's surrender, he churned out an incredible 135,000 copies. It was, boasted Bennett, "the largest issue of any newspaper that has ever been printed."[6]

Similar scenes, scarcely rivaled by those seen after Gettysburg, unfurled throughout the North and South. In New Orleans and Richmond, news-starved crowds clustered around press offices like hogs to feeding troughs, anticipating bulletin updates and new issues to roll hot off the press. In Chicago, thousands poured into the streets, swarming press offices and devouring new issues as soon as they became available. In Philadelphia, the masses outside grew so large that many could not get close enough to read the bulletins. To spread the news, those in front read the bulletins aloud, and then, like a stone striking a pond, the news rippled word-of-mouth toward the edges of the crowd.[7] "All newsdom was in ferment," remarked one historian.[8] Indeed it was. The opening shots at Fort Sumter infected the public with war fever, which incited a level of news fervor yet unseen in American history.

Historian Michael Schudson summarizes the Civil War's impact on the press when he says it intensified "the direction in which journalism had been turning since the 1830s." The forces that conspired to create the antebellum news revolution did not dissolve in 1861 only to give way to some novel and distinct era in journalism. Instead, the revolution begun in the three decades before the Civil War became amplified by it. Newspapers rose in importance, demand for them soared, and printers drew heavily on their antebellum experience to report on more news, in more places, faster than ever before. As Schudson explains, Civil War journalism "was not so much different as bigger, more prominent, and . . . more important to ordinary people."[9]

News-gathering efforts and press politicization especially grew more prominent. From the first shots at Fort Sumter through to Gettysburg and on to Appomattox, the public's taste for war news proved insatiable. To gather it swiftly along a wide and fluid front, printers exploited technology and employed field correspondents on an immense scale. De Fontaine joined hundreds of daring newsmen throughout the war who—armed with quill, ink, and paper—risked life and limb to report on the fighting firsthand. Meanwhile, war's extreme circumstances pushed press partisanship to further extremes. In both North and South, political loyalties deepened the pro- and anti-administration divide, with the most vehement anti-administration printers blurring the line between legitimate opposition criticism and treason to one's cause. Ultimately, the Civil War amplified the transformations begun by the antebellum news revolution. And in both the North and South, news-gathering efforts and press politicization formed the most prominent peaks of that amplification.

While the antebellum news revolution slingshot newspapers into the center of American life, the high stakes of civil strife made them more important than ever. The Civil War claimed some 750,000 lives and touched the lives of almost all Americans.[10] Northerners and Southerners, whether fighting on the front or fretting on the home front, depended on the press to understand the war as it unfolded. Newspapers described battles, discerned their implications, and depicted them in dramatic illustrations. Printers published maps, sketches, generals' orders, local soldiers' letters, and even casualty lists for those brave enough to search for a loved one's name.[11] Readers could not help but devoutly follow the coverage of campaigns involving friends and family. In sum, as historian George H. Douglas puts it, "the people lived by and through the newspaper during the four dreadful years of war."[12]

Contemporaries noticed the heightened obsession with newspapers. Shortly following Fort Sumter's surrender, Oliver Wendell Holmes decided, "The newspaper is as imperious as a Russian Ukase; it will be had, and it will be read. To this all else must give place." Quite often it did. When urgent war news arrived, it consumed people's attention and shelved their priorities. Holmes wrote, "Men cannot think, or write, or attend to ordinary business. . . . When any startling piece of war-news comes, it keeps repeating itself in our minds in spite of all we do."[13] Bennett's managing editor, Frederic Hudson, witnessed some priority-shelving when he came across a "scrubwoman, mop forgotten at her side, avidly reading a 'War Extra.'"[14]

Soldiers found newspapers no less irresistible.[15] Before the Gettysburg campaign, Virginia's Rappahannock River bisected the Union and Confederate armies, threatening to cut the illicit trade between opposing pickets. But some creative rebels devised a means to keep that trade open. A Southern picket explained how they "would rig up a board with sails and a rudder and send over tobacco in exchange for coffee and newspapers."[16] Apparently neither the Rappahannock nor threat of punishment for illegal trade with the enemy deterred soldiers from getting the news.

The abnormal hunger for newspapers persuaded printers to publish more frequently. Immediately following the Battle of Fort Sumter, Horace Greeley promised *New-York Tribune* evening editions until the war ended, while Bennett upped the ante with afternoon issues of the *Herald*.[17] Soon the prewar urban daily became the wartime bi-daily, and many printers swapped the weekly, the prewar staple of the country press, for the semi- or triweekly. Of course, the famed extra emerged as a familiar wartime feature. When any breaking battle news shot through the wires, printers steadied their staffs and readied their presses for a "War Extra," which often quintupled the usual daily sales of major urban papers. After receiving wired news of the fighting at Gettysburg, Greeley launched a *Tribune* extra that, in just a few hours, sold sixty-five thousand copies in New York City alone.[18]

The proliferation of Sunday editions showed how far printers would go to meet the wartime news demand. Antebellum Americans had taken the Sabbath seriously. During the Second Great Awakening a movement arose to enforce God's commandment in Exodus: "Remember the Sabbath day by keeping it holy."[19] Sabbatarians, as the movement's supporters became known, fought to end Sunday leisure, business, travel, and even the mail.[20] They enjoyed some success, both then and years later. When French hero of the American Revolution Marquis de Lafayette returned to America in 1824, he refused to travel on Sundays lest he offend his pious hosts, and in 1912 Sabbatarian successor movements finally prevailed in shuttering the post office on Sundays. To avoid offending God and provoking Sabbatarians, most antebellum printers abstained from work on Sunday.

Bennett, however, risked the wrath of both God and Sabbatarians. For nearly two decades before Fort Sumter, he published and sold the *Herald* on Sundays. Sabbatarians cried foul, but Bennett stood firm. Bolstered by a near monopoly on Sunday news in New York City, Bennett's sacrilegious *Herald* edition generated more than enough business to make it profitable. He proved that uninterrupted news, seven days a week, could succeed before the war despite opposition from Sabbatarians.

But when the Civil War erupted at Fort Sumter the lust for news suddenly made Sabbath adherence a secondary concern. Bennett's Sunday, April 14, issue—with its 135,000 copies—nearly ground New York City to a halt. Meanwhile, Philadelphians inhaled the city's few Sunday papers despite many never having purchased one before.[21] The war's opening act demonstrated that the public's thirst for uninterrupted news trumped their devotion to keeping the Sabbath. Antipathy against Sunday papers plummeted.[22] The shift encouraged major urban printers to join Bennett in supplying nonstop coverage of the war. By May the *New-York Tribune, New York Times,* Boston's *Herald,* and *Chicago Tribune* all introduced Sunday issues.[23] To the great dismay of hard-line Sabbatarians, the war did not take pauses on Sundays, and neither did its news.

Printers turned to new technology to meet the public demand for more news. While small to medium-sized tracts, such as the *Daily Register* of Knoxville, Tennessee, replaced their outmoded hand presses with modern steam ones, big-time urban printers like Bennett and Greeley installed cutting-edge lightning rotary steam presses, invented by Richard Hoe, which scraped ceilings at over thirty feet tall and discharged some twenty thousand copies every hour.[24] Greeley also introduced stereotyping, a process in which duplicate metal plates are cast from a papier-mâché mold of the original, allowing other presses to mass-produce highly sought issues (like Greeley's Gettysburg extra). Greeley perfected the process just in time for the war in April 1861. By summer's end, both Bennett and New York native Henry J. Raymond, a conservative Republican who made the *New York Times* an attractive alternative to the *Herald-Tribune* paradigm, adopted the technique.

Although the North and South shared a thirst for wartime news, the two sections differed considerably in their capacities to quench it. Of the nation's four thousand newspapers in 1860, only about eight hundred published in the eleven states that would form the Confederacy a year later.[25] But even with a smaller press the South failed to supply its own peacetime printing needs. In 1860 not one printing press manufacturer and only 24 of the nation's 555 paper mills operated in the South. Mississippi and Alabama, Dixie's center, constituted a paper desert, with just one paper mill between them. Consequently, Southern printers imported printing essentials from the North to meet their peacetime needs. For a South increasingly bent on achieving independence, some Southern newsmen found their dependency on the North beyond concerning. In 1860 the *New Orleans Bulletin* cautioned the South to "temper its opinions on secession until it became independent of Northern ink, type, presses, and paper."[26]

The South's inferior rail and telegraphic networks exacerbated these prewar concerns. In 1860 the nation's tentacles of industry, thirty thousand miles of railroad track and fifty thousand miles of telegraph wire, extended chiefly across Yankeedom. Dixie's inferior infrastructure saddled Southern printers with higher transportation and telegraphic costs while slowing Southern news gathering and distribution. James D. B. De Bow, the Fire-Eater publisher behind the New Orleans–based *De Bow's Review*, found this intolerable. Envisioning a robust and economically independent South, replete with transportation and communication grids rivaling the North, he told a Yankee audience before the war, "In my own region I would imitate very much what belongs to your character and career."[27] Despite the efforts of De Bow and others to do just that, the South's infrastructure continued to lag far behind the North before the war.

As if reopening an old wound, the Civil War brought these problems and many more to the fore. Southern secession resulted in the cessation of Northern shipments to the South, the blockade of Southern ports, and the slow but steady invasion of Southern territory by Union armies. For a South already incapable of supplying its own peacetime printing needs, meeting the higher wartime demand for news while a Yankee noose choked it and Union armies invaded it became a struggle against nearly impossible odds. The war triggered supply shortages, runaway inflation, and transportation nightmares that shot the price of printing essentials skyward. A paper ream costing three to five dollars at war's start soared to over fifty dollars by mid-1864.[28] In isolated Texas, the *San Antonio Herald* reportedly paid as high as $100 per ream as early as 1863. The initial bounce in issue frequency became unsustainable. The war forced Southern printers to conserve newsprint and ink by slashing their paper size, type size, and issue frequency—including the nascent Sunday editions. By mid-1862, a year before Gettysburg, Richmond's dailies all used half-sheets, and shortly thereafter most Confederate dailies and weeklies followed suit.[29]

The hoovering up of rags and personnel by the Confederate army further ladened Southern printers. Rags, the raw resource used to make paper, doubled as bandages for wounded Confederate soldiers. Paper mill owners competed with Confederate orderlies for the South's limited rag supply, contributing to what the *Charleston Mercury* called the "paper famine" and compounding the higher newsprint costs.[30] The Southern newspaper staffs also shrank as men left to fight, even though Confederate conscription law exempted "one editor of each newspaper . . . and such employés as the editor or proprietor may certify, upon oath, to be indispensable for conducting the publication."[31] About three-fourths of the South's printing press operators in 1863 had served or were serving in the Confederate army by mid-1864, when the South not only saw the bottom of the manpower pool, but began scraping it. War-caused labor shortages so plagued Southern newspaper offices, raising labor costs and impairing general operations, that some printers did the unthinkable: they hired women. In 1864 the *Savannah Republican* put two women in positions once held by men.[32]

While these problems strained Southern printers, the Union army stretched them to their breaking point. Federal advances so pinioned Southern printers that some resorted to using wrapping paper and wallpaper as newsprint. As Union and Confederate forces converged on Gettysburg in the summer of 1863, Union forces under General Ulysses S. Grant also tightened their stranglehold around the rebel stronghold of Vicksburg, forcing the besieged to eat local pets and local printer James M. Swords to publish six Vicksburg *Daily Citizen* issues on wallpaper. Swords had company. Some thirteen printers ran wallpaper issues just in the two war-torn states of Mississippi and Louisiana.[33]

In addition to further constricting Southern printing supplies, Union armies brought a wrecking ball to Southern rail lines, telegraph lines, and postal facilities—and thus to the South's economy. In a six-month span in 1864, as Yankee troops pierced deeper into Confederate vitals, wire rates quadrupled. Skyrocketing publishing costs forced Southern printers to raise newspaper prices throughout the war. Five-dollar annual subscriptions at war's start ballooned to over one hundred dollars by the start of 1865.[34] Some Southerners desperate for news but unable to pay offered livestock or crops in exchange for newspapers, which some bereft printers happily accepted. Unlike the Northern press, the Southern press struggled to keep its prewar commitment to broadly affordable news due to the success of Union arms.

The federal army's successes also threw Confederate papers on the run. Just before Memphis fell to Union forces in June 1862 the recalcitrant *Memphis Daily Appeal* printers, Tennesseans John McClanahan and Benjamin Dill, issued a notice: "Sooner would we sink our types, press and establishment in the bottom of the Mississippi River and [become] wanderers and exiles from our homes" than "submit to censorship under Lincoln's hireling minions."[35] They fitted action to these words. The city's capitulation impelled McClanahan and Dill on an odyssey of evasion that would last until after Confederate General Robert E. Lee's war-ending surrender at Appomattox. The *Appeal* published in Tennessee, Mississippi, Alabama, and Georgia, all the while staying one step ahead of advancing federal armies. When General William T. Sherman's Union army closed its jaws around Atlanta in the summer of 1864, the *Appeal* packed up its gear and slipped away to print another day. But on April 16, 1865—after nearly three years on the run and a full week after Lee surrendered—it all came to a dramatic close. Union cavalry finally caught up to the *Appeal* in Columbus, Georgia, and burned its equipment in the streets. By then the paper had earned the nickname, the "*Moving Appeal*."

The *Appeal*'s story, though remarkable, proved no anomaly. The *Chattanooga Daily Rebel* won a similar nickname for its grand evasion tour across the unoccupied South: the "*Rebel on Wheels*." Throughout the war many Southern printers took their staffs and equipment on the run, embracing an itinerant lifestyle in order to keep the Confederate cause alive in print and, by extension, alive in the hearts of Southern readers. One historian fittingly described these publications as stubborn refugees, defiant in the face of defeat and unwilling to succumb to the exigencies of a hard war.[36]

The vast majority, however, did succumb. By early 1862 the war had already killed off 17 of Florida's 26 newspapers and 50 of Texas's 60.[37] The following year, just before Gettysburg, Virginia's 120 papers dropped to 17, and in 1864 Mississippi's 75 shrank to 9.[38] Few Confederate newspapers covered the war from start to finish, and those that did, like the *Appeal*, intermittently suspended operations. According to historian J. Cutler Andrews, the Southern newspaper mortality rate grew so high that "by January 1865 there were not as many newspapers in the entire Confederacy as there were in the state of Virginia before the war." He estimated that "no more than twenty Southern dailies" survived to war's end.[39] The South's high newspaper mortality prompted the *San Antonio Herald* to remark, "War and blockade are death to newspapers."[40]

The Southern press confronted unique challenges that, while often rooted in the antebellum era, were exacerbated by a losing war. The antebellum South's inferior infrastructure and dependency on the North made meeting the higher wartime demand for news on its own next to impossible. Then the Confederate army's needs sowed supply and labor shortages while Union forces blockaded and invaded the South, crushing the Confederacy's capacity to both wage war and supply the news. As a result, Southern printers experienced far greater wartime hardships than their Northern counterparts. When the war inconvenienced Pennsylvania printers during the Gettysburg campaign by forcing some to temporarily use low-quality straw paper, it forced Southern printers to strip their walls for paper, flee their hometowns, or close their offices for good.[41] Ending the war required bringing the South to its knees. That process proved devastating for a Southern press unable to stand on its own before the war even began.

One might conclude that the Civil War rendered the Southern press a blunt instrument, dulled beyond all effectiveness, but this conclusion should be resisted. Southern printers continued to supply the news with remarkable resolve and resourcefulness despite facing challenges unique in the history of American journalism. McClanahan and Dill managed to offer morning and evening editions throughout much of the war, which tallied a daily circulation of fourteen thousand—seven times larger than the *Appeal*'s prewar readership.[42] Even if Southern printers failed to meet the higher wartime news demand, they often succeeded in boosting circulation amid the most trying circumstances. Strapped for supplies, stripped of staff, and driven on the run, Southern printers still found ways to keep Southerners informed with the news.

While the war intensified the challenges faced by the Southern press, it also intensified national and regional press hub development, even in the war-ravaged Confederacy. Richmond rapidly evolved into the heart of Confederate life. When Beauregard attacked Fort Sumter, the Virginia capital's population, slaves included, numbered just 38,000. But a month later Richmond became the Confederate capital, and Southerners began flocking there like ants to a new nest. The city's population more than tripled—capping at 120,000—as it drew legions of refugees, military personnel, government employees, and industrial workers.[43] Moreover, as Richmond's light in the Southern horizon brightened, other cities fell from the Confederate constellation altogether. Memphis, Nashville, and New Orleans—the latter being the only Confederate city to top one hundred thousand people when the war began—all caved to Union forces in 1862. By the end of the war's second year, no rival to Richmond remained in the Confederacy.

This only solidified Richmond as the Confederacy's news hub. The city's status as the rebel capital prioritized the inflow of war-related news. It also prioritized the city's defense, which helped Richmond papers outlive their Confederate peers. When New Orleans and its press fell into Yankee hands in the spring of 1862, only a few thousand short-term militia guarded the city, while almost seventy-five thousand soldiers defended Richmond.[44] The city's location, only one hundred miles south of Washington and ordinarily even closer to the war's bloodiest theater, kept its inhabitants on edge and its newspapermen on the edges of their seats. Richmond printers enjoyed the earliest reports from the Eastern Theater and easier access to Northern papers, which they often used to supplement their coverage. The city's population explosion provided its press with a large local market, even though Richmond's five dailies—the *Enquirer, Dispatch, Whig, Examiner,* and later in 1863 the *Sentinel*—circulated widely across the South, from tidewater Virginia to the Gulf shores of Texas.

No other Confederate city wielded the resources, esteem, and influence of the Richmond press. Bankrolled by large circulations, it could afford correspondents to report on the frontline fighting. Of the nine reporters who joined Lee's Army of Northern Virginia at Gettysburg, three worked for Richmond papers.[45] Printers the South over, and even some in the North, republished Richmond's press reports knowing they represented the best in Confederate journalism. After the war a respected Northern journalist, Ohioan Whitelaw Reid, conceded, "The northern public scarcely appreciated the amount of journalistic talent concentrated there. . . . The newspapers of Richmond . . . were in many respects the ablest on the continent. Their writing . . . shaped the public sentiment of the whole Confederacy."[46] That was high praise considering that Reid had risked his life as a Northern war reporter and later succeeded Greeley to head the *New-York Tribune.*

The war also fostered regional news hubs in the Confederacy. Before Sherman captured Atlanta, the city was home to a growing number of refugees and refugee papers. The *Memphis Daily Appeal, Chattanooga Daily Rebel,* and Knoxville's *Daily Register* banded with Atlanta's seven homegrown tracts, four of which were conceived during the war, to form an influential regional press hub.[47] A Southern war reporter professed, "Next to Richmond, Atlanta may boast of the ablest conducted Press in the country."[48]

Several other Southern cities—such as Mobile, Savannah, and Charleston—boasted papers with influence well beyond their locale. Robert Barnwell Rhett's *Charleston Mercury,* which helped push Southerners over the cliff of secession, continued shaping opinions well beyond Charleston during the war. The conflict Rhett helped kindle, however, eventually caught up to the Father of Secession in the Cradle of Secession. After making refugees of newspapers in Georgia, Sherman turned his wrath against South Carolina, forcing Rhett to go on the run in the war's waning months.[49]

Northern news hubs expanded with the war as well. The star of the Union press, New York City, burned even brighter during the conflict. With seventeen dailies, New York outshined all other cities in wartime circulation and coverage. Greeley's *Tribune* pulled in the war's largest weekly circulation, while the *Herald*'s 135,000 copies on April 14 eclipsed the circulation of the South's top five dailies combined at that time. Backed by colossal readerships, the New York press fielded more war correspondents than any other Northern or Southern city. To accompany General George Meade and the Union Army of the Potomac at Gettysburg, the *Herald, Times, World,* and *Tribune* alone supplied twenty-four of the estimated forty-five total correspondents (Northerners composed thirty-six of that sum).[50] With eyes and ears in more places, New York's wartime press coverage proved unmatched in both depth and breadth.

The news-verse recognized New York City as its gravitational center. Printers across Yankeedom and even some in Rebeldom acknowledged New York City's primacy by regularly reprinting its newspaper accounts. Phrases like "From the *Herald*" and "From the *Tribune*" appeared so often in papers from other cities that specifying New York as the origin only wasted ink.[51] Even before the war elevated New York City's press, printers North and South recognized, if often begrudgingly, that the seat of American newsdom rested there. In 1859 Rhett's *Charleston Mercury* summarized New York City's press dominance with a complaint: "We have to go to the New York papers for news of our own affairs."[52]

As in the South, the North witnessed regional press hubs develop during the war. Chicago, Boston, Cincinnati, Baltimore, Washington, and Philadelphia all had papers with large readerships across wide expanses of the North. One paper in the City of Brotherly Love gave the New York City press some brotherly competition. By 1862 the *Philadelphia Inquirer*—under local printer William Harding—amassed a circulation of sixty thousand, outpacing Philadelphia's *Public Ledger,* through the quality and quantity of its war coverage.[53] Thanks to a reporting corps second only in size to Bennett's *Herald,* Harding's *Inquirer* featured among the most detailed accounts of the fighting.[54] And, like the *Herald,* the *Inquirer* festooned its pages with some of the most impressive campaign and battlefield maps. It is little wonder why the paper became a favorite in the Union army. The *Inquirer* rose through the ranks to corral a circulation of twenty-five thousand just among Yankee soldiers.[55]

While modern war correspondence originated during the Mexican War and one city at the time, New Orleans, shouldered the reporting burden, the

Civil War saw newspapermen from across the North and the South pour vast resources into the enterprise. Between Fort Sumter and Appomattox, Bennett spent over half a million dollars to field the *Herald*'s small army of correspondents, and printers in Chicago and Philadelphia devoted tens of thousands of dollars annually to keep reporters near the action.[56] The war's massive stage, acted out in several theaters at once and combined with the bottomless demand for news, obliged newspapermen to radically expand their news-gathering efforts. Never before had American printers needed to report on more developments in more places. They met that need by employing a ragtag group of gifted and gutsy newsmen, who accompanied armies and braved battlefields armed with the humble weapons of their trade: quill, ink, and paper.

The largest papers kept correspondents permanently assigned to major armies. The New York *Times*, *Tribune*, and *Herald*, for example, always kept reporters in the field with the Union Army of the Potomac. They also readily paid for whatever their knights of the quill required. The deep-pocketed *Herald* accoutered correspondents with everything imaginable: horses, field glasses, tents, cots, bedding, and a headquarters chock-full of fine wine, food, cooking appliances, and even furniture. Although this was expensive, printers found that the benefits of maintaining field correspondents far outweighed the costs. Veteran army reporters furnished prompt and gripping firsthand battle accounts that they often acquired under fire. As one contemporary remarked, "war correspondents sought news as the soldier sought glory—at the cannon's mouth."[57]

Northern and Southern correspondents hazarded life and limb to cover the war in person. Gettysburg alone proved their dogged devotion to journalism. The campaign claimed two reporters' lives. Georgia's Virgil A. S. Parks, a Confederate captain doubling as a *Savannah Republican* correspondent, lost his life fighting on July 2, 1863—the second day of the three-day battle. Before that, John Mosby's guerrillas ambushed Massachusettsan Lynde Walter Buckingham, a *Herald* reporter who carried news of the cavalry clashes that preceded the battle.[58] A sudden crack of gunfire spooked Buckingham's horse, which threw him violently to the ground. The fall fatally fractured his skull, and the next morning a friend, sketch artist A. R. Waud of *Harper's Weekly*, buried Buckingham outside a nearby church.[59] Others, by sheer luck, avoided Buckingham's fate. The *New York Times*'s Lorenzo Crounse had his horse shot out from under him on July 2. Undeterred, the stout Crounse, originally a Wisconsinite, went on to finish his battle account.

Perhaps no reporter endured greater grief at Gettysburg than New Yorker Sam Wilkeson, Crounse's colleague at the *Times*. Wilkeson reached the battlefield early in the morning on July 2 only to learn what all fathers fear most. The day before, his son Bayard, a nineteen-year-old artillerist in the Army of the Potomac, fell holding fast against advanced elements of Lee's army. Despite this personal tragedy, or perhaps because of the raw emotion it inspirited, Wilkeson wrote one of the best and most poignant Gettysburg accounts. When the fighting ended, he curled up next to Bayard's newly cut grave and, with tears spilling down his cheeks, penned his heart-wrenching account, the most famous passage of which read: "Oh, you dead, who at Gettysburg have baptized with your blood the second birth of Freedom in America, how you are to be envied! I rise from a grave whose wet clay I have passionately kissed and I look up and see Christ. . . . His right hand opens the gates of Paradise—with his left he beckons to these mutilated, bloody, swollen forms to ascend."[60]

Not everyone respected the hardships endured by war reporters. The quantity of Civil War correspondents and their relentless hunt for news often irritated officers and even infuriated some top generals. A reporter at the Union base in Cairo, Illinois, recalled correspondents "at every step; they block up the approaches to headquarters; one of them is attached to the button of every officer; they are constantly demanding . . . things whose use and extent are only appreciated by omniscience."[61]

Even if those in command could tolerate reporters' incessant pestering, they often could not tolerate their reports. Edward Cropsey, a *Philadelphia Inquirer* reporter from Illinois, incensed General Meade for intimating he had countenanced retreat following the bloody Battle of the Wilderness in May 1864. After arresting Cropsey, Meade meted out a punishment mixing Athenian ostracism with a medieval shame walk. His men plunked Cropsey backwards on a mule, chained a placard around his neck reading "Libeler of the Press," paraded him through camp to much whooping and jeering, and then excommunicated him indefinitely from the army.[62] Although Meade relished the spectacle, the draconian punishment further stained his already tarnished relationship with the press. According to Sylvanus Cadwallader, a *Herald* reporter assigned to Meade's army, the Cropsey affair convinced every correspondent to "ignore Gen. Meade in every possible way and manner."[63]

Although the preponderance of correspondents and their tireless news pursuing angered some generals, it ensured that the Civil War's press coverage was more extensive and detailed than any war before it. Between April 1861 and April 1865, the war-crippled Southern press managed to field over one hundred reporters while the Northern press furnished roughly five times that number.[64] De Fontaine found himself one among many committed paladins of the press. Throughout the war the *Herald* alone kept at least sixty reporters on or near the front at any given time.[65] Besides feeding readers more of the war coverage they craved, the heightened emphasis on reporting made the Civil War one of the finest-covered conflicts in history.[66] News gathering, however, only began with reporters. To rush their dispatches from the war front to the home front, printers leaned more heavily than ever before on the crutch of technology.

The Civil War expanded technology's use in news gathering. Continued steamship use and wartime railroad expansion, particularly in the North, accelerated the rate at which news from correspondents on the frontlines reached printers and their audiences back home. But while steam empowered the swift movement of news from the front, steam technology could not outpace the speed of telegraphy. During a war in which readers hankered for fresh frontline news, Northern and Southern printers quite understandably exploited the near-instant news-transmitting capability of telegraphy like never before.

Civil War news transmission revolved around the telegraph. Reporters knew it best. They went to remarkable lengths just to wire their Gettysburg accounts (not to mention just to get to Gettysburg in the first place). When the fighting ended on the sweltering afternoon of July 3, a strong-willed *Herald* correspondent set out for Baltimore, nearly sixty miles away, to transmit his battle account. Frank Chapman reached the city so early the next morning that telegraph offices there had not yet opened. Rather than wait, Chapman showed his resolve. He raced to the home of telegrapher James N. Worl and dragged the man from his bed. Despite the rude awakening, it did not take long for Worl, the Independent Telegraph Company's superintendent and by then a veteran of the wartime wire, to catch Chapman's urgency.[67] With little time lost, the two had bounded like hares through Baltimore's still slumbering streets and reached the telegraph office, where Worl began transmitting Chapman's dispatch to New York City in an adrenaline-fueled flurry of dots and dashes.

Not long thereafter, a *Tribune* correspondent, T. C. Grey, barged into the office bearing his own Gettysburg account. Worl followed the "first come first serve" principle. Until he and his staff, which had arrived by that time, finished sending Chapman's dispatch, Grey would have to wait. But Chapman, a *Herald* man through and through, refused to surrender the wire to his *Tribune* rival. Before Worl completed Chapman's dispatch, Chapman withdrew his pocket Bible, opened it to Genesis I, and told Worl, "just keep your men busy sending this until I get back."[68] The ploy enraged Grey but ensured Chapman a monopoly on the line. All day he cycled in and out of the telegraph office, returning each time with the latest news relayed from Gettysburg to cable on to New York. Meanwhile, the *Herald* office hummed with incoming telegraphic news of Gettysburg, punctuated, no doubt to the curiosity of those handling it, by lengthy excerpts from the Old Testament. Luckily for Chapman, Bennett never worried about high telegraph costs. As one historian noted, "There was never any grudging scrutiny of expense accounts [at the *Herald*]."[69]

Printers eager for the latest frontline news absorbed higher telegraphic costs. In 1862 Bennett paid over a thousand dollars for telegraph news of the federal capture of New Orleans.[70] And while the worsening war situation played a large role in the high costs, in 1864 one Texas paper paid over six hundred dollars a week just for wired news.[71] The expense did not go to waste. Telegraphic news, a prewar novelty filling mere columns, became a wartime banality, taking up whole pages.[72] Non-wired news barely graced the *Herald*'s front pages during the war's first weekend in mid-April 1861. De Fontaine's wired account detailing Sumter's surrender, published April 14, consumed the majority of the *Herald*'s front page by itself.

Telegraphy's heavy use hastened the growth of press associations. The Associated Press (AP) pooled the vast resources of New York's dailies into one organization capable of fielding its own correspondents and securing lower wartime telegraph rates.[73] The AP also wired its war news to subscriber papers across the North for a fee, which only strengthened New York as the hegemon of American journalism. But in 1862 some western printers bettered their bargaining position with the New York–based AP by establishing a competitor, the Western Associated Press—headquartered in Chicago.

Meanwhile, in 1862 Southern printers east of the Mississippi created the Confederate Press Association (CPA), to help manage news-gathering costs. From its Atlanta headquarters, the CPA halved members' wired rates and hired some twenty correspondents to tender frontline reports.[74] But in late 1864 the fall of Atlanta, combined with the overall deterioration of the Confederate telegraph network, prompted Richmond's printers to abandon the CPA and launch the Mutual Benefits Press Association. Although the organization formed to improve wired communications, by then the apocalyptic symptoms of a losing war made doing so nearly impossible.[75]

Telegraphy's heavy use raised readers' expectations regarding the timeliness of war news. From the first shots at Fort Sumter, many Americans came to expect news not just after events occurred but also as they unfolded. The expectation was not without justification. Thanks to the "lightning," many Northerners and Southerners knew about the war's first battle before it had even ended. And just three months later the wire fed crowds in Washington, D.C., word of First Bull Run before that battle had ended in a Union rout. Beginning with these two war-inaugurating engagements, the punctual power of telegraphy helped establish a new precedent in wartime news gathering, one in which word from the front could be conveyed to those on the home front in real time. This power kept a public obsessed with war news, absolutely mad for it.

Oliver Wendell Holmes described how this wired news wielded the power of "divine right" because people could not resist going "out at unusual hours to get it."[76] Civilians hovered anxiously near press offices anticipating updates of ongoing campaigns to arrive by cable. Diarist Mary Boykin Chesnut and her fellow Richmonders "haunt[ed] the bulletin-board" for wired news when Yankee forces advanced on the rebel capital in 1862.[77] And telegraphic war news, once obtained, exerted a further dementing influence. Holmes explained how a friend became bewitched, "read[ing] the same telegraphic dispatches over and over again in different papers, as if they were new, until he felt as though he were an idiot."[78] Whether detailed in a paper or bulletined outside one's office, telegraph reports further stoked the public fervor for war-related news.

Of course, news punctuality and reliability did not always go hand in hand. The telegraph often empowered the former at the latter's expense. Immediately after Gettysburg, the telegraph handed Northern and Southern printers erroneous news, which, on publication, profoundly misled the public. Thanks to cabled dispatches, Northerners initially thought Lee's whole army had fled pell-mell after its defeat on July 3 and that Meade's pursuit had swallowed up over twenty thousand rebels and over one hundred cannons. The South's earliest wired reports proved even more absurd. Richmond printers ran a telegraph report that Lee's army had forced Meade to flee toward Baltimore and that the Confederates had gobbled up forty thousand prisoners.[79] Some printers found the initial spate of wired Gettysburg news so misleading that they took their frustration to print. The *Richmond Enquirer* seethed, "The infernal invention of the electric telegraph . . . makes us doubt everything we read, because we know that the chances are ten to one it is false."[80]

False wire reports prevailed in the immediate wake of large battles, when confusion ran most rampant. The lingering smoke, chaotic collection of dead and wounded, and disorganized movement of entire armies typical after large battles made ascertaining an accurate account, let alone a correct casualty count, extremely difficult. The fog of battle took time to clear. When it came to Gettysburg it took a few days for most printers to penetrate the initial haze of wired misinformation. As the *New York Times* put it before the war, the telegraph often delivered reports "too fast for the truth."[81]

While Civil War news gathering relied on the wire and the reporter, news distribution depended mainly on postal workers. Most Northern and Southern readers continued to get their newspapers through the mail as subscriptions, not in one-off street purchases from newsies. This runs against popular perceptions of Civil War news delivery. It is easy to imagine the young street urchin peddling papers while shouting "War extra! Get your war extra here!" But this image represented an urban exception in a still mostly rural America. Although the newsies saw a wartime boom in business, a more accurate image involves thousands of Northern and Southern postmen, aided by steam power, cheaply delivering the masses news in both rural and urban settings. In fact, both sides' mail services generally kept newspaper rates low, although the Confederate Post Office, which the Confederate government established in February 1861, raised rates several times due to war-related challenges. The U.S. Post Office, in contrast, not only kept newspaper postage low throughout the war but also introduced free delivery in Northern cities beginning on July 1, 1863—just in time for Gettysburg. Free intra-city postage further cemented the post as the Union's chief news distributor and undermines popular perceptions of the Civil War news hawker.

Wartime postal services benefited printers no less than readers. While the U.S. Post Office continued to support Northern printers through the exchange privilege, Confederate leaders immediately perceived the exchange's importance in supplying Southern printers, especially rural ones, with the news. Just one month after creating its post office, the Confederate government codified the printer exchange, allowing Southern "publishers of newspapers" to "send and receive to and from each other . . . one copy of each publication, free of postage."[82] While the exchange greatly assisted the Southern press, it grew increasingly unreliable as the war dragged on. In mid-1862 the *Appeal* already concluded that the exchange service was "the worst ever imposed upon a patient and suffering people."[83]

But the Confederate post suffered alongside the Confederate people. In the war's early years, it transported much of the South's mail via rail in specially designed cars. The gradual destruction of Southern railroads, however, increasingly disabled the Confederate post's ability to carry anything swiftly over long distances. By 1865 deterioration of the South's transportation network as well as the need to prioritize military communication so hamstrung the Confederate post that news from Richmond took nearly a month to reach Mobile.[84] Though the Confederate post technically survived to war's end, by the spring of 1865 it could do little more than limp along Rebeldom's few remaining routes.

Before postal workers delivered the news it first passed through the most partisan press in U.S. history. In 1860 four out of five American periodicals were, according to Census superintendent Joseph C. G. Kennedy, "political in their character."[85] But this figure included magazines. A narrowed look at just newspapers reveals even higher levels of political association. Every daily paper in the country, all of the nearly four hundred, functioned as an organ for one political party or another.[86] Almost all Northern printers backed either the Republican Party or the Democratic Party, whereas most Southern printers bolstered the Southern Democratic cause. The presses of both sections marched toward war in this state of hyper-politicization.

When the war of words became a shooting war at Fort Sumter, press partisanship intensified. The Southern press began the war largely unified behind Confederate president Jefferson Davis, but as it wore on and the South lost more men and territory, it splintered between printers who supported Davis and those who opposed Davis's prosecution of the war. Pro-Davis printers generally praised his appointments, applauded his policies, and defended his military strategy. The less numerous anti-Davis papers—the core of which by Gettysburg included Rhett's *Charleston Mercury*, John M. Daniel's *Richmond Examiner*, James McDonald's *Richmond Whig*, William Woods Holden's *North Carolina Standard*, J. Henley Smith's *Southern Confederacy* (published in Atlanta), and James R. Sneed and Frederick W. Sims's *Savannah Republican*—consistently denounced his leadership and occasionally blasted him with insults. In May 1862 the *Examiner* likened Davis to the hated "Pennsylvania Dutch Yankee," and in August 1863 it blamed "Mr. Davis alone" for Vicksburg's fall.[87] Unlike the North, the South entered the war without a competitive two-party system through which press support for or dissent against Davis could be channeled. As a result, the anti-Davis press functioned as an unaffiliated assortment of opposition papers, with its newspapermen the press equivalent of masterless samurai: ronin bound by no party.

The South's scattered opposition drew its motivation for dissent from various practical, philosophical, and even personal wellsprings. While some printers opposed Davis for what they viewed as his mishandling of military affairs, others saw his prioritizing of the war over civil liberties as the greater cause for discord. Rhett, however, proved a unique case, and combated Davis for neither of these reasons. Charleston's infamous Fire-Eater initially harbored ambition to climb the Confederacy's governmental ladder. But when his ascent stalled at the Confederate Congress, Rhett increasingly spited in print the national leaders he held responsible, particularly Davis. As Andrews wrote, Rhett "was influenced by frustrated personal ambition . . . and historians now attribute the *Mercury*'s opposition . . . to [his] jealousy of Davis."[88]

Regardless of their motivation, almost every anti-Davis printer emphatically undergirded the Confederate cause. As one historian explained, "They constituted a loyal opposition that hoped to improve the government [through dissent]." They did not wish to destroy it and the cause it represented.[89] Only a few Southern printers, such as Holden, opposed Davis out of an opposition to the war itself. This proved a key difference between the North and South's anti-administration presses. Unlike the Union, the Confederacy lacked a large block of anti-administration and antiwar printers who were committed to sabotaging the cause from within.

The Civil War amplified press partisanship even more in the North.[90] While Republican printers with their allies in the black press largely defended President Abraham Lincoln's wartime leadership, Democratic printers fractured into moderate and more extreme anti-Lincoln factions.[91] Bennett epitomized the moderate anti-Lincoln wing as well as any Democratic printer. Before Fort Sumter he condemned any prospect of war against the South, which bought him favor with the *Herald*'s large, prewar Southern audience. But Bennett reversed course when the fireworks of war exploded over Charleston Harbor. From then on, he committed the *Herald* to abetting the Union cause while criticizing Lincoln's leadership, a stance followed by most of his moderate Democratic peers.[92]

Bennett's pro-war conversion forced De Fontaine's hand. Southern respect for the *Herald* dried up, leaving De Fontaine out to dry as a *Herald* man in Charleston. Rather than return to the North, he embraced his Southern sympathies, joined the *Charleston Courier*'s staff, and worked as a Southern correspondent until the war ended. After Fort Sumter he penned among the finest accounts of such battles as Shiloh, Antietam, Chancellorsville, and Chattanooga.[93] But the South's adopted son did not accompany his fellow knights of the quill at Gettysburg.[94] Instead, his June 1863 marriage to Georgia Moore in South Carolina kept his quill sheathed for much of that action-packed summer.[95]

The most extreme anti-Lincoln printers in the Democratic press in the North became known as Copperheads. Named after the venomous snake, Copperheads often sympathized with the South and, through their persistent calls for peace, which many desired at the expense of national reunion, sought to undermine the Union itself. The unapologetic disloyalty, not to mention unabashed vituperation, of Copperheads made their venom in print easily detectable. On May 20, 1863, less than two months before Gettysburg, the pro-Lincoln *New-York Evening Post* published a litmus test for distinguishing anti-Lincoln Copperheads from their moderate anti-Lincoln peers. "[Copperheads] magnify Confederate victories and depreciate those of Union arms," explained the *Post*. "[They] parade reports from southern papers boasting of the size of their army and the skill of their generals . . . seize upon a northern reverse as a basis for demands for the end of a hopeless war [and] abuse the President and his cabinet without consistency or truth."[96]

Copperhead printers presented Lincoln with a grave challenge, for the venom they spat onto paper threatened the Union's survival from within. To extinguish what he called the "fire in the rear," Lincoln took unprecedented action.[97] In April 1861 he suspended habeas corpus, citing Article I, Section 9 of the Constitution, which allows for the writ's suspension when "in cases of rebellion or invasion the public safety may require it."[98] While he thought it required and within his powers, many disagreed. Writing for the U.S. Circuit Court for Maryland, Chief Justice Roger Taney—the Southerner who wrote the louche *Dred Scott* decision—ruled Lincoln's suspension unconstitutional. As Article I concerns legislative powers, not executive powers, Taney argued that suspending the writ required an act of Congress. Lincoln ignored the ruling, and the legal controversy mostly faded once Congress passed the Habeas Corpus Suspension Act, which he signed into law on March 3, 1863.

Two months later, just before the Gettysburg campaign and just as Grant got the ball rolling against Vicksburg, Lincoln's new power helped remove the political voice of Midwest Copperheads in perhaps the war's most extraordinary civil liberty case. Clement Vallandigham was an outspoken pro-peace Democrat from Ohio. His blistering anti-Lincoln and antiwar rhetoric wooed the Copperhead press into supporting his bid for the Democratic nomination for Ohio governor. But on May 5 Vallindigham's zealotry caught up with him. At 2:00 a.m. a company of federal soldiers, under orders from Department of the Ohio commander General Ambrose Burnside, broke into his Dayton home and arrested him in his bedroom for subversive speech. His May 11 application for a writ of habeas corpus was denied, and on May 16 he received a two-year prison sentence.

The Copperhead press hissed loudly. The Pennsylvania-born Samuel Medary, running the *Crisis* out of Columbus, Ohio, condemned the arrest and warned that further actions against civil liberties might bring the war to the

Midwest.[99] The combustible situation grabbed Lincoln's attention. Sensing the fire in the rear growing hotter, Lincoln hoped to reduce the flames to embers and commuted Vallandigham's sentence. Rather than imprisonment, Lincoln exiled him to the Confederacy.

The attempt at damage control initially backfired. With help from the Confederate army, Vallandigham slithered his way across the South, boarded a blockade-runner to Bermuda, and then took passage to Canada, where he managed his campaign for Ohio governor in absentia from a hotel in Windsor, Ontario. In September the Ohio Democratic State Convention, presided over by Medary, unanimously nominated Vallandigham for governor. His general election campaign enjoyed support from the Copperhead press, including Medary's *Crisis*. But the circus ended in October when Vallandigham lost the general election in a landslide to his pro-war opponent, John Brough. To say that the result relieved Lincoln would be an understatement. The president wired Brough, "Glory to God in the highest; Ohio saved the Union."[100]

The Vallandigham episode demonstrated that support for the Copperhead cause rose and fell inversely with the Union tide of war. Vallandigham's support peaked in midsummer, when Vicksburg still stood defiant and Lee's invasion still threatened the North. But after Grant captured Vicksburg and Meade rebuffed Lee at Gettysburg, support for Vallandigham and his peace platform tanked like a lead weight. That Vallandigham lost the election to Brough is only partially true. His defeat should also be credited to Grant and Meade.

The Vallandigham episode also convinced Lincoln that less equaled more when containing the Copperhead scourge. When the wife of currency comptroller Hugh McCullough requested that Lincoln suppress the Copperhead *Chicago Times* in late 1864, he replied, "I fear you do not fully comprehend the danger of abridging the liberties of the people. . . . A government had better go [to] the very extreme of toleration, than to do aught that could be construed into an interference with . . . the common rights of its citizens."[101] Although Lincoln told his department commanders to act cautiously and "only arrest individuals, and suppress . . . newspapers, when they [might] be working palpable injury," at least three hundred Democratic newspapers—including the *Chicago Times*—faced some measure of suppression during the Civil War.[102]

Davis did not venture as far as Lincoln in suppressing opposition papers. One historian believed he relied "on an imagined spirit of unity to guide press behavior" rather than on his authority as a wartime president to stomp out internal dissent.[103] Davis's general disinclination to suppress disloyal papers occasionally inspired Confederate soldiers to take matters into their own hands. Two months after Gettysburg, Lieutenant General James Longstreet, of the Army of Northern Virginia, traveled by train with the Confederate First Corps to reinforce the Army of Tennessee in northern Georgia. On the way he switched trains in Raleigh, North Carolina, where Georgia soldiers destroyed the office of Holden's *North Carolina Standard*—the anti-Davis paper perhaps most critical of the war.

Soldiers knew that bias and misinformation pervaded the press. "We have learned not to swallow anything whole that we see in the papers," mused a Yankee officer. "If half the victories we read of were true the Rebellion would not have a leg to stand on." Johnny Reb proved no less aware than Billy Yank. "I have been so often deceived by [newspaper reports]," remarked one rebel, "that I've lost confidence in our press and believe nothing coming through that channel unless I know it is so."[104] Their suspicion bore warrant. Pro- and anti-administration newsmen made neutral reporting during the war even rarer than before it. To undermine the administration they opposed, the most extreme anti-administration printers downplayed victories and overstated defeats. Conversely, to pillar the administration they supported, pro-administration printers exaggerated victories and dismissed defeats. After Gettysburg, for example, the pro-Lincoln *Philadelphia Inquirer* cheered "Victory!!" and declared "Waterloo Eclipsed!!"—as if Meade's triumph over Lee surpassed even the Duke of Wellington's war-ending triumph over Napoleon Bonaparte.[105]

Political bias was not alone in influencing how pressmen portrayed the war. North and South, newsmen catered to local tastes, which led to coverage that highlighted the contributions of their own state's soldiers. The Richmond press, for example, stressed Virginia's men at arms, which marginalized the contributions of other Southern soldiers in the Confederacy's most-read papers. After Gettysburg, North Carolinians protested the home state bias of the Richmond press, which praised Virginians involved in the battle-ending assault known as Pickett's Charge while all but ignoring the sacrifice of Tar Heel soldiers. The Virginia–North Carolina feud over Pickett's Charge spawned such resentment that it continued in various media forms for over a century after the war.[106]

Regional partisanship plagued the Northern press as well. For holding a home state bias, New York City's powerful printers often angered their Northern peers in other states. In covering Gettysburg, Pennsylvania printers complained that the New York press privileged its soldiers over the Keystone State's. "It is time that the New York journals should cease to sneer and cavil at everything Pennsylvanian," snarled the Philadelphia *Press*. "They misrepresent the actions and sentiments of our people." As if to offset New York's home state bias, the *Press* reveled in the fact that the Gettysburg victory came about in Pennsylvania at the hands of Meade, a proud Pennsylvanian.[107]

The Civil War further rived an already bitterly divided press. Alexis de Tocqueville's 1831 observation—"All the political journals of the United States are . . . arrayed on the side of the administration or against it"—rang even truer when the war erupted thirty years later.[108] Like a violent earthquake, the Civil War deepened the pro- and anti-administration fault lines that preceded it and emboldened some printers to blur the boundary between legitimate criticism and subversion. Ultimately, the war's high stakes made tempers run hot and the ink flow hotter, intensifying partisanship in an already intensely partisan press.

The Civil War amplified the transformations begun before it. As the peoples' primary means for understanding the conflict as it happened, newspapers went from merely important before the war to utterly indispensable during it. Demand spiked, and the Civil War press drew heavily on its antebellum experience to ensure that the news-hungry masses did not go without. Edition frequency, technology usage, and reliance on the mail increased, press hubs and associations grew more rapidly, and news gathering from a wide and fluid front depended more than ever on the wire and the reporter. Rather than flip journalism on its head, the Civil War and its bloodiest battle, Gettysburg, as Michael Schudson explains, "intensified the direction in which journalism had been turning since the 1830s" by making it "bigger, more prominent . . . and more important" than ever before.[109]

CHAPTER THREE

The Blood That Dried in Ink

Washington, D.C., looked "like a city besieged as after Bull Run" on the evening of June 30, 1863. "All night long troops were marching; orderlies with clanking sabres clattering along the streets; trains of wagons grinding over the bouldered avenue; commissaries were hurrying up their supplies; [and] the quartermaster's department was like a beehive," observed *Cincinnati Daily Gazette* reporter Whitelaw Reid. "Every thing was motion and hurry."[1]

Indeed it was and for good cause. The capital had slipped into a war-induced fever as the principal army of the rebellion now trampled on Northern soil and its cavalry arm stretched within a dozen miles of the city's gates. The temperature in Washington heated Reid's blood to a boil. As a veteran war reporter, he could see the writing on the wall as well as anyone. With the Confederate Army of Northern Virginia slashing through Yankeedom and the Union Army of the Potomac "sweeping splendidly up to meet them," "a great battle, perhaps the greatest of the war, was daily if not hourly impending," and Reid not only intended to witness it but also to capture it in exquisite detail.[2]

Getting there would be its own odyssey. Like a storm chaser tracking a tornado yet to touch down, Reid searched for a battle yet to begin. Where would war's hammer and anvil meet next? Rather than grope blindly in the dark, he determined to hitch himself to the Union army, for the tornado of battle could not touch down in its absence. Intercepting the blue host, however, presented a litany of challenges. Enemy cavalry still lurked "about the very gates of the Capital," and although the Union army widened its berth, "spreading out like a fan to make use of every available road," it marched through Maryland with a "rapidity of movement unprecedented in the East" to meet the invader at a still undetermined point. Reid gathered that portions of the army were "reported to be concentrating at Westminster," directly north of Washington. In less pressing circumstances he might have played the role of the diligent reporter, flagging down every boat for information before casting his own into uncertain waters. But the hour of crisis grew late. To ensure he did not miss the "great battle," Reid set off for Westminster in all haste.[3]

"It was not to be a solitary trip." The capital had drawn to it an all-star journalistic cast, Northern knights of the quill who could sense, as Reid had, a battle building like the sea drawing back before a tsunami. Samuel Wilkeson, "the well-known brilliant writer on the New York *Tribune*, lately transferred to the *Times*," and Uriah H. Painter, "chief Washington correspondent of the Philadelphia *Inquirer*" would join Reid on his course of interception, while a talented New Englander, Charles Carleton Coffin of the Boston *Journal*, "had telegraphed an appointment to meet [Reid]" later with the Union army."[4]

The trio rode the iron horse that night to Baltimore, a city that—like Washington—had fallen to fear thanks to a near brush with Confederate cavalry. From there they hoped to take the train on to Westminster, "but this had been abandoned in terror by the Company, and the rolling stock was all in Philadelphia." Thus, reasoned Reid, "There was nothing for it but to hasten [west] to Frederick, then mount and follow the track of the army."[5]

The night train to Frederick was "crowded to overflowing with citizens . . . willing to take the risks" of venturing into a region that just eighteen hours earlier "the rebels had swarmed across." Luckily it passed without incident, and once in Frederick the threesome found "the *debris*, the offscourings" of their fast-moving quarry. In fact, the town crawled with Union laggards either unable or unwilling to keep pace with the "brilliant forced marches" of their commands. Reid grew incensed. Their presence, especially when "there was sore need for every musket," rubbed coarse every patriotic fiber in his body. He condemned the men as "cowards," "bullying vagabonds," and "the worst elements of a great army."[6] The reporters passed the night in Frederick. Come morning, refreshed and restocked, they would mount the galloping horse and overtake the true men of the blue army.

But when the sun rose on the fateful morning of July 1, Reid's "little party broke up unceremoniously." His "companions thought it better to go back to Baltimore and up to Westminster by rail on the expected Government trains" while Reid "adhered to the original plan of proceeding overland [by mount]." Whether due to luck or his sixth sense as a reporter, Reid chose wisely. After putting spur to steed and covering some distance, he noticed, "The army had moved up the valley of the Monocacy [River] through . . . pleasant little Maryland villages—where in peaceful times Rip Van Winkle might have slumbered undisturbed, [but] the direction seemed too far north for Westminster." And a rider shortly brought word "that [Union] headquarters were not there but rather at Taneytown, a point considerably farther north and west" and much closer to the Maryland-Pennsylvania border. Reid knew what the change in direction meant: "Our movements to the northwest were based upon news similar of a concentration by the rebels. The probabilities of a speedy battle were thus immensely increased, and we hastened the more rapidly on."[7]

Reid prodded ahead. By afternoon he reached Taneytown, "a pleasant little Maryland hamlet" Reid assumed was "named in honor of the Chief Justice of the United States." The courier had spoken the truth. The blue host, at least in large part, tossed about there like a vast, angry ocean. "Army trains blocked up the streets; a group of quartermasters and commissaries were bustling about . . . [and as] far as the eye could reach, rose the glitter from the swaying points of bayonets . . . marching northward."[8]

Reid drew rein and dismounted at army headquarters. "In a plain little wall tent . . . pen in hand, seated on a camp-stool and bending over a map [was] the new 'General Commanding' for the Army of the Potomac": George Gordon Meade. The commander (as of four days earlier) appeared "tall, slender, not ungainly, but certainly not handsome or graceful," Reid wrote. "[He was] apparently between forty-five and fifty years of age—altogether a man who impresses you rather as a thoughtful student than a dashing soldier." Reid had "chanced to hear the President say a few days after [the Union defeat at Chancellorsville back in May], 'I tell you, I think a great deal of that fine fellow Meade.'" Now Reid related the president's comment to Meade's recent promotion: "Here was the result of that good opinion. There is every reason to hope that the events of the next few days will justify it."[9]

With all of the commotion, "clearly something was in the wind." Either the tornado of battle had already touched down nearby, or it would at any moment. Then Lorenzo L. Crounse, "the well-known chief correspondent of the New York *Times* with the Army of the Potomac," the man who wrote the battle's first published words, strode up and "hastily dismounted" next to Reid. The two "exchange[d] hurried salutations" before Crounse explained he had "just returned from a little post village in Southern Pennsylvania, ten or fifteen miles away." There "a fight, of what magnitude he [could not] say, [was] going on."[10]

The battle had at last begun, and Reid stood—armed with quill, ink, and paper—at its threshold. He learned that the "little post village," the place that would "decide the invasion" and "decide whether the war should henceforth be fought on Northern or Southern soil," bore an altogether unassuming name with a suffix as stock as any in the nation: Gettysburg. At that, Reid leapt into his saddle. With Crounse in the lead and history's wind at their back, "Mount and spur for Gettysburg [was], of course, the word." And Reid raced off to record his account.[11]

In late June 1863, the third summer of the American Civil War, Robert E. Lee and his Confederate Army of Northern Virginia marched onto Northern soil with hopes to end the conflict. Meanwhile, the Union Army of the Potomac rushed to meet the invaders under its new commander, George Meade. The two colossal armies, each the largest for their side, were once again set on a collision course. All roads led to the then-unremarkable town of Gettysburg, Pennsylvania, where three days of unparalleled bloodshed produced one of the most remarkable battles of the Civil War.

The Army of the Potomac set out against a disappointing backdrop. Over the preceding year it had lost every major battle to Lee's Confederates save one at Antietam Creek in Maryland. Northern servicemen, politicians, and printers searched high and low for a scapegoat. Ultimate blame fell not on the army's soldiers but instead on the shoulders of its top commanders. President Abraham Lincoln, desperate for a worthy commander, removed four different generals before finally appointing Meade on June 28, just three days before the battle began. The defeat-inspired command changes threatened to smother the army's morale just when the need for victory grew most urgent. The Northern press and public anxiously hoped for the army to reverse what the *New York Times* dubbed its "history of misfortune" and repel Lee's invasion.[12] The federals marched to battle roughly eighty-eight thousand strong.

The Army of Northern Virginia had shined where its counterpart did not. Victory proved the primary variable. The army's triumphant history not only bloated Lee's confidence in his soldiers but also the soldiers' confidence in Lee. After Marse Robert, a nickname favored by his men, beat the Union army back from Richmond's doorstep in 1862, a Georgia soldier wrote to the *Southern Confederacy* that he placed his faith in two sources: "God and Gen. Lee."[13] The Confederate press and public put their trust in Lee almost as much as his men. His successes after taking command in mid-1862—from the Seven Days, Second Bull Run, and Fredericksburg to his latest handiwork at Chancellorsville—got Southern printers to bandy around the word "invincible" and Southerners to attach, in one historian's words, "magnificent expectations" to Lee and his army.[14] The old man hoped to deliver on those high expectations with a smashing victory on Union soil.[15] The opportunity would weigh heavily on his judgment. With morale high, the Army of Northern Virginia departed its namesake with about seventy-five thousand men.

The clash to come was but one scene in a grander drama. While Lee and Meade converged in the Eastern Theater, war's flames raged on elsewhere without waver. In the Volunteer State, the outnumbered rebel Army of Tennessee backpedaled toward northern Georgia, ceding swaths of Southern territory to its Union adversary, the Army of the Cumberland. In the Palmetto State, Union forces marshaled their strength for a new campaign aimed at prying Charleston, the seedbed of secession, free from Confederate hands. And in the southwest, along the Father of Waters, Yankee and rebel forces found themselves locked in a bitter siege for Vicksburg, the Confederate Gibraltar, as well as its smaller cousin, Port Hudson, Louisiana, 150 crow-flight miles southward. Squeezed by the Union anaconda on all fronts, Lee's invasion took on increased importance for the Confederacy. Many looked to it as a valve to relieve the constrictive pressure as well as a beacon to light a path to victory through a summer of darkness. The *Richmond Dispatch* wrote in June, "We look to the future [of Lee's invasion] with increased hope."[16]

That invasion, however, nearly stumbled off its starting block. At dawn on June 9, Union major general Alfred Pleasanton splashed twelve thousand sabers over Virginia's Rappahannock River in a surprise attack aimed at penetrating Lee's cavalry screen. What followed proved the war's largest cavalry battle. Caught off guard, Confederate major general J. E. B. ("Jeb") Stuart and his ten thousand mounts fled in a brume of confusion before Pleasanton's jubilant troopers. But, by midday, surprise's reward turned into a sponge wrung dry. Stuart rallied and ordered a vicious counterattack that by early afternoon drove Pleasanton spattering back over the Rappahannock. The Battle of Brandy Station cost nine hundred federals and five hundred Confederates.[17]

Although Stuart glanced Pleasanton's blow, Brandy Station struck a stinging blow to his pride. Jeb had been caught pants down. "All [reports] seemed to concur," reproached the Richmond *Daily Dispatch*, "our forces were surprised and did not know of the enemy's presence until reports of his artillery were heard."[18] The headline-sensitive Stuart ached for a shot at redemption, and when on June 23 Lee gave Stuart discretion "to judge whether you can pass around their army without hindrance, doing them all the damage you can," he saw his shot.[19] Stuart proceeded to circumnavigate Meade's army on a raid that busted up rail lines, chewed through telegraph wires, and set off tremors of trepidation through Northern cities like Washington and Baltimore. But Lee's discretionary order handed Stuart just enough rope to hang himself and perhaps the rebel army with him. While Stuart's foray won him some of the flattering press he craved in the South, it left Lee fumbling blindly in the North. Reid called it "the most ill advised raid of the war."[20]

Meanwhile, both armies filed through some of the most beautiful landscapes in the country. Starting in early June, the rebels blazed an arcing route northward through the Shenandoah Valley. Girdled by the Blue Ridge and Allegheny Mountains and nourished by the Shenandoah River, this lush land saw fresh water careen down mountainsides to picturesque farms below. Soldier-reporter Captain Virgil A. S. Parks of the Seventeenth Georgia Infantry Regiment and the *Savannah Republican* admired the "deep shady dells and green hills . . . and the towering grandeur of the Blue Ridge."[21] It was the type of scenery that weaved its way into folk songs and, for those fortunate enough to pass through unscathed, became a nostalgic escape amid a terrible civil war.

To head the Confederates off, the Yankees tracked a no less compelling path north through Maryland and southern Pennsylvania. Most of that fertile land remained unmarred by the scars of war. Generations of what Reid called "improvements" saw the region cleared and revealed as rolling farmland. As he traveled with the Union army, Reid appreciated the charm of this "billowy country"—framed in the distance by the Blue Ridge's South Mountain—which "loomed" to the west "amid the morning mists."[22] For a time the Blue Ridge supplied federal soldiers with a stirring backdrop for sunsets and kept, like an inviolable veil, the two armies blissfully apart.

On June 14, the Confederate army dispensed with the only Union obstacle threatening their route onto enemy soil. Lieutenant General Richard Ewell, who filled Stonewall Jackson's cavernous shoes as commander of the Confederate Second Corps, steamrolled the federal garrison at Winchester, Virginia, in the northern Shenandoah. In addition to garnering sorely needed supplies and thousands of Yankee prisoners, the Southern victory at Winchester further dilated the confidence felt within and without Lee's army. One Southern soldier boasted, "The *morale* of the troops was never more favorable . . . victory will inevitably attend our arms."[23] The Richmond *Sentinel* remarked, "Truly, Lee has delivered a good blow, and Ewell has made an admirable start as the successor of the great Jackson."[24] Time would tell whether Ewell would adorn his brow with further laurel wreaths. For now, however, his victory removed the only Union hurdle checking Lee's advance and in so doing, as a pair of historians put it, "opened the door to Gettysburg."[25]

Yet Gettysburg became the battle site not out of some premeditated design but instead out of unpredictable circumstance. Lee planned to concentrate his army on Harrisburg, some forty miles to the northeast, before falling upon, one piece at a time, a strung-out Union army gasping its way northward. But that all changed when the rebels sighted Yankee scouts near South Mountain on June 28, much nearer to Lee's own strung-out army than previously supposed. The old man acted swiftly. To prevent the piecemeal destruction of his own army that he'd had in mind for Meade, Lee ordered the Confederate army to concentrate not on Harrisburg but rather just east of the

Blue Ridge Mountains.[26] From there it was quite simple. Like spokes traced to the center of a wheel, the rebels rendezvoused where the nearest roads of their extended army united: Gettysburg. Union major general Abner Doubleday said Gettysburg functioned as a "junction of seven great roads leading to Hagerstown, Chambersburg, Carlisle, York, Baltimore, Taneytown, and Washington."[27] The clever Charles Carleton Coffin, the *Boston Daily Journal* correspondent who aimed to link up with Reid at the battle, expressed Doubleday's point more creatively: "If you have a map, you will see it [Gettysburg] is a focus for roads north, east, south, west, from nearly all points of the compass. You are reminded of a spider, or a bug, or an old daddy long-legs, with its numerous limbs reaching in all directions."[28] Plainly put, fate favored Gettysburg due to circumstance and its convenience as a crossroads.

On Wednesday, July 1, the earliest spoke tracers collided northwest of Gettysburg. Major General Henry Heth's division of Confederate infantry, after rounding the southern toe of South Mountain, approached the town's outskirts from the northwest. Meanwhile, Major General John Buford's two Union cavalry brigades thundered toward Gettysburg from its southeast, where a series of prominent hills and ridges stippled the farm-checkered landscape like lumps in a great quilt. Buford immediately sensed their importance. Despite being outnumbered nearly two to one, he resolved to stall Heth long enough for Union infantry, whom he urged forward, to arrive and secure the position. Then followed the most famous battle in American history.

Northwest of town, along McPherson Ridge, Buford dismounted his troopers and ensconced for a fight. At 7:30 a.m. it came. The rebels drew within range, and the Yankees rang war's bell with fury. "The division had not advanced more than 100 yards before it became hotly engaged," Heth later recalled.[29] Buford's men plied their repeating carbines with a vigor that inflated their strength, but the fighting wore on and exhaustion exacted a demanding toll. A hail of lead and iron bent and pocked the thin Yankee line as if it were a sutler's tin plate. Without reinforcements Buford risked being overrun before the heights beyond Gettysburg could be secured.

Help arrived just in time. In fact, Buford and his troopers delayed the rebel advance long enough for the Union army's First Corps, under Major General John Reynolds, to arrive in force. Reynolds skillfully swung his infantry into Buford's crumpling line, transforming warped tin into unbent Yankee steel. As if a predator made prey in mid-pounce, Heth was baffled by fortune's reversal. The Union line had just teetered on the brink of collapse, yet now Heth stared down a blue line shored up by fresh infantry who outnumbered his own. The rebels desperately needed reinforcements to maintain the offensive.

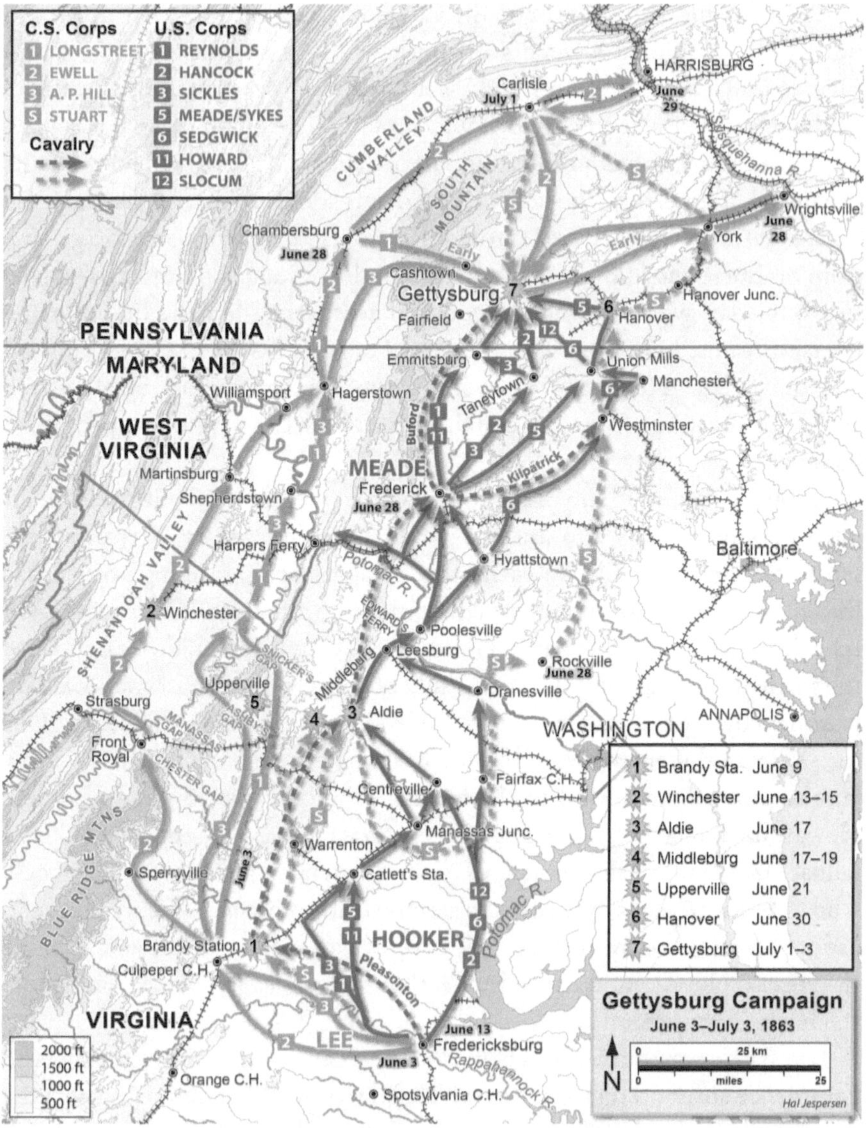

MAP 1 Gettysburg campaign, June 3–July 3, 1863. (Map by Hal Jespersen, www.cwmaps.com)

Then fortune smiled again on the Confederate cause. From the north and northwest, additional elements of the newly formed Third Corps, under Lieutenant General A. P. Hill, and Ewell's Second Corps fell upon the battlefield like a gray avalanche. Reid would lament, "The old, old game was playing. The enemy was concentrating faster than we."[30] After relieving Heth's exhausted Southerners, the larger Confederate force began to overwhelm the federals. A Minié ball ripped through Reynolds's neck, toppling the general from his horse and killing him before he hit the ground. Command devolved to Doubleday, who did what he could to avert crisis, but the tide of battle coursed against him. Even with the arrival of Major General Oliver Howard and the federal Eleventh Army Corps, the mounting Confederate attack could no longer be kept at bay, and the spine of the Union line snapped under its weight.

A rout ensued. With no prearranged path to guide their flight, the blue fugitives poured blindly into the grid-patterned town from a variety of points. Hosts of men slammed into each other at right angles, forming bottlenecks that all but caused the blue stampede to clot into a standstill. Meanwhile, the rebels fanned the flame of panic. Omitting opportunists who broke off to loot the town, they hounded the rattled Yankees block by block and swallowed up prisoners by the thousands. The *Richmond Dispatch* would soon beam, "Our forces drove the enemy from the town that afternoon."[31] The Union survivors scrambled southward to the heights scouted earlier by Buford where Howard had detached a portion of his federals to secure Cemetery Hill as a fallback position. With the help of Major General Winfield Scott Hancock, who rode ahead of his own corps to assume field command, reserve units and artillery batteries crowning the hill covered the Union retreat and stopped the rebels cold. As Reid fancied it, "A thunderbolt leaped out . . . and smote them where they stood."[32]

Lee had reached the battlefield hours earlier and given Ewell orders to commence an attack on Cemetery Hill "if practical."[33] But unlike Jackson, the man he replaced, the recent champion of Winchester hesitated to exploit Lee's open-ended instructions. Ewell seemed indecisive just when the moment demanded Stonewall's trademark tenacity. An officer who served under Jackson before Ewell is said to have howled, "Oh, for the presence and inspiration of Old Jack for just one hour!"[34] But Ewell declined to press the attack, and Cemetery Hill went untaken.

Whether or not Ewell missed a golden opportunity, the Confederates had already achieved a stunning victory.[35] Much happened that first day. Of the roughly twenty-four thousand Confederate and nineteen thousand Union

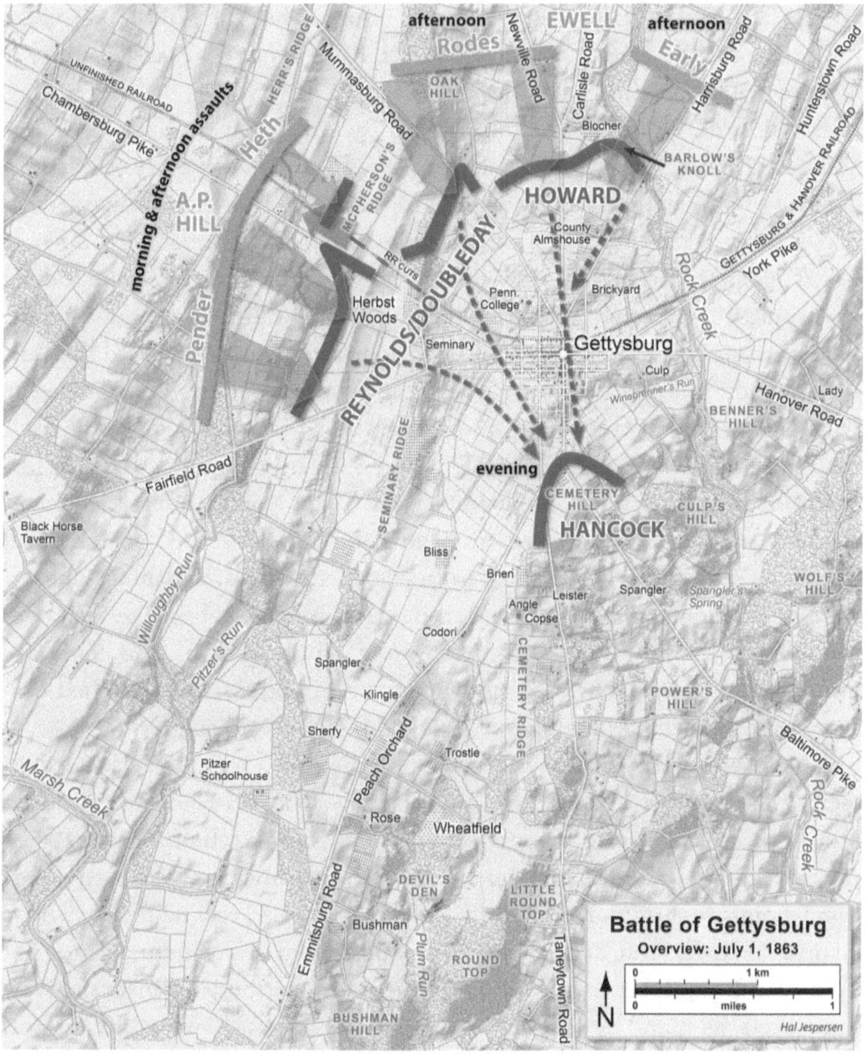

MAP 2 Battle of Gettysburg, overview: July 1, 1863. (Map by Hal Jespersen, www.cwmaps.com)

soldiers engaged, over ten thousand lay dead or wounded—a grisly milestone matched or exceeded only thirteen times during any single day of the war.[36] Although each side eclipsed five thousand killed and wounded, the rebels bagged, according to Lee, "more than four thousand prisoners."[37] And although Heth suffered a bullet-grazing wound to his head, one that left him indisposed for the remainder of the battle, Reynolds suffered a life-ending wound that left the federals deprived of one of their senior officers. Once again Marse Robert had dealt a hammer blow to the Army of the Potomac. Reporting for the *Cincinnati Daily Gazette*, Reid wrote charitably, "Today it had opened for us—*not* favorably."[38]

But Buford, Doubleday, Howard, and Reynolds rendered Lee's victory hollow. Their sacrifice, albeit costly, endowed Meade with a priceless gift: a defensive battle with the advantages of high ground and interior lines. South of Gettysburg, the Union line ran along the brows and intervening saddles of Culp's Hill, Cemetery Hill, and Cemetery Ridge. Its concave shape looked like a great bow drawn tight before loosing an arrow. Lee's army, meanwhile, took position to Gettysburg's south and southeast—where it faced the Yankees already industriously employing the spade on Culp's and Cemetery Hills—as well as to Gettysburg's southwest along Seminary Ridge, where it eyed the Yankees entrenching on Cemetery Ridge. The Southern army's orientation boded ill. The Confederate First Corps commander, Lieutenant General James Longstreet, regretted how the army assumed an "elliptical curve" spanning several miles just to face its foe.[39] The disadvantage of exterior lines not only spread the soon-to-be outnumbered rebels like seed over too much soil but also threatened to impair communication and coordination between the ends of their sprawled wings. In brief, Lee's stretched-thin army risked its left hand not knowing what its right hand doeth.

That evening the Confederates debated their next move. Lee favored attack, while Longstreet, who had outranked even the beloved Jackson as the army's second-in-command, preferred maneuvering to better ground. Lee pressed his commanders, "If the enemy is there tomorrow, we must attack him." Longstreet demurred. "If the enemy is there, it will be because he is anxious that we should attack him—a good reason in my judgment for not doing so." Longstreet then countered Lee's proposition with his own. Why not, asked the man Lee knighted as his "Old Warhorse," swing the Army of Northern Virginia around Meade's left to interpose it between the enemy and Washington? Doing so would compel Meade to attack on ground chosen by the Confederates, not the other way around. After all, added Longstreet, "Meade's army, not its position, was our objective."[40] But his plea fell on deaf ears. The army's July 1 success narrowed Lee's thinking like scoping a target narrowed one's sight. Only by renewing the attack, thought Marse Robert, could he consummate the greater victory now underway.[41] Coffin agreed. He wrote of July 1, "[Lee] was flushed by success. He was confident. He had beaten us. . . . He felt he could always do it."[42] Though no decision came that evening, Longstreet left convinced Lee had fixed his mind on attack.

Confederate command reconvened at sunrise on Thursday, July 2. Longstreet again advised slipping around Meade's left to sever the Union artery to Washington and spare the rebels a costly attack against an entrenched enemy on high ground. But this time Lee vetoed the idea outright. The wheel of war then turned in the opposite direction: suggestions of attack against the enemy's present position. Ewell and his top-ranking division commander, Major General Jubal Early, asserted that the federal position on Cemetery and Culp's Hills was unassailable. Lee agreed, noting that an initial attack by Ewell on the enemy's right "would not do."[43] The growing consensus called for an attack elsewhere to divert Union forces from these heights. All eyes fell on Longstreet. His corps remained unsullied at Gettysburg due to its later arrival on July 1. At 11:00 a.m. on July 2, after some haphazard reconnaissance thanks to Stuart's continued absence, Lee ordered Longstreet to spearhead the initial attack on the enemy's left.

The Confederate plan that day seemed simple enough. After Longstreet's First Corps launched its offensive on the Union left, Ewell's Second Corps would strike the Union right, while Hill's Third Corps performed an ancillary demonstration to occupy the Union center. The sequenced flank attacks might first soften the Union defenses on Cemetery and Culp's Hills by dredging up bluecoats from their right to buttress their left. But once Ewell untethered his attack, Meade's troops would be pinned down on both sides by the clamping jaws of two Confederate corps. If all went well, Longstreet and Ewell would roll up and over the federal army's flanks like ocean surf. With Longstreet's last division, that of Major General George Pickett, still en route to the battlefield, a division from Hill's corps would support Longstreet's assault.

About one mile away the Yankees consolidated their position. Throughout the night of July 1 and predawn morning of July 2 they proved their stereotype for ingenuity true. Tirelessly and methodically, they stacked rocks, felled trees, and excavated the dew-sodden earth. At Hancock's behest, Meade arrived on scene from Taneytown at 12:00 a.m. on July 2. By sunrise, six of his seven infantry corps stood ready to defend the heights south of Gettysburg. The absent Sixth Corps—with nearly fifteen thousand men under the capable command of Major General John Sedgwick—camped southeast of Gettysburg near Manchester, Maryland, on the evening of July 1. At dusk Sedgwick received a dispatch from Meade, ordering his corps to hasten at once to Gettysburg. The blue army, indicated Meade, would make its stand there. Sedgwick wasted no time. His men marched a remarkable thirty-two miles nonstop in order to play a role in the battle to come.

Meanwhile, Lee sent Longstreet orders to move discretely beyond sight of federal signal stations with one of Lee's handpicked engineers leading the column.[44] The Confederate First Corps cut south from Seminary Ridge and carved a path parallel to the Emmitsburg Road. The Union army's position on Cemetery Ridge rose to the east separated by an innocuous wheat field and peach orchard. To the southeast loomed a pair of sister peaks: Little Round Top and Big Round Top.

The Confederates made sluggish progress. Crossing unfamiliar ground with twenty thousand men while upholding Lee's order to keep them unexposed postponed Longstreet's offensive. Georgia's Peter Wellington Alexander, reporting for the *Savannah Republican*, complained, "Much time was lost before the movement upon the enemy's flank could be executed."[45] The delay on the heels of his appeal for a different attack plan made Longstreet an easy target for blame after the battle. He opened the offensive at 4:00 p.m. that day, five hours after Lee issued the order.[46]

When the federal signal station on Little Round Top spotted the rebels, the need for speed replaced the need for stealth. Major General John Bell Hood's division sidled toward the federals' far left flank near Little Round Top. Meanwhile, Major General Lafayette McLaws's division veered east toward Cemetery Ridge's tapered edge. Musket and cannon fire instantly erupted and not where the rebels expected it. McLaws advanced no farther than the Emmitsburg Road before encountering stiff resistance. Major General Dan Sickles, commanding the Union Third Corps, disputed his passage. In a wild gamble, Sickles had abandoned his Meade-assigned post at the southern end of Cemetery Ridge and took position in the wheat field and peach orchard to his front. Although the unauthorized move afforded Sickles higher ground on which to plant his artillery, it laid bare a perilous vulnerability. As if exposing a limb to wolves, Sickles had created a salient in the Union line. Longstreet sensed an opportunity and threw his men forward in force.

The once erratic musket fire now roared constantly like the sound of tearing sheets. "It was furious," jotted Coffin. The rebels "came with cheers, yells like Indians sounding a warhoop."[47] Though Sickles made a determined stand, the Confederates flooded forward and engulfed his lone corps. His gamble had backfired. Even with support streaming in from the Fifth Corps and elements of the Eleventh Corps, the federal line imploded. The Southerners unlimbered their artillery, trundled several pieces into the peach orchard, and, from the very heightened spot Sickles thought advantageous, showered the fleeing Yankees in a gale of shot and shell. Screaming like banshees, Confederate infantry spilled down the backside of the orchard in pursuit. As artillery splintered trees into fragments and shattered bones like glass, many bluecoats ditched their firearms to accelerate their flight. The rebels welled forward.

But, as afternoon gave way to early dusk, the Confederate momentum began to stall. Union major general George Sykes, commanding the Fifth Corps, helped secure Little Round Top and a boulder-ladened gorge fringed by woods to its northwest since known as Devil's Den.[48] Sickles's retreating men, trussed by reinforcements ordered up by Meade, formed a new defensive line that melded with Sykes's. When the rebels reached Devil's Den, the base of Little Round Top, and the southern bank of Cemetery Ridge, they found themselves fighting uphill against fresh federal troops. "We felt at every step the heavy stroke of fresh troops," recalled Longstreet, "the sturdy regular blow that tells a soldier instantly that he has encountered reserves or reinforcements."[49]

"Hotter grew the fire," bayed the *Boston Daily Journal* five days later.[50] Hood's men pushed into Devil's Den with heavy loss as sharpshooters and artillerists checked their advance. The blue line reeled to the nape of Devil's Den, but it inflicted irreparable damage along the way. Confederate soldiers dragged Hood from the battlefield after an artillery blast severely injured his left arm. And the rebel soldier-reporter Captain Parks lost his life valiantly charging into battle alongside his men.[51] At Little Round Top, near battle's edge, one Confederate line after another clawed up a labyrinth of pine, boulders, and scree to beset the federals infixed on its summit. Although the Yankees parried each attack, every collision chipped away at their defense. It remained unclear whether the federal left would hold or roll up like a rug.

Colonel Joshua Lawrence Chamberlain, commanding the Twentieth Maine, anchored the outermost edge of the Union line on Little Round Top's crest.[52] The fighting at this critical location raged so furiously that Chamberlain's regiment completely exhausted its ammunition. Suspecting Hood's men to be spent, Chamberlain ordered a risky bayonet charge down Little Round Top. Unlike Sickles's gamble, Chamberlain's paid off. The shocked rebels either bolted or hoisted their hands in surrender. Heroism abounded as the fighting crescendoed to its denouement like a manic chorus. Coffin exclaimed, "What deeds of valor were performed! There were many heroes that day."[53] Longstreet's men made progress, but the federals now dug their heels in deep. The Southern onslaught could not be sustained without help.

To worsen the rebels' situation, Sedgwick's Sixth Corps began arriving via the Baltimore Pike. Their backbreaking trek took a toll. Matilda Pierce, a

MAP 3 Battle of Gettysburg, overview: July 2, 1863. (Map by Hal Jespersen, www.cwmaps.com)

teenage Gettysburg native, noticed at least one "worn-out soldier crawling along on his hands and knees" as he neared the battlefield.[54] Meade could not afford to wait for the Sixth Corps to catch its breath. He ordered Sedgwick's men instantly into the fray to support Sykes and Sickles. The tired troops still had plenty of strength left to fight. A *New-York Tribune* correspondent said that when "the situation flashed into the minds of these weary soldiers, the fire and zeal . . . was kindled anew in their hearts."[55] Sedgwick's timely arrival helped thwart Longstreet's final lunge. The Confederates withdrew to the peach orchard, ending the fight on the Union left.

At about six thirty that evening, Ewell sprang his offensive against the Union right. The Confederate Second Corps charged the Union defenders on Cemetery and Culp's Hills with great loss and little success. Since Ewell did not coordinate his attack with Longstreet, but instead began just as Longstreet's subsided, Meade pivoted reinforcements from the left of his interior line to support the right. As the *New-York Tribune* explained, "The 1st and 6th Corps came up promptly to the [right flank's] support [and] repulsed [Ewell] with terrible slaughter."[56] Though Ewell won a foothold at the base of Culp's Hill, the federal position remained mostly intact. The fight ended at about ten that night.

Much occurred that second day, yet little changed. Each side endured an estimated nine thousand casualties. A *New York Herald* reporter saw that an artillery shell had "so badly shattered" Sickles's right leg "that it hung merely by a shred."[57] Hood's injury left his left arm to hang limp for the remainder of his life, and he was replaced for the remainder of the battle. Similar to the first day, the Confederates broke through the initial federal position like a battering ram. But after reforming their line, the Yankees halted the Confederate ram and heaved it back in retreat. The federals' defense on July 2 both ensured and strengthened their terrain advantage. In contrast, the Confederates failed to achieve their objective to uproot and rout the Yankees. While Longstreet saw this as irrefutable proof that the Union position could not be taken, his commanding general saw the situation differently. Lee explained in his report, "Longstreet succeeded in getting . . . the desired ground. Ewell also carried some of the strong positions which he assailed. . . . These partial successes determined me to continue the assault next day."[58]

That night the stage already appeared set for one more act of violence. A combined 130,000 men—the entirety of both armies after two days of decimating combat—now bivouacked in their respective conurbations, which fanned out as thick as carpet on the fields, ridges, and hills south of Gettysburg. Sedgwick's timely entrance onto the stage of battle made the Army of the Potomac whole. Meade's seven corps now clung to a three-mile-long position shaped like an inverted fishhook. The eye stood watch over both round tops, a vantage that commanded the battlefield's southern edge. From there the fishhook extended its shank north along the backbone of Cemetery Ridge, then swerved east to form its clockwise bend over Cemetery and Culp's Hills, before finally jutting south to sink its barbed point at the Baltimore Pike. Meade consolidated this position throughout the night and, following military convention, shuffled reinforcements to patch up the bludgeoned wings of his army.

Yet Meade remained apprehensive. Over the preceding two days, the federal First, Eleventh, Third, Fifth, and even portions of the Second Corps had confronted a rebel Scylla and Charybdis and survived only by teeth's skin. Combined they had suffered no less than eighteen thousand casualties, more than the entire army had suffered in its defeat at Chancellorsville two months earlier. Only the Sixth and Twelfth Corps, the former of which had just now caught its breath, could be considered anything approaching fresh. Kneeling to caution, Meade convened a late-night council of war.

The Army of the Potomac's corps commanders met in the dark, cramped quarters of a nearby farmhouse. Meade put to them the ultimate question: should the Union army, after two days and five bruised corps, stay put or withdraw to a stronger position nearer to Washington? Meade's council of war refused to take counsel of its fears.[59] The vote was unanimous. The Army of the Potomac would "stay and fight it out."[60]

The Army of Northern Virginia strung itself out in the shape of a horned moon in order to face the blue fishhook. But the rebels could take heart, for the night of July 2 also saw their army made whole. Pickett's division of Longstreet's corps, which made up the last note in the army's staccato march into Pennsylvania, strode into camp at about the same time as Stuart's much-anticipated cavalry. After reproving Jeb for a raid that left him blind in enemy country, Lee turned his mind to the fight yet to come. He saw in the arrival of both men a pair of untapped and unblunted weapons—swords fresh from the whetstone—and, although he had not yet disclosed the plan concreting in his mind, Lee intended to use these up to the hilt in a masterstroke that would make Gettysburg for him and the Confederacy what Austerlitz had been for Napoleon some six decades earlier.

On Friday morning, July 3, Ewell and Longstreet prepared to renew the attack as outlined the day before. Ewell would storm the federals' right on Culp's Hill while Longstreet reignited the flame of battle on the enemy's left. This time, however, Longstreet planned to pass around both round tops to gain the federals' flank and attack them from reverse.[61]

Just before Longstreet put the plan in motion, Lee rode up with new orders. Longstreet was to organize the divisions of Major Generals Pickett, Heth, and William Dorsey Pender for a concentrated offensive against the linchpin of the federal position: Cemetery Ridge. (Due to injuries suffered by both Heth and Pender, however, command of their divisions fell respectively to Brigadier General James Pettigrew and Major General Isaac Trimble.)[62] Lee's reasoning seemed sound. The fight the day before would have compelled Meade to reinforce his overtaxed flanks at the expense of his untouched center. Cemetery Ridge, the Union line's radial point, would be a muscle stripped to the sinew. Concentrating a three-division, fifteen-thousand-man charge at that under-defended point would be like driving a heavy lance through an overlooked chink in armor. The force of the focused thrust would collapse the Union center and take Meade's entire position with it in a *coup de maître* worthy of Napoleon. So Lee thought. But, as with anything Napoleonic, risk matched reward. The plan called for Southerners to cross nearly a mile of open ground, uphill and under constant fire, just to breach the Union line.

Longstreet shuddered at the image. He saw nothing sound in Lee's reasoning and offered an alternative before expressing his doubts. "General, I have had my scouts out all night, and I find that you still have an excellent opportunity to move around to the right of Meade's army and maneuver him into attacking us." Lee interdicted. The old man raised one hand, pointed directly at Cemetery Ridge, and stated sternly, "The enemy is there, and I am going to strike him." With his alternative buried, Longstreet questioned an assault on Cemetery Ridge with a bluntness he hoped might move his commander. "General, I have been a soldier all my life. I . . . should know, as well as any one, what soldiers can do. It is my opinion that no fifteen thousand men ever arrayed for battle can take that position."[63] But Lee, known before the war as "the Marble Man" for his statue-like facade, refused to budge from his plinth. Longstreet acquiesced. Rebuked for the last time, he began preparing for an offensive against the Union center.

Meanwhile, Ewell renewed his attack on Culp's Hill, attempting to finish the work he began the day before. A vicious carnage, which would be overshadowed by events to come, consumed the Union right. With an ocean-like relentlessness, wave after wave of Confederates roiled forward and crashed against the federal defenses on Culp's Hill. Every ebbing attack uncovered more misery in its wake. A rebel infantryman recalled a wounded comrade "between the lines, asking for friends to take him out," but because "no one could get to his relief," they left him to die "or at best, become a prisoner."[64] According to Coffin's report for the *Boston Daily Journal*, Ewell's men "held on with dogged pertinacity."[65] But after a federal counterattack, his corps suffered a grievous repulse. The Second North Carolina Battalion alone lost 200 of its 240 men.[66] The fighting here ended around 11:00 a.m. Thereafter an unnerving lull, the pause between breath's draw and truth's moment, fell upon the battlefield.

To complement Longstreet's impending assault on Cemetery Ridge, Stuart's cavalry jockeyed behind the Union army. Lee hoped the move might divert some of Meade's forces from the main battle site and position Stuart to exploit a possible federal retreat. At noon, Union and Confederate cavalry sparred three miles east of Gettysburg. The spectacular contest featured bold charges and horrific moments of hand-to-hand combat. Major General David Gregg's federal cavalry, with the help of an intrepid twenty-three-year-old brigadier general named George Custer, successfully defended the Union rear. The Confederate diversion failed. Each side lost around 240 men.

Back at the main battle site, just after 1:00 p.m., the unsettling recess abruptly ended. One hundred seventy Confederate cannons, the war's largest concentration of field artillery, opened fire on the Union position at Cemetery Ridge to pave the way for Longstreet's infantry. Not to be outdone, federal artillerists answered the Confederate challenge. Soon a dueling chorus of hundreds of cannons briefly deafened those nearby, caused the ground to quake, and kicked up clouds of blinding smoke and dust that temporarily obscured the battlefield. Virginian Jonathon W. Albertson, reporting for the *Richmond Enquirer*, painted the scene: "The very earth shook beneath our feet and the hills seemed to reel like a drunken man. For one hour and a half this most terrific fire was continued. . . . [It] made a picture terribly grand and sublime, but which my pen utterly fails to describe."[67]

At about two thirty the federals slowed and then ceased their firing. Meade wanted to preserve ammunition for any forthcoming attack while fooling the rebels into thinking that they silenced the Union guns. Even though the Confederates mostly overshot their targets, the ploy worked. Perceiving success, the rebels reined in their artillery and prepared to advance their infantry. The temperature, meanwhile, climbed toward a humid ninety degrees Fahrenheit.

Pickett, who helped lead the assault, asked Longstreet, "General, shall I advance?" Longstreet, overcome with emotion—the need to order an attack he deemed doomed—did not speak but merely nodded in reply. Three Confederate divisions emerged from the shelter of the woods along Seminary Ridge. Their line stretched a mile wide. Federal troops on Cemetery Ridge peered over a stone wall in bewilderment at the flawlessly arrayed column. Reid gaped at the rebels, "'dressed to the right' as if for a parade before some grand master of reviews."[68] Some 5,750 Union infantrymen initially stood ready to face the 15,000-man Southern charge. As Lee expected, Meade fortified his army's extremities at the expense of its vitals. Only elements of the Union Second Corps, commanded by Hancock, at first defended Cemetery Ridge. Coffin called it "our weakest point" and feared a "break through" against "the thin line of men at the second corps."[69] Meade recognized the danger as well. The Union commander ordered Doubleday's division and General George Stannard's brigade to support Hancock.[70] With interior lines, the movement did not take long.

Once in the open it became obvious that the Confederate artillery had failed to silence the Union guns. Muzzle-loading twelve-pounder Napoleons, named after French Emperor Napoleon III, pitched into the charging Confederates from the apices of Cemetery Ridge. The cannon fire punched small holes in the rebel line, which the Southerners filled like running water into breaks. "On came the Rebels," penned a *New-York Tribune* correspondent.[71] It seemed the men in gray would reach the federal line intact.

But as the Confederates hurtled themselves across the rolling country of southern Pennsylvania, nearing the federal line, Union artillerists swapped the twelve-pounders for canister and let fly a raking fire. The once picturesque Confederate column, a portrait of military precision all witnesses found unforgettable, began to crumble. Southerners fell in bulk, sometimes by the dozens, and their line began to bunch like schooling fish. Longstreet's artillery, drained of ammunition from the earlier barrage, could not mask the waning rebel charge. Albertson cried in his report, "Why do not our guns reopen fire . . . our batteries are silent as death!"[72] Then Hancock's men loosed their muskets at two hundred yards from behind the stone wall.[73] According to Reid, the rebel assault "literally melted away."[74]

A few hundred Confederates, led by Brigadier General Lewis Armistead, did puncture the initial Union line, briefly flying Confederate flags on Cemetery Ridge. But these men found themselves drowning in a sea of Union blue as their own comrades fled across the bloodstained ground whence they came. The day was lost. Like Icarus, Lee had flown too close to the sun. His vision of a Napoleonic victory vanished before his eyes in less than half an hour.[75] Reid said, "It was not a rout, it was a bitter crushing defeat."[76] Pickett's Charge left seventy-five hundred rebels on the field.

As the mangled mass of survivors staggered back to Seminary Ridge, Lee confessed, "It is all my fault." Southern soldiers, first by the hundreds and then by the thousands, collapsed in a traumatic state of exhaustion upon reaching the presumed safety of their line. The Confederate mindset soon

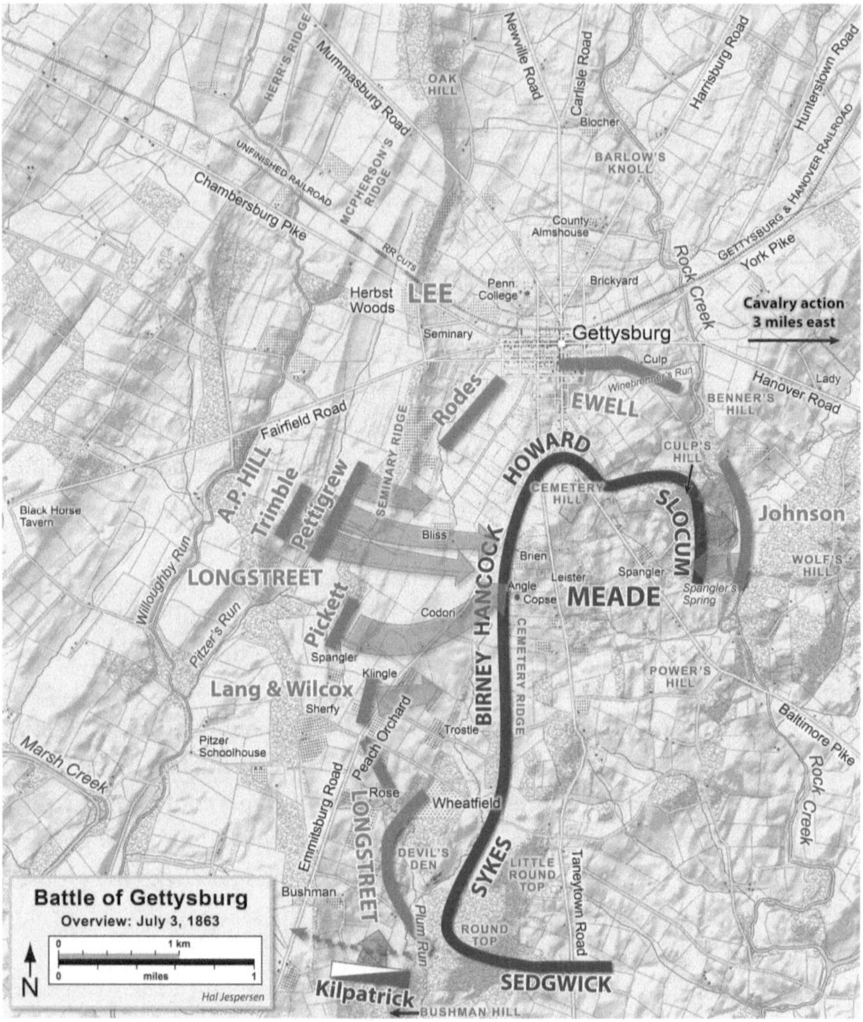

MAP 4 Battle of Gettysburg, overview July 3, 1863. (Map by Hal Jespersen, www.cwmaps.com)

switched, however, from self-deprecation to self-preservation. The magnitude of their failure handed Meade a prime opportunity to counterattack. Longstreet and Lee began rallying all able-bodied men and spare artillery to form a defensive line. Lee shouted, "It is I who have lost this fight, and you must help me out of it the best way you can. All good men must rally."[77] He even instructed Pickett, who had just lost nearly two-thirds of his division, where to place his few remaining men. In tears, Pickett keened, "General Lee, I have no division now." Recognizing Pickett's anguish, Lee replied gently,

"Come, General Pickett, this has been my fight and upon my shoulders rests the blame."[78] The broken rebels mustered what little defense they could. Fortunately for them, Meade's counterattack never came.[79]

One mile to the east, *New York Times* reporter Sam Wilkeson cheered, "Our troops hold the field . . . the enemy has been magnificently repulsed." The rebels had indeed been magnificently repulsed, the question now became whether or not they would be pressed to ruin's end.[80] Despite taking a bullet to the thigh while defending Cemetery Ridge, Hancock pleaded with Meade to throw forth the army's reserves and chase down Lee's battle-blighted divisions. But Meade had commanded the Army of the Potomac for just six days, half of which he spent simply trying not to lose the war.[81] Attacking Lee, the master of so many battlefields, troubled Meade, who feared replicating Lee's mistake by flinging federal forces at the Confederate guns lining Seminary Ridge. Why, thought Meade, reward the rebels' recklessness with like rashness?

Meade faced a dilemma, one complicated by Lee's reputation and a shortage of information. He knew the Southerners had suffered a heavy blow, but he knew not to what degree or that their artillery ammunition was critically low. Moreover, Meade knew that Stuart threatened his rear but remained unaware in the moment that Gregg had neutralized the threat. Over-respecting his enemy and fearing the unknown, Meade played the conservative hand. He told his officers, "We have done well enough."[82] With the exception of some minor skirmishing, the Battle of Gettysburg ended around 3:00 p.m. on July 3.

Like hieroglyphs carved into an ancient temple, that day forever incised Gettysburg as a Confederate defeat. The rebels attacked and were hurled back with appalling loss. Pickett's division virtually no longer existed. Four thousand rebel soldiers fell into Yankee hands, and Lee reported another five thousand missing. Unable to accommodate its wounded, the Confederate army left thousands behind for tending by Union surgeons. Regarding the decision to assault Cemetery Ridge, Alberton's colleague at the *Richmond Enquirer*—an unidentified reporter writing under the pseudonym "X"—perceptively remarked, "I believe Gen. Lee was led to this by overweening confidence in his troops."[83] Lee himself told Longstreet, "It is all my fault, I thought my men were invincible." For his part, Lee's "Old Warhorse" saw Gettysburg as a lost opportunity, reflecting later, "great results would have been obtained had my views been thought better of."[84] All told, the Army of the Potomac lost more than a quarter of its strength—some twenty-three thousand casualties out of eighty-eight thousand. But the South fared far worse. The Army of Northern

Virginia suffered an irreplaceable twenty-eight thousand casualties out of seventy-five thousand, over a third of its strength.[85] This great human cost distinguished Gettysburg as the bloodiest battle of the American Civil War.

On the following day, July 4, the Union had more to celebrate than just Gettysburg "four score and seven years" after the nation's founding.[86] Nearly a thousand miles to the southwest, the war's longest campaign finally ended. Union general Ulysses S. Grant accepted Vicksburg's surrender, along with its garrison of thirty thousand men. The capture of the rebel river fortress, followed shortly by Port Hudson, not only reopened the Mississippi to commerce from tail to mouth but in so doing also rent the South in two at the hip. The rupture would paralyze coordination between the Confederacy's two halves until war's end. While a blithe Lincoln felt free to write "The Father of Waters goes again unvexed to the sea," the crestfallen *Richmond Dispatch* printer felt compelled to concede, "The fall of Vicksburg is a heavy blow."[87] Indeed it was. Vicksburg's loss forever shifted the winds of war in the Western Theater against the South.

The day the Confederate Gibraltar fell, Lee began his retreat to Virginia. Torrential rains added insult to the march home. Roads muddied into all but impassable bogs, and the Potomac River, which separated the rebels from the safety of Southern soil, swelled to seemingly uncrossable levels. Traveling with the Army of Northern Virginia, Alexander described the situation as "vexatious": "[Should Meade attack and cause a] disaster to our arms [the] Potomac . . . would render escape impossible."[88] But rather than accept nature's helping hand, Meade again played the conservative one. On July 13, the Potomac floodwaters receded, and the tattered rebel army escaped into Virginia, as Lee put it, "without molestation."[89]

Meade's tepidness reaped the excoriation of Lincoln. Though he never sent it, the president wrote in a letter intended for Meade, "[Lee] was within your easy grasp, and to have closed upon him would, in connection with our other late successes, have ended the war. As it is, the war will be prolonged indefinitely."[90] The press soon caught wind of Lincoln's frustration. Reid wrote in his report, "The President declares Lee's escape the greatest blunder of the war."[91]

Despite the campaign's conclusion, Gettysburg—especially when considered with the strategic Union victory at Vicksburg—was the high-water mark of the Confederacy and a major turning point of the war in Union favor. The Confederacy lost one of its last opportunities to gain foreign recognition and resuscitate the prospect of peace on the grounds of Confederate nationhood.

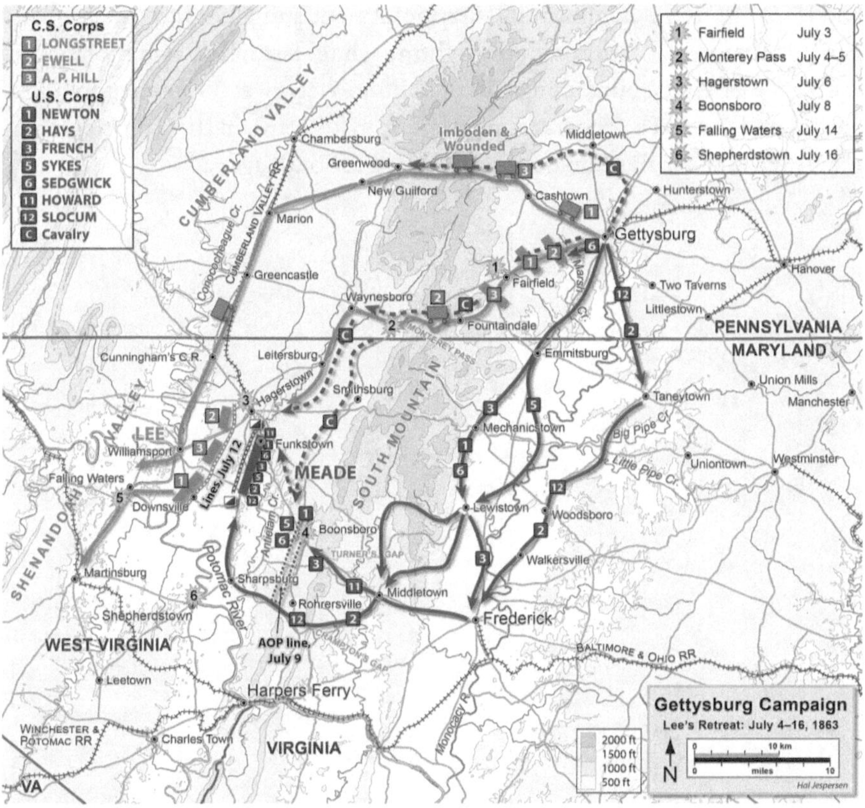

MAP 5 Gettysburg campaign, Lee's retreat: July 4–16, 1863. (Map by Hal Jespersen, www.cwmaps.com)

Lee's army never recovered its pre-Gettysburg strength. After the battle the *North Carolina Standard* observed, "We are weaker today than when he crossed the Potomac into Maryland. . . . Our fighting population is well exhausted."[92] The manpower loss not only closed off the possibility of another major Confederate invasion of the North but also forced Lee to fight the defensive war of attrition that he feared ruinous. As long as Northerners could stomach a slow and costly march to victory, they would achieve it. As it was, Gettysburg revived Northern morale to that end. Talk of peace faded, at least for a time, and morale skyrocketed. The *Richmond Enquirer* admitted, "Nobody at the North *now* speaks of peace, save on the terms of submission to the Union."[93] The "history of misfortune" burdening the Army of the Potomac was lifted with the North's morale. The *New York Times* declared that the army had leapt "from the depths of its disappointment and gloom to the height of glory and success."[94] Although the fighting would last nearly two more years, the Battle of Gettysburg alongside the Union victory at Vicksburg are often considered the war's watershed moment, for afterward, in the words of historian Allen Guelzo, the "sun never shone for the South again."[95]

President Abraham Lincoln
(1809–1865)

The sixteenth president of the United States knew well the power of newsmen to shape public opinion toward the war. Lincoln read newspapers religiously and gave interviews sparingly, knowing he would likelier say something self-defeating than self-promoting. In contrast to his Southern counterpart, the Illinoisan was not above placating the press. When a *New York Herald* correspondent complained that Navy Secretary Gideon Welles had refused him passage down the Potomac, Lincoln not only intervened on the correspondent's behalf but also personally wrote Bennett a letter of apology. With the assassin's bullet less than two years off, he was fifty-four during the Gettysburg campaign. (Photograph by Alexander Gardner, Library of Congress)

President Jefferson Davis
(1808–1889)

If the Confederacy's first and only president knew the power of the press, he did not act accordingly. The elitism of a great planter followed him to the Confederate White House like a dark shadow. Unlike his Northern counterpart, Davis viewed any effort to propitiate pressmen as beneath his high office. He gave even fewer interviews than Lincoln, and, whereas Lincoln could at least feign warmth toward opposition printers, he could not hide his icy disdain. Had he Lincoln's Midwest humility, the Mississippian might have harnessed more of the Southern press behind his vision for the Confederacy. Instead, the opportunity passed him by. He turned fifty-five when the Gettysburg campaign began. (Brady-Handy Photographic Collection, Library of Congress)

General George Meade
(1815–1872)

Born in Cadiz, Spain, and raised in Philadelphia, Pennsylvania, Meade graduated nineteenth of fifty-six from the U.S. Military Academy at West Point in 1835. When war broke out in 1861, he commanded a single brigade. At Gettysburg two years later, he commanded the largest army in the Union. He distrusted newsmen even more than he distrusted politicians. The aftermath of Gettysburg only exacerbated the sentiment. When he crossed swords with Lee on the soil of his home state, he was forty-seven years old. (Brady-Handy Photographic Collection, Library of Congress)

General Robert E. Lee
(1807–1870)

Hailing from one of Virginia's great families, Lee graduated second of forty-six from West Point in 1829 without a single demerit to his proud name. He won national notoriety in 1859 for mopping up John Brown's raid on the federal arsenal at Harpers Ferry. When he took command of the Confederate army in 1862, the Southern press mocked him as "Granny Lee," "Evacuating Lee," and "the King of Spades." A year later, he became "Marse Robert," "the Great Tycoon," and, with affection, "the Old Man." He rode to Gettysburg fifty-six years old. (Photograph by P. E. Gibbs, Liljenquist Family Collection, Library of Congress)

Major General J. E. B. Stuart
(1833–1864)

One of Virginia's great cavaliers, Stuart graduated West Point thirteenth of forty-six in 1854. Lee, then the college's superintendent, sensed his promise. Before the war, Stuart served under Lee at Harpers Ferry and did not disappoint, nor did he in the war's first two years. But the summer of 1863 proved exceptional. His fragile ego and taste for theatrics led to an ill-timed raid that, as Lee saw it, forced the Confederate army's hand at Gettysburg. When the thirty-year-old cavalry chief belatedly cantered into camp on July 2, his old superintendent gave him a scathing. Apart from Brandy Station, however, the Southern press largely let him off unscathed. (Joseph H. Taylor Album, National Archives)

Lieutenant General Richard Ewell
(1817–1872)

Another scion of the Old Dominion, Ewell graduated West Point thirteenth of forty-two in 1840. He proved his mettle early in the war serving under Stonewall Jackson in the Shenandoah Valley. In August 1862, he took a bullet that forced surgeons to take his left leg. Outfitted with a wooden prosthetic and driving his own one-horse buggy, he returned to action in the spring of 1863—just in time to succeed the late Stonewall as commander of Lee's Second Corps. But his corps-command debut at Gettysburg proved no less disappointing than Stuart's handling of the Confederate cavalry. Some Southern pressmen noticed; more should have. "Old Baldy," as his men warmly called him, came to Gettysburg forty-six years old. (Library of Congress)

Major General Dan Sickles
(1819–1914)

Even among a band of wartime characters, New York's Dan Sickles stuck out. Before the war he shot his wife's lover, Philip Barton Key (son of "Star-Spangled Banner" author Francis Scott Key), in cold blood and in broad daylight. At the trial, he pled temporary insanity and literally got away with murder. During the war, he won a command not through professional soldiering but instead through savvy politicking. It showed. At Gettysburg, Longstreet broke him and broke his corps. Yet as litter bearers ushered the injured forty-three-year-old from the battlefield, he lived up to his larger-than-life character: he reportedly struck a match, lit a cigar, and waved his men onward. Of all the Union commanders who least deserved positive press, he received the most. (National Portrait Gallery, Smithsonian; Frederick Hill Meserve Collection)

Lieutenant General James Longstreet
(1821–1904)

Unlike Dan Sickles, James Longstreet was a professional soldier. The ample Georgian, despite graduating in the bottom quarter of his 1842 West Point class, proved a skilled commander during the Civil War. More a man of action than words, Lee's "Old Warhorse" preferred to fight on the defensive and failed to find the words to convince Lee to do so at Gettysburg. After the battle, Southern printers rarely blamed him for the defeat. But after the war, he became a Republican, and Southern apologists made him their Gettysburg scapegoat. He came to the battle forty-three years old. (Brady-Handy Photographic Collection, Library of Congress)

Major General George Pickett
(1825–1875)

George Pickett graduated dead last in the West Point class of 1846. During the war, he personified the Virginia dandy. He wore pristinely tailored uniforms, curled his hair in ringlets, and spritzed himself in rare colognes. Before charging Cemetery Ridge, he stuck a steel beam down his division's spine: "Don't forget today that you are from old Virginia!" But whether his men remembered as canister and musket fire mauled their ranks is unclear. The Virginia press, however, did not forget. He stormed Cemetery Ridge a thirty-eight-year-old man. (Brady-Handy Photographic Collection, Library of Congress)

Major General Winfield Scott Hancock
(1824–1886)

A proud son of the Keystone State, Hancock graduated West Point eighteenth of twenty-five in 1844. Tall and handsome, he not only played the part of an able general during the war, he looked it as well. He assumed command of the Union Second Corps two months before Gettysburg. Unlike Sickles, he deserved his command and the positive press he received after the battle. His defense of Cemetery Ridge was almost as celebrated as Pickett's repulse was memorialized. His celebrity helped win him the Democratic nomination for president in 1880 (though he lost the election to Republican James A. Garfield). When he crushed Lee's *coup de maître*, he was thirty-nine years old. (Brady-Handy Photographic Collection, Library of Congress)

General Ulysses S. Grant
(1822–1885)

Graduating West Point twenty-one of thirty-nine in 1843, the Ohio-born Grant struggled in all professions except one: war. In early 1862, he took Forts Henry and Donelson along the Tennessee and Cumberland Rivers, stripping Kentucky and western Tennessee from rebel hands. In April that year, he snatched victory from defeat's jaws at Shiloh. His next labor, Vicksburg along the Mississippi, proved a much tougher nut to crack than either Henry or Donelson, but his persistence paid off. He won Vicksburg the day after Meade won Gettysburg. Coverage of the latter often outshined that of the former. If he cared, he did not show it. He went on to defeat Lee, win the war, and not long after win two terms as president. He captured the Confederate Gibraltar at age forty-one. (Brady-Handy Photographic Collection, Library of Congress)

Printer Frederick Douglass
(1818–1895)

After finding the pathway to freedom, Douglass took it. In 1835, he stole head, body, and limbs from his Maryland master and trekked north. For a time, he lived in Massachusetts working with abolitionist printer William Lloyd Garrison, but he yearned to try his own hand at newspapering. In 1847, he moved to upstate New York and launched the weekly *North Star*, which he later renamed *Frederick Douglass' Paper*. When his friend John Brown attacked Harpers Ferry in 1859, he fled the country, fearing he might be implicated. Returning in 1860 after the imbroglio cooled, he turned his paper into a monthly. He published the last issue of *Douglass' Monthly* in early August 1863, right after Gettysburg. But like many black printers, the cause of racial justice took precedence. He left the campaign unremarked upon. He was forty-five at the time. (Liljenquist Family Collection, Library of Congress)

Printer James Gordon Bennett
(1795–1872)

Propelled by a dream of fortune through revolutionizing news, the cross-eyed Scottish-born New Yorker founded the *New York Herald* on May 6, 1835. The dream came true. His ingenuity made the *Herald* the most circulated daily both before and during the war. His Democratic slant and wide readership, not just in America but also in Europe, drew Lincoln's delicate attention. The president never missed a chance to compliment him and went above and beyond to remove red tape in his path. Lincoln's white glove treatment helped keep the moderate Bennett from sliding into the Copperhead cleft. While he remained anti-administration, he never turned antiwar. He covered Gettysburg at age sixty-seven. (Photograph by Matthew B. Brady, Library of Congress)

Printer Horace Greeley
(1811–1872)

Despite later popularizing the expression "Go West, young man, and grow up with the country," he grew up in New England and moved no farther west than New York City. Bald and bespectacled, his appearance impressed no one, but his paper, the *New-York Tribune*, impressed friend and foe alike. As a radical wartime Republican and shrewd businessman, he met Bennett head-on both editorially and innovatively. The president also paid him mind. When Greeley called on Lincoln to free the slaves in his editorial "The Prayer of Twenty Millions," the president personally replied just two days later. After the war, he sought to shape the nation's politics directly rather than editorially. In 1872, after undergoing a political transformation, he ran for president as a Democrat-endorsed "Liberal Republican" against Grant. His election loss proved uglier than Hancock's. He covered Gettysburg at age fifty-two. (Library of Congress)

Printer Benjamin H. Day
(1810–1889)

Like Greeley, Benjamin Day grew up in New England and moved no farther west than New York City. In 1833, he won renown by igniting the penny paper revolution with the nation's first one-center, the New York *Sun*. But affordability superseded quality. In 1835 he ran a series of articles about a civilization discovered on the moon. The "Great Moon Hoax," as it became known, gained him readers but cost him credibility. Bennett and Greeley wisely imitated him in price, less in fakery. Despite his departure from the paper in 1837, the *Sun* remained hotly circulated up to and during the Civil War. As a Republican sheet, it stood by Lincoln. (National Portrait Gallery, Smithsonian)

Printer Henry J. Raymond
(1820–1869)

After cutting his teeth at James Webb's New York *Courier and Enquirer*, Henry Raymond followed Frederick Douglass's example and cut his own path. In 1851, despite looking more like the captain of an ironclad than a newspaper, the New York native launched what became America's paper of record: the *New York Times*. Both before and during the war it proved a first-rate operation, worthy of utterance in the same breath as the *Herald* and the *Tribune*. As a conservative wartime Republican, Raymond stood to Bennett's left and Greeley's right but always by Lincoln's side. In 1864, as chair of the Republican National Committee, he oversaw the president's successful reelection campaign. He was forty-three during the Battle of Gettysburg. (Brady-Handy Photographic Collection, Library of Congress)

Printer Benjamin Wood
(1820–1900)

Few, if any, stood to Benjamin Wood's right. Like his brother, New York City mayor and Democratic congressman Fernando Wood, he was about as antiwar and anti-Lincoln as anyone in Yankeedom. His *New York Daily News,* which he bought in 1861, frothed with so much Copperhead venom that the post office forced its suspension that same year. In 1862, while his publication remained out of operation, he wrote an antiwar, pro-secessionist novel: *Fort Lafayette, or, Love and Secession*. It sold few copies, but the *Daily News,* which he restarted in 1863, sold quite well. Wood was forty-two when Meade met Lee at Gettysburg. (Brady National Photographic Art Gallery, National Archives)

Printer John W. Forney
(1817–1881)

With sideburns to rival those of Henry Raymond and perhaps even Ambrose Burnside himself, Forney began publishing the Philadelphia *Press* in 1857. During the war, the Pennsylvanian backed the Union president so tenaciously that he won repute as Lincoln's dog. The president rewarded his loyalty. When Forney's bid for clerk of the House of Representatives foundered, Lincoln made sure he became secretary of the Senate instead. Alongside fellow Philadelphia printer William Harding, Forney guaranteed that the City of Brotherly Love stood second only to New York City in the newspaper industry. He was forty-five when Lee invaded his home state. (Brady-Handy Photographic Collection, Library of Congress)

Printer Joseph Medill
(1823–1899)

Born in New Brunswick, Canada, his family immigrated to the U.S. West and grew up with the country. After some publishing success in Ohio, he moved to the rising jewel of the Midwest: Chicago. In 1855, after helping establish the Republican Party following passage of the Kansas-Nebraska Act, he purchased the *Chicago Tribune*. As reform-minded as Greeley and as loyal to Lincoln as Forney, he proved a vital voice against the wartime paroxysms of Midwest Copperheads. After the war, he tried his hand in politics. Although he did not reach as high as Greeley or Hancock, he grasped more success. In late 1871, after the Great Fire, Chicagoans elected him mayor. He covered Gettysburg at age forty. (National Library of Medicine)

Printer Wilbur Storey
(1819–1884)

Born in New England, Wilbur Storey too went west to grow up with the country. After stint running the *Detroit Free Press*, he moved to Chicago in 1861 and bought the *Chicago Times*. If his westward trek, peppered beard, and brushed back hair resembled Medill, the similarities ended there. Storey was a Chicago Copperhead opposed to the war and to Lincoln, and his newspaper became the ideological foil to Medill's Republican *Tribune* Like Wood, he frothed with enough venom to attract the government muzzle. He covered Gettysburg at age forty-three. (*Daily Graphic*, November 22, 1876)

Clement Vallandigham
(1820–1871)

Before the war, Vallandigham went from Ohio legislator to U.S. congressman. During the war, he became the head of the Copperhead snake. If one did not know who the author was, his anti-Lincoln speeches would lead one to think him likelier a rebel than a Yankee. As a peace Democrat, he was willing to sacrifice the Union on peace's altar. The circus of his arrest, banishment, and campaign for Ohio governor in absentia painted the political backdrop to the Gettysburg campaign. Union victory not only dashed his gubernatorial hopes but also sank the rising tide of Copperheads. He was a month shy of forty-three during the battle. (Brady-Handy Photographic Collection, Library of Congress)

Printer Samuel Medary
(1801–1864)

If John Forney was Lincoln's dog, then Samuel Medary was Clement Vallandigham's. Through the Columbus *Crisis,* the Ohio Copperhead campaigned tirelessly for Vallandigham's election and against Lincoln's war. Few printers fanned the fire in the rear more. Ironically, that fire engulfed him. In May 1864, U.S. marshals arrested him for conspiracy against the government. He was released on bond, and a trial date was set for later in the year, but he never saw his day in court. Overstressed and depressed, he died before the trial on November 7. The next day, the president he had fought so hard against won reelection. Medary was sixty-two when Lee invaded his neighboring state. (*New Ulm [Minn.] Review,* September 1, 1909)

Printer James Cowardin
(1811–1882)

In 1850, Virginian James Cowardin founded the first penny paper below the Potomac: the Richmond *Daily Dispatch*. At war's start, only two New Orleans printers could boast a higher circulation, but after the Crescent City's capture, Cowardin claimed the highest circulation in the Confederacy. He supported Davis and the war yet toed the line less than most of his Southern peers. By and large, Cowardin was to the South what Raymond was to the North: a dependable mast to which patriotic readers clung through war's choppy seas. He covered Gettysburg at age fifty-one. (Courtesy of the Library of Virginia)

Printer John M. Daniel
(1825–1865)

Before the war, Virginian John M. Daniel served as a U.S. diplomat to Sardinia but resigned after a letter leaked in which he said his hosts reeked of garlic. On war's eve, he returned to Richmond to helm the *Richmond Examiner*. His wartime coverage proved as irreverent and sarcastic as "the garlic letter." Despite supporting the war, he despised Davis and bludgeoned him with one caustic editorial after another. Perhaps he just enjoyed picking fights. Throughout his short life he fought nine pistol duels (and nearly a tenth against a drunk Edgar Allan Poe), yet dueling did not cut his life short. He died from acute tuberculosis on March 30, 1865. Nine days later the Confederacy followed him to the grave. He covered Gettysburg at age thirty-seven. (National Portrait Gallery, Smithsonian)

Printer Robert Barnwell Rhett (1800–1876)

The Fire-Eater who fanned the flames of secession before the war remained no less fiery during it. Cut from the same cloth as John M. Daniel, the South Carolinian backed the war but spurned Davis without restraint and without relent. His spite likely sprang from a sense that Davis had sidelined him from the government that his extremism helped create. Thus, the *Charleston Mercury*, which he ran with his sons, became an anti-administration cudgel—one wielded with great effect. His editorial bite could puncture the thickest skin and did in the aftermath of Gettysburg. He covered the campaign at age sixty-two. (Library of Congress)

Printer William Woods Holden (1818–1892)

Thin-lipped, beady-eyed, and bald, his appearance impressed little more than Greeley's, but like Greeley, he proved an editorial force with which to reckon. Opposed to the war and to Jefferson Davis, the native Tar Heel wielded his *North Carolina Standard* like a rapier, slicing holes in the Southern rationale for war against growing odds. Politically, he was to Davis what Vallandigham was to Lincoln. In 1864 he ran for governor on a peace platform. Although he lost to pro-war incumbent Zebulon Vance, time's passage vindicated him. After the South's defeat, he became a Republican and was not only appointed governor in 1865 but also elected in 1868. He covered Gettysburg at age forty-four. (Image courtesy of University of Georgia Library)

Correspondent Whitelaw Reid
(1837–1912)

The thickly mustached Ohioan Whitelaw Reid reported for the *Cincinnati Daily Gazette* and freelanced on occasion for Horace Greeley's *New-York Tribune*. He rose to journalistic stardom for his thorough and candid account of the Battle of Shiloh. His Gettysburg report proved no less impressive. After the war, his star kept rising. When Greeley died in 1872, Reid took over the *Tribune* and won favor in the Republican Party it supported. He served as U.S. ambassador to France, a delegate to the peace conference that ended the Spanish-American War, and—until his death—U.S. ambassador to Britain. He rode to Gettysburg via Taneytown at just twenty-five years old. (Brady-Handy Photographic Collection, Library of Congress)

Correspondent Charles Carleton Coffin
(1823–1896)

The correspondent whom Whitelaw Reid aimed to meet at Gettysburg, Charles Carleton Coffin hailed from New England and cut his prewar teeth reporting for Boston papers. During the war, he reported for the *Boston Daily Journal* and performed the job as if born to it. Combining Reid's frank thoroughness and Sam Wilkeson's artistic flair, he produced one of the finest accounts of Gettysburg. Only resolve matched talent. To submit the account he rode horses of flesh and iron two days straight. With grateful Bostonians cheering him through the finish, he staggered into the *Journal* building on July 6. After his account went to print, he slept an entire day. He came to Gettysburg a month shy of his fortieth birthday. (Liljenquist Family Collection, Library of Congress)

Correspondent Sam Wilkeson
(1817–1889)

The son of Buffalo's fifth mayor, Sam Wilkeson rode the wave of prosperity ushered in by the Erie Canal. After whetting his appetite in Buffalo's burgeoning news business, he moved to the nation's emerging news mecca: New York City. There he reported for Greeley's *Tribune* before taking up with Raymond's *Times*. If Lorenzo Crouse, his *Times* colleague, was a better summarizer, he was a better storyteller. The loss he suffered at Gettysburg inspired the most moving account of the battle, which helped inspire one of the greatest speeches in American history. He came to Gettysburg forty-six years old. (Courtesy of the Missouri Historical Society)

Correspondent Peter Wellington Alexander
(1825–1886)

The South's "Prince of Correspondents" hailed from the Peach State and reported for the anti-Davis *Savannah Republican*. Generally honest and thorough, he was to the Confederacy what Reid was to the Union. Unsurprisingly, he wrote one of the finest Southern accounts of the Gettysburg campaign. The absence of his chief reporting rival, Felix Gregory De Fontaine (whose writing style mirrored Coffin's), only increased its value. He traveled to Pennsylvania with Lee's army at age thirty-eight. (Peter Wellington Alexander Papers, Rare Book & Manuscript Library, Columbia University)

Part II

CHAPTER FOUR

"Look to Glorious Lee"

While the Confederate Army of Northern Virginia blazed a path to Pennsylvania, the Confederate Military Telegraph Service attempted to run that path with wire. Supervised by Major J. T. Coldwell, a special work detail sweated through eleven long days and nights stringing up an impressive fifty-seven miles of new telegraph cable.[1] Their herculean effort connected the Confederate capital with Martinsburg, just below the Potomac River in the northern Shenandoah Valley. At scarcely fifty miles from the action at Gettysburg, Coldwell became the first Southern source to transmit news of the battle to Richmond. That news, however, triggered one of the greatest misinformation debacles in the history of Confederate journalism.

On July 6, a stream of dispatches, signed "C." for Coldwell, poured into the Richmond telegraph office from Martinsburg.[2] The news was spectacular. On Sunday, July 5, a major battle had erupted at Gettysburg, resulting in the total dissolution of the Union Army of the Potomac and the capture of innumerable prisoners. One telegram reported, "[Lt.] Gen. [A. P.] Hill, whose corps occupied the centre of our line, fell back, causing the enemy to believe he was retreating." The gullible Yankees "promptly took the bait and advanced when Ewell and Longstreet advanced with right and left wings, thus completely surrounding the enemy."[3] Lee had reproduced Hannibal's genius at Cannae.[4] The brilliantly orchestrated attack, revealed the dispatches, not only yielded the heights south of Gettysburg but also a jaw-dropping forty thousand prisoners. As if this were not enough, an ironic jewel ornamented victory's crown. According to Coldwell, "The prisoners refused to be paroled," and Pickett's division, after wrapping itself in the laurels of victory, won the honor of "guarding them to Richmond."[5]

The reports from Martinsburg sparked two days of jubilee in Richmond. Marylander John B. Jones, a clerk in the Confederate War Department, watched as word of the enemy's destruction latched onto Richmonders' hopeful hearts "as if by some sort of magnetism." Thousands emptied their homes and workplaces, spontaneously hugging, cheering, and whirling wildly about until the streets themselves seemed to churn like rivers with excitement. To confirm the celebratory news, Southern Telegraph Company president Dr. William S. Morris tracked down the city's largest Confederate flag and hung it outside his office window.[6] Shortly thereafter, an ecstatic Morris released Coldwell's dispatches to the press.

Southern printers spread the story like a virus. Beginning on July 7, just one day after Coldwell wired the news from Martinsburg, some of the South's most-read papers ran some of the war's most exhilarating headlines. The *Savannah Republican* proclaimed "The Best News of the War!"—"Overwhelming Defeat of the Yankees at Gettysburg!"[7] The *Richmond Enquirer* trumpeted the capture of forty thousand Yankees as if its veracity matched that of the law of gravity.[8] The incredible news even prompted some papers to predict an end to the war. While the *Republican* saw a wide-open door to Washington, the Richmond *Daily Dispatch* saw on the South's horizon "the glimpses of peace" even if the wired account were to "prove only half true."[9]

But it proved far less true than that. On July 8, word began reaching Southern news offices that Vicksburg had fallen just as the telegraph in Martinsburg pulsed with some sobering updates to the Gettysburg story. The Confederates had not achieved the Union army's total dissolution on July 5, thereby opening the door to Washington.[10] Instead, the rebels had fled toward Hagerstown, Maryland, after a costly rebuff on Friday, July 3, that had stripped Pickett's division of its laurels by chewing it to pieces.[11] Also, the Confederates had not quite captured the host of prisoners reported.[12] Rather than forty thousand federals, the rebels had bagged only four thousand.

The whiplash in fortune squelched all jubilation. Slumped Richmonders aimlessly roamed the streets, unable or unwilling to swallow the disorienting news. Others, feeling cheated, boiled with indignation. "The news from Lee's army is appalling," wrote Jones. "The accounts from Martinsburg now state [that] he fell back to Hagerstown . . . [and] instead of 40,000 we have only 4,000 prisoners." The taste of ashes made Jones eager to point the finger. The war clerk faulted Coldwell for propagating the misinformation that ultimately duped the Confederate nation. "Our telegraph operators are great liars," he fumed.[13]

Southern printers, who cringed at having to walk back the story, shared Jones's ire for the man at the Martinsburg wire. "[Coldwell likely] hear[d] a flying rumor to the effect of what he wrote," deduced the *Dispatch* on July 10, "but is that the sort of information to be so gravely transmitted to the press and War Department?"[14] The *Richmond Enquirer*, the staff of which touted its ability to discern factual from fictional reports, raged at the telegraph more generally.[15] "We may as well give up the attempt to know anything about the fate and fortunes of our armies," grunted the paper on July 10. "[The telegraph] brings intelligence quick; yet . . . it is always so obfuscated by these quick-coming reports, all destroying one another, that the true story is generally longer in being ascertained than it was before."[16] At perhaps the most critical juncture in the Civil War, the "lightning" had prematurely struck the South. In early July 1863, the *New York Times*'s prewar concern looked less like pithy commentary and more like prophecy. The telegraph was simply "too fast for the truth."[17]

Although the South did not win the mythical victory Coldwell claimed, its pro-administration press refused to accept that the Gettysburg campaign had resulted in failure. Indeed, from the start of the campaign in early June to the weeks that followed the sobering revelation of July 8, the pro–Jefferson Davis press continued to cast Gettysburg in an auspicious light. Each day of the battle was overhauled. The Wednesday success became an unparalleled victory, Thursday's draw became another Confederate triumph, and the tragic Friday charge became a romanticized setback affected only by the enemy's position and numerical advantage. This new and improved Gettysburg, which pro-Davis printers further enhanced by skewing casualties in Confederate favor, armed them with the means to sustain morale and distinguish the "success" of Gettysburg from the disaster of Vicksburg. The pro-Davis press covered the war to augment the Confederate president and the cause of Confederate nationhood. That bias proved irrepressible and coated every column of its Gettysburg coverage.

As the Army of Northern Virginia sallied north in mid-June, throwing Yankeedom into panic, pro-Davis printers began pinning to it high hopes and the usual "magnificent expectations."[18] Virginia printer James Cowardin took the lead. His Richmond *Dispatch*, one of the South's first penny papers before the war and its number one daily during it, saw the army's new course as a harbinger for brighter days. "One thing we are sure of," opined the *Dispatch*. "Our army will do all that man can do and we look to the future not only with undiminished but with increased hope and confidence."[19]

Confidence in the rebel army centered on its commander, General Robert E. Lee. Virginia native Nathaniel Tyler, helming Richmond's original Davis organ—the *Enquirer*, took comfort knowing that the rebel invasion rested in Lee's competent hands.[20] "He knows, if any man knows, what war is, and how to wage it," the *Enquirer* dotingly asserted.[21] Cowardin reminded his thirty-thousand-strong readership that the invasion was in good hands before the settling dust at Gettysburg could suggest otherwise.[22] "Gen. Lee is a great General . . . [with] wisdom and sagacity" and a "prudent," "cautious," and "careful" temperament, fawned the *Dispatch*.[23] And Cowardin did not stop there. In case this praise parade inadequately expressed his own confidence in

Lee, he added that of the entire South. "Throughout the whole Confederacy the highest degree of confidence is felt in Gen. Lee," remarked the *Dispatch*. "The people feel he is bent upon some enterprise which will have a most important bearing upon the issue of the war."[24]

Confidence in Lee and his new enterprise only seemed commensurate with his sterling military record. By dazzling Southern printers with victories in his first year of command, Lee all but positioned himself beyond the bite of their ink. Lee's latest victory, at the Battle of Chancellorsville in early May, was a key reason why. In what became his magnum opus, Lee had trounced the Army of the Potomac despite it dwarfing his own force at the time two to one.[25] President Lincoln, on hearing of yet another defeat at Lee's hand, reportedly turned pale as a corpse and bellowed "My God! What will the country say!"[26]

The country said its worst.[27] But while Northern printers groaned about the Union army and its then-commander General Joseph Hooker—whom George Meade would replace on June 28—Southern printers extolled Lee to the point of blurring the boundary between deserving positive press and groveling, cult-like worship. "No leader on earth today has won so many battles . . . [as] the Glorious Lee," truckled Tyler after Chancellorsville. "[His army banners] glow with a purer lustre than any other standards that in this generation have been given to the winds over all lands and all seas."[28] With Chancellorsville at his back, Lee could almost do no wrong. His shining reputation cast a blinding glare into Southern newspaper offices, and although he had not yet acquired the demigod status of the late Stonewall Jackson, who died from a wound received at Chancellorsville, by the Gettysburg campaign no other living general in the Confederacy seemed above press criticism quite like General Lee.[29]

Pro-Davis printers' faith in Lee and his new enterprise was soon rewarded. On June 14, while en route to Pennsylvania, the rebel van under Ewell overwhelmed the seven-thousand-man federal garrison at Winchester, Virginia—some twenty miles southwest of Martinsburg. The victory, albeit ancillary, reaped the rebels an impressive harvest. Losing just forty-two soldiers killed, Lee acquired hundreds of horses and loaded wagons, stores valued at over a million dollars, twenty-three cannons, and an estimated four thousand Yankee prisoners.[30]

Winchester's low-cost, high-yield harvest demanded the attention of pro-Davis printers. But their coverage proved wholly disproportionate, both in quantity and quality, to the victory's bearing on the war. Tennessean Francis Paul, the newspaperman behind the nomadic *Chattanooga Daily Rebel*, claimed that Ewell captured nine thousand Yankees, two thousand more than had defended Winchester.[31] Cowardin also lathered the triumph in exaggeration. "The capture of Winchester is . . . one of the most important, events of the war," celebrated the *Dispatch*. "It seems to be the first in a projected series of operations, which . . . will result most beneficially to the cause of the Confederacy."[32]

With the first fruit of Lee's invasion in hand and the rebel army poised to penetrate Pennsylvania unopposed, pro-Davis printers began forecasting an all-but-inevitable Confederate victory. John McClanahan and Benjamin Dill, still on the run with their refugee paper, the *Memphis Daily Appeal*, claimed Winchester had upheld the Army of Northern Virginia's invincible reputation and put Washington within its sights.[33] Tyler envisioned Lee accomplishing much more than merely threatening Washington. The *Enquirer* told readers that Lee would sweep aside the Army of the Potomac, envelop Washington with his right arm and Harrisburg with his left, and then press his standards—through Baltimore and Philadelphia—all the way to the Delaware River.[34] Cowardin hyperventilated no less than Tyler. Before learning of Meade's promotion, the *Dispatch* blustered like a peacock, "We should not be surprised to hear that Lee has bagged Hooker."[35]

Pro-Davis printers saw Winchester as the opening act to a show that would drop the curtain on the Union, further ballooning the already "magnificent expectations" they had fastened to Lee and his Army of Northern Virginia.[36] The ramifications of this were at least threefold. For one, it created a context in which Coldwell's dispatches could be viewed credibly. After all, "the Glorious Lee"—champion of Chancellorsville and now Winchester—looked predestined to strike a major, if not war-ending, blow to the enemy on his own soil.[37] The heavy breathing of pro-Davis printers also backed them into a corner wherein Lee's campaign results needed to at least resemble, if not match, the hyperbolic reports published before it. To do otherwise risked a loss of face among pro-Davis printers and a war-crippling plunge in morale among Southern readers. By preordaining its success, then, the South's pro-administration press set the stage for Gettysburg's favorable treatment. Lastly, whether a primary motivation or not, the expectation fanning by pro-Davis printers facilitated a boon in business. Tyler announced in late June, "There never yet was such devouring eagerness for news. Undoubtedly the chief interest centres on the fortunes of our army on the Potomac."[38]

That highly sought news became scarce the moment Lee crossed the Potomac. By venturing beyond that watery boundary, the rebel army not only left the Confederacy itself, it also left itself untethered from Coldwell's telegraphic outpost in Martinsburg. Communication became dubious. Southern printers hoped that express riders might maintain contact with Lee's advancing host, but in hostile territory the effort proved fruitless. Even as Lee charged Cemetery Ridge at battle's end, the Southern press remained—apart from the misleading light of rumors—totally in the dark. Tyler admitted on July 3, "We have nothing fresh from General Lee's army." But to retain the public fervor for news, he added, "Stirring events are in brief futurity . . . and upon them hangs the destiny of the campaign."[39]

The lull in news did not stop the pro-Davis press from anticipating Lee's victory. In fact, as the silence lengthened, confidence in Lee stiffened. Even in outlying Texas, Vermont-born printer Edward H. Cushing stayed buoyant with confidence in Lee. Operating the state's chief administration organ, the Houston *Tri-Weekly Telegraph*, Cushing wagered, "Lee is marching in triumph on the North, as though we had authentic accounts of it in telegraphic dispatches."[40]

Although Coldwell supplied Richmond with its first news of Gettysburg from a Southern source, the first news of any kind to reach the Confederate capital steamed in via flag-of-truce boat from the North. On the night of July 4, the Gettysburg accounts of Northern papers began filtering into Richmond's press offices. That any battle news, let alone the much-anticipated climax to Lee's invasion, should come first from the Yankees had always exasperated Southern printers and automatically placed those accounts under suspicion. On June 12, as the Gettysburg campaign got underway, Cowardin addressed the issue and its galling implications. "It is to be regretted that the reading public is so much dependent for detailed accounts of battles . . . upon Northern journals," croaked the *Dispatch*.[41] "Although we know them to be the most shameless liars in the world, their fables, when unaccompanied by note or comment, are apt to have some effect."[42]

Unsurprisingly, the pro-Davis press treated the North's initial Gettysburg accounts with incredulity. A July 6 editorial in the *Dispatch* attempted, without any controverting evidence, to discredit a Union victory report from the *Philadelphia Inquirer* by playing on the mendacious Yankee stereotype. "Our troops have gained a great victory," asserted the *Dispatch* flatly. "The Philadelphia *Inquirer* cannot conceal the fact, although it lies with an ardor and an earnestness that deserved better success." The *Dispatch* justified its own victory claim by glomming on to the word "indecisive," which the *Inquirer* had used to describe some of the fighting. "It is proof enough that they [the Yankees] have been badly beaten," charged the paper. "Had it really been indecisive they would have claimed a decided victory."[43]

Initially starved for Southern news, pro-Davis printers resorted to low-brow retorts to triumphant Gettysburg reports from the Northern press. Given that the victorious accounts of "the most shameless liars" belied weeks of their own glorious predictions, this is unsurprising.[44] Pro-Davis printers were more or less honor bound to publish face-saving refutations, even if done underhandedly. What raises eyebrows is that despite being inundated by Northern victory proclamations, pro-Davis printers devoutly clung to the belief that Lee's masterstroke remained imminent. On July 6, in the same issue as his attempted defenestration of the *Philadelphia Inquirer,* Cowardin surmised, "In a few days we expect to hear that Meade's army has been defeated, and probably annihilated."[45] Annihilated! In the face of Northern papers rejoicing over Lee's defeat, pro-Davis printers dug in their heels. Like blind disciples, they stood unfazed by contrary evidence and remained ever faithful that Marse Robert would prevail.

And for a fleeting moment it seemed he had. The awkward window in which Southern printers possessed only Northern Gettysburg news closed almost as soon as it opened. Within hours of the *Dispatch* running its hatchet job on the *Inquirer,* Coldwell's cables started spilling into the Richmond telegraph office. Rather than trivializing Northern victory accounts, the pro-Davis press began trumpeting—using a Southern source—the brilliant Confederate triumph they expected all along. Front pages brimmed with soaring headlines. On July 8, the *Chattanooga Daily Rebel,* under the headline "The Greatest Battle of the War," declared: "General Lee Victorious!"[46] A day later North Carolina's *Fayetteville Observer* roared, "Gen. Lee Again Victorious!"[47]

Of course, the victory proved utterly mythical. Coldwell had relayed information significantly more misleading than anything published in the *Philadelphia Inquirer.* His updated telegram, sent from Martinsburg on the morning of July 8, eviscerated his original dispatches and that U-turn poured cold water on the fire of elation sweeping the South. The next day Cowardin lamented, "The public feeling must undergo a painful revulsion from the state of exaltation produced by the telegram of yesterday morning." Yet over the next few weeks, as they sifted through reports trickling in from different sources, including their own correspondents, pro-Davis printers endeavored to keep the flames of "exaltation" from extinguishing by overhauling each day of the Battle of Gettysburg.[48]

Richmond's pro-administration press led the way. Tyler and fellow Virginian Richard Smith, who ran the newly minted *Sentinel,* overstated the already compelling Southern victory of July 1. Despite the rebel army possessing a numerical edge that day, both men fattened the Wednesday victory by claiming that the odds had been stacked against it. The *Enquirer,* which posted two correspondents to Gettysburg, averred, "We had attacked a superior force; had driven him over three miles." The rebels had inflicted a grave loss while their own loss "was not heavy."[49] Smith took Tyler's ante and upped it. Using a report forwarded by his sole Gettysburg correspondent, Smith not only repeated the victory against long odds angle, he also overshot the number of Yankees bagged by the Confederate Second and Third Corps. "After a fierce battle against fearful odds," harped the *Sentinel,* "[Ewell and A. P. Hill] captured between five and six thousand prisoners."[50] These misrepresentations lent the impression that the Confederates achieved an even greater victory on July 1 than had actually resulted.

Coverage of the July 2 battle proved no less misleading. Richmond's pro-Davis triarchy—the *Dispatch, Enquirer,* and *Sentinel*—transformed the inconclusive Thursday fight into another conclusive Southern victory. Despite rebel and Yankee casualties totaling about nine thousand each, the *Enquirer* boasted, "The enemy's loss during this day's fight was very heavy. . . . Our own loss was slight."[51] While Tyler toyed with casualties, Smith overstressed the inroads made by Ewell and Longstreet against the Union army's flanks. "The enemy was driven in on the right and left" so much so that the Army of the Potomac "assume[d] very much the position of a V," reported the *Sentinel.*[52] Cowardin distorted the July 2 battle no less than his colleagues. By conflating Wednesday's success with Thursday's draw, the *Dispatch* turned the latter into another victory. The paper vowed, "The fights of the two first days are represented to have been very decidedly in our favor."[53]

Conflations of July 1 and 2 became ubiquitous. One of the Old Dominion's rural publications, the *Abingdon Virginian,* insisted that on both Wednesday and Thursday the rebels had routed the Yankees with unprecedented carnage.[54] After conversing with Confederate officers, the Richmond correspondent for the *Memphis Daily Appeal,* a John Barton who wrote under the pseudonym "Dixie," reported that the Yankees suffered three to one losses on both days.[55] Paul seconded these sentiments. In fact, Paul's *Chattanooga Daily Rebel* recycled one of the most regurgitated lines used by the Southern press in its Gettysburg coverage. "In the fights of Wednesday and Thursday," parroted the *Rebel,* "we whipped the enemy badly."[56]

Lumping the first two days into one indistinguishable "whipping" reinforced the uplifting battle narrative pro-Davis printers wanted told. These newspapermen understood that Wednesday had shined brightest for Confederate forces at Gettysburg. Even candid Northern journalists like Whitelaw Reid acknowledged that Wednesday went "*not* favorably" for the Union army.

But the teetering Thursday firefight clanged to a different key. Reid called the July 2 battle straight when he wrote, "On the whole the Confederates were unsuccessful, but we had not quite held our own."[57] By melding the unambiguous rebel success of July 1 with its ambiguous successor, the South's pro-administration printers engineered something akin to a victory by association. Thursday rode to victory on Wednesday's triumphant coattails. Regardless of how they covered July 3, pro-Davis printers gave the impression that Lee won at least two days of the three-day Battle of Gettysburg. As Cowardin put it before addressing the critical Friday fight, Lee reigned "victorious in two days of the battles."[58]

But July 3 handed pro-Davis printers a reporting nightmare. Lee had suffered horrendously, with no offsetting gain. In what became known as Pickett's Charge, the failed assault by three rebel divisions against the Union center on Cemetery Ridge, Lee sustained seventy-five hundred casualties—fully half of his attacking force. The butcher exacted an especially steep bill from Lee's officers. Command in Pickett's division effectively ceased to exist. While Pickett miraculously escaped unscathed, the same could not be said for his three brigadier generals, two of whom perished and the third of whom fell prisoner, nor could it be said for a staggering fourteen of his fifteen regimental commanders.[59] Friday's costly fiasco prompted a soldier in Longstreet's corps to reflect, "Gettysburg was . . . as clear a defeat as our army ever met with."[60]

The Friday battle left Lee's army recoiling and left pro-Davis printers scrambling for some way to wring a dry sponge. Excuses ran rife. Rather than blame Lee for ordering a futile charge, the pro-Davis press much preferred to sidestep him and blame Meade's position instead. The *Abingdon Virginian* claimed that Pickett's Charge "was checked by certain hills, entrenchments and rifle pits, behind which the enemy took refuge."[61] If this excuse left Southern readers craving more, the pro-Davis press frequently offered another: Meade's numerical superiority. The *Sentinel*'s lone correspondent, who shielded his identity behind the alias "Gwen," used both excuses to downplay the Confederate blunder. "The failure of Gen. Pickett to take the position . . . was due to the strength of the enemy's fortifications and want of support," explained Gwen.[62] "With no help at hand, we are driven out of their fortifications and forced back by overwhelming numbers."[63]

These excuses went on ad nauseam. Paul highlighted the "heights, which he [the enemy] had fortified," Cowardin underscored the Union army's possession of "fortified heights," and Tyler considered seizing Cemetery Ridge against the dual disadvantages of ground and numbers an exercise in "human impossibilities."[64] The pro-Davis press seldom deviated from these talking points to point a critical finger at Lee, but one of Tyler's two correspondents refused to handle the general with velvet gloves. Writing under the pseudonym "X," the unidentified reporter dispatched his battle account on July 14 from Martinsburg. A week later Tyler published it in the *Enquirer,* and Southerners began reading rare censures of Lee in a paper that, following Chancellorsville, had prostrated itself before him like a serf unto his lord.

X blamed Marse Robert for Friday's grim outcome. Lee had erred by directly assaulting the enemy and by doing so after that enemy had firmly ensconced himself on high ground.[65] X could therefore not help but find the Friday charge unjustifiable and could not help but think that "Gen. Lee was led to this by overweening confidence in his troops." X linked the unjustified Friday assault to the rebels' inability to press their advantage on Wednesday by commandeering the heights south of Gettysburg. "By leaving the enemy in possession of these heights," he explained, "they were enabled to fortify and render them quite impregnable to our efforts made during the second and third to storm them." Whether responsibility for that "great mistake," as X termed it, should fall on Lee, Ewell, or the star-studded shoulders of both men remains a disputed topic in historical circles. For X, however, the answer was clear. This "great mistake," penned the correspondent, "was made by Gen. Lee."[66]

X's astute analysis distinguished his report. With the possible exception of two reporters for the anti-Davis *Savannah Republican,* X supplied the Southern press with its most incisive analysis of Lee's generalship at Gettysburg. But even X recognized that criticizing Lee, the paragon of the South, required a countervailing gust of praise. After all, X worked for a pro-administration paper committed to bolstering Confederate authority, and no other living authority figure loomed larger in the public's imagination than Lee. Consequently, X followed his analysis with some equipoise. The correspondent dashed off the postscript: "But, suppose [Lee] has made one failure, let us acknowledge it, and in doing so, let us thank Heaven that we have so great and good a General."[67]

While criticizing Lee for the July 3 charge proved rare, romanticizing it proved commonplace. Indeed, pro-administration printers felt obligated to soothe grief-stricken Southerners by idealizing Pickett's ill-fated charge.[68] No state's pro-administration press took up this mantle like Virginia. With two reporters at Gettysburg, Tyler's *Richmond Enquirer* stood uniquely positioned to capture that hapless foray in the quixotic and quasi-poetic prose historian Carol Reardon calls "the real soul of this journalistic era's craft."[69] Like his colleague X, the second *Enquirer* correspondent wrote his Gettysburg account under a byname, in his case "A." But unlike the mysterious X, historians easily identified A as the veteran war reporter Jonathan W. Albertson, who also contributed to the Confederate Press Association. Using Albertson's eloquent account, Tyler offered Virginians these consoling words: "Though many a Virginia home will mourn the loss of some noble spirit, yet at the name of Pickett's division and the battle of Gettysburg, how the eye will glisten and the blood course quicker, and the heart beat warm, as among its noble dead is recalled the name of some cherished one. They bore themselves worthy of their lineage and their state. Who would recall them from their bed of glory? Each sleeps in a hero's grave."[70]

Richard Smith also gave grief-stricken Virginians solace by eulogizing the sacrifice of Pickett's men. Thanks to the report furnished by Gwen, the *Sentinel* lauded, they "won for themselves an immortal name . . . the country must ever be grateful to the heroes who there so nobly illustrated Southern valor." The Richmond tract went on to salute "the *gallant dead*" and asked readers: "What pen can do them justice? Can express in language sufficiently warm, a nation's gratitude, or in strains sufficiently mournful the agony and the grief that now breed around many a hearthstone in Virginia." The *Sentinel* concluded its paean, "But such is war."[71]

Virginia's *Staunton Spectator* trailed its kin in the capital by rhapsodizing the Friday charge. "It is believed that a more gallant and noble charge was never made on this continent," venerated the *Spectator*. "[Those who sacrificed,] your country will cherish the memory of your deeds and sufferings with a gratitude and affection which time can never obliterate."[72]

And time never has. Pickett's Charge, like some inexorable pickaxe, mined its way into America's collective consciousness, where it has existed in a state of limbo between the two poles of history and myth. Reardon writes, "The endurance in the nation's historical consciousness of Pickett's Charge suggests that it inspired—and still inspires—reflections and emotions that spring from a source far removed from respect for historical truth."[73] Pro-Davis printers almost immediately seized on the emotional appeal of Pickett's Charge. Rather than print the honest facts of that direful repulse, they ran embellished accounts wrapped in romantic imagery. Forsaking the former for the latter not only provided Southern readers with succor in the face of trying circumstances, it also began the gradual drift of Pickett's Charge away from the annals of history toward the pseudo-historical inventions of mythology.

The obsessive focus on Pickett's division by Virginia's pro-Davis printers exposed their home state bias. Not only was Pickett the progeny of Virginia, so too were the soldiers under his command. In fact, all fifteen regiments in his three brigades at Gettysburg came from the Old Dominion. Richmond's pro-Davis printers refused to let the sacrifice of Virginia's sons, many of whom called the Confederate capital home, pass without special recognition. On July 13, the *Richmond Dispatch* led its front-page with a story titled, "DESCRIPTION OF FRIDAY'S FIGHT—THE FIRST VIRGINIA REGIMENT AT GETTYSBURG."[74] It proved no coincidence that Cowardin bestowed this unique honor, one he denied non-Virginia regiments involved in the Friday assault, on the First Virginia specifically. In addition to suffering dearly in the July 3 charge, the First Virginia had been mustered in Richmond.

Cowardin continued to manifest his hometown and home state biases, even though his readership's wingspan swathed the whole Confederacy. Throughout the week of July 13, the *Dispatch* published several Gettysburg casualty columns spotlighting the regiments in Pickett's division, including the First Virginia. That two other divisions participated in the Friday charge, those of Major Generals Henry Heth and William Dorsey Pender, seemed inconsequential. Perhaps that had something to do with the fact that only one of the eight infantry brigades in those two divisions originated from the Old Dominion. The other seven came plucked from a mixed bag of Southern states, including three from North Carolina. The exalting of Pickett's division by the Richmond pro-Davis press infuriated printers in other states, especially North Carolina, who felt the contributions of their states' soldiers marginalized in the most-circulated Confederate papers. But while this marginalization caused friction with printers from other states, nothing fanned that friction to flame like the offense of soldierly malignment.

Of Richmond's pro-Davis triarchy, no paper maligned the actions of non-Virginians in the Friday charge quite like the *Richmond Enquirer*. Albertson bore much of the blame. In the same account in which he gave bereaved Virginians a eulogy honoring Pickett's division, he also gave excuses explaining why Pickett's men failed to wrest away Cemetery Ridge. In addition to citing the usual apologetics of the enemy's superior position and numbers, Albertson unapologetically indicted Pickett's co-chargers. According to his account, Pickett's men scaled Cemetery Ridge intact, scattered its defenders, and planted their flags securely on its crest. But as Pickett's Virginians shouted in triumph, the command of North Carolinian James Pettigrew, the brigadier who led Heth's division in the assault, broke and took to flight like terrified deer. Without Pettigrew's support, Pickett took fire from all sides. The Virginians faced no choice, bemoaned Albertson, but to cede Cemetery Ridge in retreat, thereby ending the fighting on July 3.[75]

Albertson's denigration of Pettigrew and his command, whether warranted or not, sparked a fiery backlash from the Tar Heel press. Not only did Pettigrew hail from North Carolina, so too did his brigade, which Albertson impugned for deserting Pickett's Virginians at the eleventh hour. The *Raleigh Register* speedily issued a rebuttal. "[The *Enquirer*'s reporter] does the grossest injustice to Gen. Pettigrew's [command]," snapped the *Register*. "He represents it as breaking at a critical point in the battle, and flying to the woods . . . [but] we believe this account to be wholly untrue." That Albertson hid his identity behind a pseudonym further irked the *Register*. An unnamed correspondent, from its perspective, unduly besmirched the good name of Pettigrew and his valiant North Carolinians. The paper vented, "It is hard, that when they have suffered, and toiled, and fought, and fallen, their reputation should be tarnished by an anonymous newspaper correspondent."[76]

The malignment and marginalization of non-Virginians in the Friday charge provoked a long and bitter press feud between Virginia and North Carolina. The *Richmond Enquirer* and the *Raleigh Register* fought a vitriolic and heated exchange that sizzled for well over a month. Tyler never retracted the portion of Albertson's account blaming Pettigrew and his North Carolinians for the Friday failure. Instead, the *Enquirer* stood by "the statement made by . . . correspondent 'A,' that Pettigrew's command failed to efficiently support Pickett." It added, "Here is probably to be found the real cause [for the failure] of our unfortunate assault."[77] This only amplified the furor of Tar Heel printers. Eventually their uproar caught the ear of North Carolina governor Zebulon Vance, who vainly demanded of the War Department that a newspaper correspondent from his state remain with Lee's army "to see that justice was done the North Carolina troops."[78]

But that justice went undone, at least during the war and in the several decades that followed. For the Confederate press, the interpretative battle between North Carolina and Virginia over July 3 was like David battling Goliath without divine help. Against the towering might of Richmond, where pro-Davis printers boasted the South's most reprinted and circulated papers, no real victory was attainable. Cowardin, Tyler, and Smith ignored their non-Virginia audiences across the South and, as Reardon writes, "put the priorities of their local readers first."[79] Together they helped establish a Virginia-centered narrative of the Friday charge that became so entrenched that no stone slung by the presses of other Southern states could topple it. The Southern press's Goliath prevailed. The very fact that the July 3 assault became broadly known then and remains securely known now as "Pickett's Charge"—rather than "Pettigrew's Charge" or the less palatable but more suitable "Pickett-Pettigrew-Trimble Charge"—testifies to the incredible, narrative-establishing power wielded by the biased printers of the Confederacy's only national news hub.[80]

For discerning readers of their papers, the press infighting over Pickett's Charge signaled just how disastrous it was for Lee's army. Successes in battle discouraged finger-pointing. Unequivocal disasters, meanwhile, stimulated the scourge of scapegoating. Pickett's Charge proved as near to an unmitigated disaster as the Army of Northern Virginia ever met with, and, for Southerners willing to read between the lines, the ensuing press wrangle confirmed it.

At his desk in the War Department, John B. Jones processed a slew of Gettysburg-related information, including material pertaining to the Virginia–North Carolina press feud over Pickett's Charge. On July 30, he handled an angry letter from Vance after the War Department denied the governor's request to place a Tar Heel correspondent with Lee's army.[81] And on August 1 he learned that, due to unfair press treatment, fifty North Carolina soldiers had deserted Lee's ranks. Although Jones's work exposed him to extensive Gettysburg content, the aftershocks of the press feud helped inform his view of the Friday battle. The war clerk later journaled, "Gen. Pickett's division (decimated at Gettysburg)."[82]

Many pro-administration printers would have bristled at Jones's entry. In fact, many balanced their excuse-making for Pickett's repulse by downplaying its severity. Cowardin believed, "[The Friday] charge resulted in a repulse, but nothing else. The enemy did not leave his fortified heights to try a battle in the field again that day."[83] Using a report forwarded by "Dixie," printers McClanahan and Dill actually claimed Lee meted out at least as much punishment as he took in the Friday battle. The *Memphis Daily Appeal* chimed, "On Friday, when we carried their entrenchments, their casualties were at least equal to, if not greater than our own."[84]

Pro-Davis printers twisted casualties in Confederate favor. Gettysburg proved no exception. Before Lee submitted any estimates to President Davis, they made it seem as though Lee had triumphed at Gettysburg by lowballing his casualties and overshooting Meade's.[85] Tyler's knights of the quill warped the Gettysburg numbers like their jobs depended on it.[86] Despite his sharp analysis of Lee's generalship, X set overall rebel losses at no more than fifteen thousand—nearly half the true sum.[87] But X's undercount paled before that of his *Enquirer* colleague. Albertson, the man who stoked the coals of bitterness between Virginia and North Carolina, reported a three-to-one Gettysburg casualty disparity: thirty thousand for Meade and less than ten thousand for Lee.[88]

The Richmond triarchy sang in one voice. While Cowardin estimated Confederate losses at no more than twelve thousand, he assessed Union casualties at twice that number.[89] In an article headlined "Losses of Gen. Lee's Army," Smith brandished a Gettysburg receipt almost as generous as Cowardin's. "Our entire loss . . . in killed, wounded and prisoners will not reach fifteen thousand," maintained the *Sentinel*. "There cannot be a doubt as to the enemy's losses far exceeding ours." Smith assured his readers, who doubtless found the article palliating, that the information came from a highly credible source.[90] Who that source was, however, Smith never divulged.

Pro-Davis papers across Rebeldom sang the same biased tune. Virginia's country press spun the numbers no less flatteringly than those in Richmond. Agreeing that the bluecoats had suffered far worse, the *Abingdon Virginian* and the *Staunton Spectator* tallied Confederate losses at just twelve thousand and fifteen thousand respectively.[91] Meanwhile, over a thousand miles from Virginia, Houston's *Tri-Weekly Telegraph* printer Edward H. Cushing sat in the dark. When Union general Ulysses S. Grant cleaved the South in two at Vicksburg, he also cut the last telegraph line connecting the eastern Confederacy with the trans-Mississippi. Gettysburg news in Texas became even scarcer than reams of paper. Although Cushing later established an express service to hasten news between the South's severed halves, he spent the month of July piecing the Gettysburg story together as if working a jigsaw puzzle blindfolded. Finally, on July 31, he felt the picture complete enough to publish casualty figures. The *Telegraph* put Lee's bill at "ten thousand, and four thousand prisoners," while Meade's tipped the scales at "fully twenty-five thousand killed and wounded, and twelve thousand prisoners."[92]

These reader-gratifying casualty estimates sharply contrasted those published in Northern journals. In fact, while pro-Davis printers spun the numbers favorably for the South, Northern printers often added more muscle to the Union victory narrative by swelling Lee's losses and shriveling Meade's. Of course, both sides' estimates could not be correct, although both sides could be and were often wrong. When the conflicting casualty reports of Northern papers sieved Southward through the lines, pro-Davis printers once more took to their favorite pastime: discrediting "the most shameless liars in the world."[93]

Cowardin again threw his columns to the task. When several Northern papers estimated Lee's casualties at thirty-three thousand, the *Dispatch* scoffed, "A more monstrous falsehood was never published even in a Yankee newspaper." To invalidate the Yankee estimate, Cowardin called attention to an aspect of the Gettysburg campaign commonly used by Southern apologists to discount Union victory claims: Lee's successful retreat. The *Dispatch* asked, "If the loss of Gen. Lee was so great, how comes it that a single man of his army was allowed to cross the Potomac? Why was it not pursued sword in hand, and . . . why was Gen. Lee allowed to withdraw without the loss of a gun or a caisson?" After launching this interrogatory salvo, the *Dispatch* charged, "The loss of 33,000 men . . . would have dissolved [Lee's army] like a snow wreath in the warm rains of Spring." It concluded, "[The federal troops] did not follow Lee because they could not. They had been so badly beaten that pursuit was impossible."[94] Smith shared the same view as Cowardin. At Gettysburg, argued the *Sentinel*, Lee "struck the enemy a most awful blow, that they should fear to molest him . . . at Hagerstown [Maryland]."[95]

Lee's mostly unharried retreat through Pennsylvania and Maryland and successful Potomac crossing on July 13 said less about what happened at Gettysburg and more about Meade's mindset afterward. Critical Northern printers used adjectives such as "overcautious" and "hesitant" to explain how Meade allowed Lee to escape unmolested.[96] It had nothing to do, they argued, with the "badly beaten" state of the Army of the Potomac.[97] But this explanation did not wash in the South. Many Southerners saw Lee's unbadgered withdrawal beyond the Potomac through the same lens as the *Dispatch* and the *Sentinel*: as further proof that Lee gave at least as good as he got at Gettysburg. Edmund Ruffin, a Virginia Fire-Eater surpassed only by Robert Barnwell Rhett in influence and invective, believed that if Meade had triumphed over Lee at Gettysburg, then the Union general would have "followed upon the rear of Lee's very slowly retreating army."[98]

If pro-Davis printers were right and Lee had crippled Meade at Gettysburg, rendering him incapable of aggressive pursuit, then why did Lee retreat from the battlefield in the first place? That Lee suffered defeat, one so severe it necessitated a full-scale retreat on July 4, supplies the obvious answer. But most pro-Davis printers refused to entertain this noxious notion. Rather than taint Lee's record in defeat, they gave him the benefit of the doubt. "Opinions are various with regard to the motives which induced Gen. Lee to withdraw his army to the Virginia side of the Potomac," remarked Cowardin's *Dispatch*. "All seem, however to agree that the movement was proper . . . being guided in their opinions entirely on the profound confidence which they repose in the Commander's professional skill." According to the *Dispatch*, Lee's undeniable competence combined with two circumstances, sustained flooding of the Potomac and the need to maintain communications with Virginia, to amply explain the retreat without invoking defeat.[99] Tyler agreed with Cowardin but made his case more succinctly.

Lee's retreat, declared the *Enquirer*, "was a prudential move, not occasioned by any success on the part of the enemy."[100]

With Lee back on Southern soil for reasons supposedly unattributable to defeat, the pro-Davis press attempted to quash any lingering concern over Gettysburg's outcome by putting a positive face on the condition of Lee's army. "All accounts represent our army as in most excellent condition and the best of spirits," assured Smith after learning of Lee's withdrawal south of the Potomac.[101] Tyler and Paul drank from the same optimistic cup. The *Enquirer* dispelled any cause for alarm following the army's return to Virginia by asserting "The army is in fine spirits and excellent condition" while the *Daily Rebel* announced, "Our army was not whipped, and we are ready for another fight."[102]

These optimistic reports made an impression. On July 17, South Carolinian Emma Holmes repeated pro-Davis press talking points when she diarized, "Lee has recrossed the Potomac, in admirable order, and the army in splendid trim without loss." On July 25, North Carolinian Catherine Edmondston journaled the oft-repeated press line, "Gen. Lee's army said to be in fine condition."[103] Even though Gettysburg had cut through Lee's army like a scythe through grass—leaving more than one-third of his men killed, wounded, or missing—the pro-Davis press peddled a narrative that hope-hungry Southerners eagerly latched on to, a narrative in which the Army of Northern Virginia suffered fewer casualties than its adversary and returned to the Confederacy's warm embrace both undaunted and unbeaten.

The relative inaction on the Virginia front following the Gettysburg campaign gave Southern newspapermen a chance to catch their breath and reflect on its fruits. While most pro-Davis printers refused to label the campaign anything analogous to failure, they also acknowledged an awkward reality: the results did not fully measure up to expectations. After pouring nearly all of his Gettysburg coverage through a propitious funnel, Smith conceded that the campaign's results fell short of its aspirations. "We must cheerfully make up our minds to accept a less telling campaign than we had hoped at its commencement," acceded the *Sentinel*. "[It proved not] as glorious and crushing as we had expected."[104] Tyler concurred. After forecasting in late June that Lee's invasion would have the North "thirsting and hungering for peace," the *Enquirer* admitted otherwise in mid-July: "All hope of a speedy peace depended on a decisive success of Lee's army; and that success has not been decisive."[105]

But the lack of decisive success did not render the campaign unsuccessful. Pro-Davis printers generally viewed the Gettysburg campaign as a double-edged sword but one that sliced in the South's favor. McClanahan and Dill, two printers who initially doubted the wisdom of a Northern invasion, regretted that it helped Union recruitment efforts but applauded its capture of thousands of horses and livestock alongside provisions capable of supplying Lee's army through the next winter.[106] Cowardin seconded the *Appeal*'s peripatetic chiefs. After proclaiming Gettysburg "an overwhelming victory" on July 13, five days later the *Dispatch* confessed that the campaign had brought both "good and evil" but believed the former outshined the latter.[107] The evil referred to the post-Gettysburg spike in Northern morale drawing in new federal recruits. The outweighing good of Lee's campaign, however, relieved war-starved Virginia from supporting two massive armies, procured vast supply stores by stripping Pennsylvania to its husk, and showed Yankeedom that, like Dixie, it too lay vulnerable to invasion.[108]

Time only hardened Cowardin's conviction: Lee's invasion left the Confederacy in the black. Its gains more than offset its losses. On July 28, the *Dispatch* considered Gettysburg a "drawn battle" but dignified Lee's invasion as "one of the wisest, grandest, and most imposing schemes ever conceived by the mind of man." The South could hang its hat on the fact that the campaign yielded "immense stores of every kind . . . relief to our overburdened land by the transfer of the war . . . [and] the moral advantage obtained by proving to the enemy that his dominions were open to invasion."[109]

Such rationalization reeked of disappointment. When Lee's army marched onto Northern soil in late June after Winchester, pro-Davis printers had prophesied a total Confederate victory. After Lee dispensed with the Army of the Potomac, it was said, Harrisburg, Washington, and even Baltimore and Philadelphia would fall like dominoes and a Confederate peace dictated at the point of Lee's triumphant sword. This vision, however, never materialized because, as Tyler confided, Gettysburg had "not been decisive."[110] The gulf between their expectations for the campaign and its actual results drove pro-Davis printers to grasp whatever straws they could find. Whether it be Lee's hefty haul or his turning of war's table against the North, pro-Davis printers shifted the goalpost of success in order to keep the Gettysburg campaign from sliding into the cleft of defeat. It was, wrote historian J. Cutler Andrews, "the best solace the Confederate press could offer for the disappointing sequel to magnificent expectations."[111]

Regardless of how they viewed the campaign, the South's pro-administration printers stood unflinchingly behind Lee. All across the South, from the Rappahannock to the Rio Grande, they reaffirmed their faith in Lee following Gettysburg. "No one in the army has had his confidence in Gen.

Lee in the slightest degree impaired," commented Tyler's *Enquirer*. "His fair fame will not receive a single blot by this campaign."[112] Cowardin dittoed his Richmond colleague. "Victorious in two days of the battles, he failed but in one instance to rent the enemy, and then fell back in perfect order, induced to do so by the want of provisions alone," argued the *Dispatch*. Even as Lee's wounded swamped Richmond's hospitals and the hair-raising shrieks of dying men carried into nearby homes, the paper remained as loyal to Lee as ever before. "The people of the Confederacy may place, as heretofore, the most implicit confidence in him. Wherever he is there they may be assured everything will be done that should be."[113]

Declarations of faith in Lee washed over the South like a religious revival. North Carolina's *Fayetteville Observer* testified, "We have faith in Gen. Lee."[114] Atlanta's *Daily Intelligencer* affirmed, "The confidence of our community in the ability of Gen. Lee to thrash this boastful enemy . . . remains as strong as ever."[115] The *Charleston Daily Courier*, the city's pro-administration counterweight to Rhett's anti-Davis *Mercury* and the paper that took in Northern reporter Felix Gregory De Fontaine, expressed unwavering faith in Lee after Gettysburg. "We feel no uneasiness concerning that great captain and his invincible army," professed the *Courier*.[116]

Perhaps no newspaper reiterated its belief in Lee more devoutly than Cushing's Houston *Telegraph*. "We have full faith in his generalship," kowtowed the paper on July 20. "No man ever gave better evidences of consummate generalship than has Lee since he took command of the army about Richmond."[117] The following day the *Telegraph* sermonized on faith in Confederate leadership: "Confidence in the powers that be must be maintained. President Davis has made the world confess his greatness and his statesmanship. Gen. Lee is today as great a General as breathes the breath of life. Trust to their judgment. Have confidence in their foresight and wisdom. Do not be discouraged because you do not understand the moves upon the military chess-board. FAITH, FAITH, FAITH. We have reason to rejoice that in this great struggle we have had such gallant leaders as God has raised up."[118]

Propping up the Davis administration became all the more necessary following Confederate cataclysms in the Southwest. On July 4, Vicksburg—the South's linchpin on the Mississippi—surrendered to Grant. With the Confederate Gibraltar went Port Hudson, and with the two went nearly forty thousand rebel prisoners and all remaining rebel control of the Mississippi. The blow struck Southerners like a sledgehammer. When Mary Boykin Chesnut heard the news she literally fainted: "I felt as if I had been struck a hard blow on the top of my head, and my heart took one of its queer turns."[119]

The news hit Jones hard as well. "Vicksburg capitulated," he yelped. "This is a terrible blow, and has produced much despondency."[120]

Pro-Davis printers had laid the kindling for that despondency. For weeks prior to July 4, while they busily predicted Lee's coup de grace, they also assured the South that Vicksburg was a whale the Yankees would never harpoon. The *Dispatch* gloated on June 16, "We do not believe that the Yankees will ever take Vicksburg."[121] And on June 30, four days before the fortress raised the white flag, the *Dispatch* crowed, "That she [Vicksburg] will ever be reduced by Grant, we cannot find it in our hearts to believe."[122] Even papers close to the action pledged that all remained well along the Father of Waters. On June 16, the Jackson *Mississippian* promised that Vicksburg contained enough rations to hold out for two more months.[123] And on July 3, the day before the citadel surrendered, the *Mississippian* assured Southerners they need not worry because the garrison remained well provisioned.[124]

In addition to these sureties, pro-Davis printers spun victory fantasies that bore no resemblance to the military reality. According to one widely circulated delusion, Confederate general Joseph E. Johnston—who hastily organized an army in Jackson—would not only break Grant's siege but also unite with Vicksburg's defenders to deliver Grant his fatal blow. But neither this fantasy nor the assurances of the pro-Davis press ever materialized. Instead, the "key" to the South, as President Lincoln likened Vicksburg, fell into federal hands. And by heightening expectations that never came true, pro-Davis printers fed into Southerners' growing disillusionment and mounting distrust of the news they depended on to make sense of an unintelligible war.[125]

The fall of Vicksburg threw the pro-Davis press into damage control, but shock ensued first. On July 9, the *Sentinel* claimed the news came "unexpectedly": "We had just received such assurances . . . as to have given confidence in its safety."[126] But once the truth sank in, the South's pro-administration printers turned to their favorite crutch for support, one they often used to save credibility and save Southern morale from nosediving after unexpected setbacks: downplaying military disasters. The *Staunton Spectator* minimized the reverse by telling readers, "[Vicksburg] fell with the least possible damage to us."[127] The *Chattanooga Rebel* shrugged off the defeat by claiming the Yankees "gave fifty thousand lives for an elephant which [could not have been] . . . appropriated to any valuable purpose."[128] To many pro-Davis newspapermen the Union capture of Vicksburg left Billy Yank holding an empty bag. The loss did not entail a war-paralyzing forfeiture of the Mississippi. The *Fayetteville Observer* promised, "The loss of Vicksburg is not the loss of the Mississippi . . .

[because Confederate] light artillery from a hundred other points can effectually prevent [Northern] commerce on that great river."[129]

Despite this wishful thinking, the pro-Davis press characterized Vicksburg in ways it never did Gettysburg. The *Dispatch* called it "a heavy blow," the *Observer* "calamitous," and the *Telegraph*, alongside many others, "disaster."[130] As if two different species, Vicksburg and Gettysburg could not be classed together. The former, argued pro-Davis printers, constituted an unambiguous defeat in Rebeldom's heartland, whereas the latter proved no worse than a draw, one that sullied the North's second-most-populous state with the turpitude of war. McClanahan and Dill maintained, "The loss of Vicksburg is really the only serious reverse that our arms have met with during the past twelve months."[131] Meanwhile, Richard Smith worried not about Gettysburg and Lee but rather about Vicksburg and the gale it put behind Union sails in terms or morale. As "easy as we feel in regards to LEE," commented the *Sentinel*, "it is not to be overlooked that the enemy will be vastly encouraged by the capture of Vicksburg."[132]

Whether they knew it or not, pro-Davis printers reflected the view of Davis himself. In a late July letter to Lee, the president expressed no concern over Gettysburg but a mountain of worry over Vicksburg and developments out west. "I have felt more than ever before the want of your advice during the recent period of disaster," wrote Davis. "You know how one army of the enemy has triumphed by attacking three of ours in detail, at Vicksburg, Port Hudson and Jackson."[133] Not only did Davis exclude Gettysburg when listing July's setbacks, he also asked Lee for advice in its costly aftermath. Ultimately, the pro-Davis press and President Davis himself drew a sharp line between the Vicksburg disaster and Lee's hard-won "success" at Gettysburg.

Some pro-Davis printers tried lifting spirits sunk by Vicksburg by pointing to Lee. Before dissecting the sobering details of Coldwell's July 8 telegrams, Francis Paul wanted Southerners focusing on Lee, not Vicksburg. "[We] are entirely comforted for any disaster on the Mississippi by the great exploits of our great Captain 'over the border,'" remarked the *Rebel*. Cushing believed that those "great exploits" more than compensated for the loss of Vicksburg.[134] And on July 24 his *Tri-Weekly Telegraph* demanded "Faith, Faith, Confidence, Confidence" and directed Southerners thirsting for hope to "look to glorious Lee."[135]

Pro-Davis printers looked to Lee and Gettysburg throughout July and into much of August.[136] Logistics partially explain the prolonged focus. Since Gettysburg occurred deeper in Northern territory than any other major Civil War battle, it necessarily took longer for the reports of Southern correspondents to make it into print. Of course, the bare bones of the battle, information that could be easily bulletined outside newspaper offices, rode the "lightning" throughout Dixie and heralded word of Gettysburg with little delay. But wired news left cracks in the Gettysburg story that only correspondents could fill. To spread their accounts, printers relied on the Confederate post's newspaper exchange, which by the war's third summer was more backlogged than Richmond's hospitals. The disruption in mail services, complained McClanahan and Dill in mid-July, had prevented them "from obtaining detailed accounts of the capitulation of Vicksburg."[137] Gettysburg proved even worse. Thanks to sluggish mail distribution, the details of Gettysburg—a battle already beyond the South's reach—spread through Southern newsdom like water through a kinked hose. Southern printers resorted to patching the Gettysburg story together one column at a time throughout most of July.

At least two other factors kept Gettysburg in the press spotlight. For one, the feud over which state's soldiers bore blame for July 3 kept Virginia and North Carolina printers at each other's throats. Neither side gave ground. For nearly a month and a half after the battle they kept the debate over Pickett's Charge alive and thus kept Gettysburg alive in the news. Another reason for Gettysburg's staying power involved the objectives of the pro-Davis press. Andrews once wrote, "Southern newspapers exalted the spirits of their readers . . . to keep the South fighting against long odds for four years."[138] This rang especially true for the patriotic printers of the pro-Davis press. But to sustain morale these biased cheerleaders of the Confederate president and his increasingly desperate war effort needed pliable content, war-related news that could be molded like clay to positively affect Southern readers' hearts and minds. In the gloomy summer of 1863, Gettysburg—a battle that starred a man who figured warmly in Southern hearts and minds—seemed far more malleable than the solid reverse of Vicksburg. As a result, pro-Davis printers stayed glued to Gettysburg and Lee to provide Southerners a beacon of hope in a dark season of war.

But eventually the dark summer showed rays of light. General P. G. T. Beauregard thwarted Union efforts to capture Charleston and its surrounding forts; Clement Vallandigham, the banished Copperhead king, started his in absentia campaign to be Ohio's antiwar governor; and New York City, the Union's news hub and largest metropolis, erupted in violent resistance to Lincoln's new military draft. To say that pro-Davis printers ate these stories up would be an understatement. They ate them up and sucked the marrow dry. The riots, according to many, would spread like wildfire to every Northern city, prevent Lincoln from adding a single soldier to his ranks, and shorten the war.[139]

These stories gave pro-Davis printers something meatier to chew on than the lean scraps of the Gettysburg campaign. And the sudden influx of even more pliable content encouraged them to begin transitioning Gettysburg away from the limelight—a process mostly completed by mid-August.

The South's pro-administration printers overhauled the Gettysburg campaign from start to finish. Buoyed by Lee's reputation and a campaign inaugurating victory at Winchester, they greeted the invasion with forecasts of a war-finishing blow on Union soil. At first, thanks to Coldwell's telegrams, they thought that blow had been delivered. But once they saw that Gettysburg fell short of expectations, they rolled up their biased sleeves and got to work remolding and varnishing the clay of defeat. Pro-Davis printers made the Wednesday triumph even more striking, conflated the indecisive Thursday fight with the prior day's victory, and downplayed, excused, and romanticized the Friday disaster. Gettysburg became nothing worse than a draw, if not another hard-won victory for Lee and his still "invincible" army, a point supposedly confirmed by a lower casualty count, successful retreat, and a multitude of post hoc rationalizations—such as the rebels' hefty supply haul or their shifting north the stage of war.[140] By sharply contrasting the "calamitous" result at Vicksburg, this revamped version of Gettysburg gave hope-thirsty Confederates something to sustain them through a draught-ridden season of war.[141]

Pro-Davis printers covered the Civil War with a bias about as barefaced as any in the history of journalism. To stay the administration and the morale needed to win Confederate independence, they cast war-related events in the most favorable light possible. Victories were overblown and defeats minimized, for pro-Davis printers understood that "the principal determinant of morale was victory or defeat," as historian James McPherson writes. "Victory pumped up morale; defeat deflated it."[142] But with Gettysburg, pro-Davis printers did not merely minimize a defeat to bolster morale. Instead, they inverted that defeat, transforming Gettysburg—a battle that ought to have shaken the Confederacy's foundations and dulled Lee's shining name in the umbra of defeat—into yet another success for Lee and his veteran Army of Northern Virginia. Rather than turn from Lee in one of his darkest hours, the South's pro-administration printers used his name like a pillar to buttress the Confederacy in one of its darkest hours, and they called on Southerners to "look to glorious Lee" for hope that the war remained winnable.[143]

CHAPTER FIVE

"Waterloo Eclipsed"

As the sun dipped toward the western horizon on July 2, 1863, a travel-worn *New-York Tribune* reporter dismounted outside a hotel in Hanover, Pennsylvania, and rushed inside. Homer Byington sensed history in the making. Hanover sits thirteen miles east of Gettysburg, and he could hear low rumbling artillery in the distance like faint thunder. A great battle raged there, and its news needed to get out. Byington implored the hotelman for the town telegrapher. With finger raised, the man replied, "There he is, over yonder."[1] To Byington's shock, telegrapher Daniel Trone literally lay within reach, casually sleeping on a nearby bench, resigned to joblessness ever since rebel cavalry had swept through like a pack of wolves and mauled the town telegraph wire. But Byington aimed to remedy that. After rousing Trone to fetch his gear, Byington assembled a local crew and, with the help of a handcar, repaired the line with an urgency equal to the moment's magnitude. Their work paid off. Trone linked his battery to the newly mended wire and, waving his hat with abandon, shouted, "We've got Baltimore!" The reporter mounted his horse and raced off toward the thunder emanating from Gettysburg.[2]

Byington quickly found what he needed. On reaching the battlefield he scored a description of the July 1 fight from Union major general Oliver Howard. Shortly thereafter a fellow *Tribune* reporter, Josiah Sypher, intercepted Byington, bearing an account of the July 2 battle. With the first two days' news in hand, the duo made off like jockeys for the Hanover telegraph. Sometime before 11:30 p.m., they wired their accounts to the *New-York Tribune* office by way of Washington. Byington's signature authenticated the dispatch.

Horace Greeley leapt into action. He once said "The paper that brings the quickest news is the thing looked to," and now he possessed among the first Gettysburg news to get through to the press.[3] On the morning of July 3, Greeley ran a *Tribune* extra featuring Byington's and Sypher's accounts. New Yorkers devoured it. While the fighting at Gettysburg banged on like a tempest, *Tribune* newsies hawked sixty-five thousand copies in New York City alone.[4]

Meanwhile, back in Hanover, the telegraph chirped with an incoming message. It came not from the *Tribune* office in New York but instead from the War Department in Washington. Trone deciphered the cable, turned to the man of the hour, and said "The President wants to know 'Who is Byington?'" Apparently the news wired that night proved not only among the first Gettysburg reports to reach the press but also the first Gettysburg report of any kind to reach President Lincoln. Byington, reveling in his moment, told Trone to tap three words in response: "Ask Uncle Gideon."[5]

Navy Secretary Gideon Welles, after waiting in vain all day for news, had left the War Department at 11:00 p.m. for a much-needed night's rest. Scarcely thirty minutes later, however, a courier stirred Welles from bed carrying Byington's message.[6] To all who remained at the War Department, including Lincoln, the correspondent was an unknown and, therefore, unreliable commodity.[7] But Byington had singled out Welles for a reason. Both men came from the Nutmeg State, and Welles knew Connecticut pressmen better than most generals knew their own staffs.[8] The secretary told Lincoln, "The telegram was reliable. Byington is the editor . . . of a weekly paper in Norwalk, Connecticut . . . is sometimes employed by the New York *Tribune*, and is doubtless so employed now."[9]

After learning his identity, Lincoln made Byington an offer he could not refuse. In exchange for the War Department's use of the line to communicate with Union general George Meade, Byington could continue to use it to forward reports to Greeley. He accepted. As historian J. Cutler Andrews noted, "Byington had no choice in the matter—the request was tantamount to a military order."[10] While other correspondents combed the countryside for a working wire, Byington continued to supply the *Tribune* and President Lincoln with the latest from the Battle of Gettysburg.

Over the next four days, as Byington and his fellow knights of the quill heralded victory at Gettysburg, the North's pro-administration press erupted in euphoria. "Victory!!"—"Waterloo Eclipsed!!" roared the *Philadelphia Inquirer*.[11] "The Rebellion Receives Its Death Stroke," boomed the Harrisburg *Evening Telegraph*.[12] The news landed like manna from heaven. From Boston to Chicago, Northerners rejoiced. Church bells tolled, cannons growled in salute, bands struck up patriotic tunes, and strangers embraced and agreed: "This ends the Rebellion." As if the storm of war had passed altogether, thousands poured into New York City's Union Square waving flags and shooting off fireworks. "A memorable day," journaled New Yorker George Templeton Strong on July 5, "even should its glorious news prove but half true."[13]

Unfortunately it did. The North's initial post-Gettysburg excitement, like that in the South, was drummed up by an initial wave of exciting but extremely inaccurate reports.[14] Depending on the newspaper, the Confederate corps commanders—Lieutenant Generals James Longstreet, Richard Ewell, and A. P. Hill—had ended up dead, wounded, captured, or both of the latter two. Many also claimed that Meade had bagged twenty thousand graybacks, sent the remnants of General Robert E. Lee's rebel Army of Northern Virginia flying like bleating sheep into the mountains, and gobbled up nearly half of Lee's estimated 270 guns.[15] The fog of battle fell thick upon the North and South after Gettysburg, obscuring fact from fiction. But even after that fog lifted as more detailed correspondence reached Northern press offices beginning on July 6, pro-Lincoln printers continued to stuff their pages with overly favorable coverage of the Gettysburg campaign.

Gettysburg gave the nation the victory it craved, and pro-Lincoln printers made certain their coverage satisfied every appetite. To magnify the triumph, they miscalculated casualties, misconstrued each army's strength, and even mischaracterized the enemy. Pro-Lincoln printers also rubbed smooth the battle's rough edges. While Wednesday's rout became an orderly withdrawal, Thursday's bloody exchange became a clear-cut victory wherein Major General Dan Sickles's unauthorized gamble proved anything but a costly mistake. The pro-Lincoln press took the decisive Friday triumph, which needed no dressing to make palatable, and suffused it with exaggeration and sentimentalism. The overstated defeat of Lee persuaded most pro-Lincoln printers to value Gettysburg on par or above Vicksburg and to predict that Meade, the nation's new hero, would finish off the rebel army before it reached Southern soil. When this failed to materialize, the pro-Lincoln press turned on Meade for "hesitating" to crush Lee and then turned elsewhere to feed the public hunger for uplifting war news. Ultimately, pro-Lincoln printers spun the war with an eye toward maintaining morale and sustaining support for Lincoln's administration. That bias blanketed every column of their Gettysburg coverage.

"The Empire City of the New World" pointed the way.[16] Greeley and Henry J. Raymond, the leading pro-Lincoln printers in New York City, twisted each day of the battle favorably. Greeley, who dispatched eight reporters alongside Byington to Gettysburg, denied that the federals had been routed on Wednesday. Union troops stood their ground like sentries all afternoon, argued the *Tribune*, until they merely "retired" to the advantageous heights south of town.[17] Raymond's *New York Times*, which placed four correspondents at Gettysburg, saw things likewise.[18] Chief *Times* correspondent Lorenzo Crounse reported that the federals simply withdrew and "in good order."[19] Crounse, the first reporter at Gettysburg and thus the man who supplied its first published words, even gave reason to admire the outcome. "There is no cause whatever for discouragement at the result," he explained,

"It was simply an advance of two corps engaged with, two whole corps (two-thirds) of the rebel army."[20] But Crounse overdrew his bowstring. Although the Confederates possessed a numerical advantage on July 1—roughly twenty-four thousand against nineteen thousand—less than one-third of Lee's army fought that day.[21]

Greeley and Raymond also painted a positive portrait of the Thursday battle, which in truth left neither army a firm peg on which to hang a triumphant hat. Both printers gave no hint of a close contest, claiming the Yankees repulsed every attack heaved at them.[22] And neither criticized Sickles for his forward gamble that nearly cost him his life and the Union army a costly defeat. In fact, Greeley did the opposite. After acknowledging the injury to Sickles's right leg, which forced its amputation, the *Tribune* asserted that Sickles "successfully prevented" Longstreet's attack against the Union left, which otherwise "might have turned the tables on Meade's army."[23] These misrepresentations helped persuade the Northern public that July 2 resulted in a resounding Union success rather than an indecisive draw.

The Friday battle handed both Greeley and Raymond the ideal war story: a victory so convincing it needed no sprucing up to make appetizing. Yet both printers sprang at the chance to garnish that already savory triumph. The *Times* hurrahed the "magnificent success" of July 3 for yielding "the complete discomfiture of the entire rebel army."[24] The *Tribune* trumpeted a brilliant triumph that, when combined with the previous two days, resulted in thirty-five thousand rebel casualties—almost half of Lee's army.[25]

This uncurbed victory narrative trickled down to the city's other pro-Lincoln papers. The New York *Sun*, which proudly continued the penny tradition of its founder, Benjamin H. Day, promised that July 3 was even more conclusive than the initial wave of already hyperbolized reports suggested.[26] Meanwhile, Massachusetts-born printer William Cullen Bryant turned ebullient over the Friday victory. Bryant's *New-York Evening Post*, which closely tracked its hometown peers in circulation, swanked after receiving the news, "It is impossible to overestimate the importance of the victory at Gettysburg."[27]

Pennsylvania's chief pro-Lincoln printers covered the battle as propitiously as their New York City colleagues. As if conspiring to shield the public from negative news, native Pennsylvania printers William Harding and John W. Forney, alongside the German-born newspaperman George Bergner, all but ignored the Confederate army's transparent July 1 success. Instead, they shifted to the more ambiguous July 2 battle and styled it an unambiguous Union victory. Despite there having been no involvement from much of Lee's army, Bergner's Harrisburg *Evening Telegraph* dubbed Thursday a "substantial success" for the federals: "[Lee's] entire army was engaged, and suffered a signal service."[28] Harding's *Philadelphia Inquirer*, which fielded three reporters at Gettysburg, erroneously claimed the federals confronted "twice their number" while inflicting losses "four-fold that of ours."[29] Forney swam in the same spurious waters. With its own trio of Gettysburg reporters, Forney's Philadelphia *Press* maintained that Longstreet and Hill's corps smashed into the Union left with a phalanx of fifty thousand bayonets.[30] The actual figure, however, barely topped twenty thousand. Together these false reports helped fashion the same illusion peddled by Greeley and Raymond: July 2 resulted in a clear Union victory.

Coverage of Sickles in the Thursday battle only added to that illusion. Both Harding and Forney omitted that Sickles had nearly dealt the Union army a defeat by uprooting his corps from its Meade-assigned post. Instead, both printers made Sickles out as a major reason why the Union army staved off defeat. The *Inquirer* congratulated Sickles and his Third Corps for fighting "nobly" and creating a "stonewall," even though Longstreet toppled that wall and forced Sickles from the salient he foolishly created.[31] To the likely frustration of Meade, however, Forney inoculated Sickles against any wrongdoing. The *Press* insisted that the corps commander was "ordered forward to develop the enemy's attention."[32] Not only did Meade issue no such order, he also worked like a Trojan repairing the damage it caused.

Sickles fought for his reputation after Gettysburg harder than he fought at the battle itself. Beginning on July 5, while he still roamed between life and death in a D.C. hospital post-amputation, Sickles used the outpouring of sympathy he received to his advantage.[33] He explained to none other than President Lincoln, who left his own sick wife to see the wounded general, that circumstance had forced him to leave his designated post for the higher-elevated peach orchard.[34] Sickles's power of persuasion remained intact even if his body did not. An aide to the general wrote, "He certainly got his side of the story of Gettysburg well into the President's mind . . . and this doubtless stood in good stead afterward."[35] Indeed it did. When Meade considered court-martialing Sickles for disobeying his orders, Lincoln emphatically objected, "No, no, we can't do that. General Sickles may have erred . . . but at any rate he fought superbly! He gave his leg—his life almost—for the Union!"[36]

Lincoln's favor and the loss of a limb convinced the pro-Lincoln press to cast the Gettysburg fool as a great hero. Raymond swiftly took up the mantle. On July 6, the *New York Times* gushed, "The misfortune of no one whose lot it has been to be smitten in this war has excited livelier sympathy than the painful injury sustained . . . by Gen. Daniel E. Sickles, [who] literally carved his way to fame with his sword." While most pro-Lincoln printers gave Sickles the same positive press, Raymond harbored a reason beyond the general's injury and relationship with Lincoln to do so. Raymond, like Sickles himself, hailed from New York. Civil War newsmen coveted the chance to spotlight their own, and Raymond proved no exception after Gettysburg. "When the roll call of heroes is written for this war," cooed the *Times*, "one of the highest on the list will be that of Gen. Daniel E. Sickles, and New York will justly claim him as her own."[37]

The press also worked in Sickles's favor because he actively ensured that it did. At least one perceptive publication, a weekly titled the *Round Table*, noticed the game Sickles so craftily played. The paper intuited, "We know that he [Sickles] has accomplished more by personal address, adroitness, and cunning management of newspaper correspondents [to establish his Gettysburg image] than by actual display of military ability."[38] Sickles used his persuasive powers as effectively on the press as he had on Lincoln. Thanks largely to his shameless self-publicizing, pro-administration printers gave Sickles the benefit of the doubt and gave his Gettysburg contribution an unwarranted scrubbing. Sickles spent his life safeguarding the hero image established by the press after Gettysburg. As one biographer wrote, "The national press began to develop the one-legged war hero image that Dan would spend the next fifty years cultivating."[39]

Like Greeley and Raymond in New York, Pennsylvania's pro-Lincoln printers overstated the already trenchant July 3 victory. Harding not only thought that the Friday victory eclipsed the Duke of Wellington's at Waterloo but also that it left the Confederates with more casualties than they actually suffered. The *Philadelphia Inquirer* estimated Southern losses over all three days at thirty-five thousand—almost seven thousand more than the best estimates.[40] Forney performed even greater overreach. After celebrating an absurd thirty thousand rebels captured, the Philadelphia *Press* believed Friday's "Complete Triumph" had so decimated Lee's army that it would never "again dare to meet that army [the Army of the Potomac] in battle array."[41]

Although bruised and battered after Gettysburg, like a boxer after twelve pulping rounds, Lee's army remained unbroken. Under the old man's command, the Army of Northern Virginia won further laurels battling the Army of the Potomac for nearly two more years. But Forney saw Lee's Friday defeat as evidence instead of an undeserved reputation. "Lee is not the great man we are all apt to imagine him," chortled the *Press*. "He is but shorn Samson."[42]

The Pennsylvania press took the victory on its own soil as an opportunity to gloat. Forney radiated with home state pride. "The most gratifying feature of the [Gettysburg] victory," reasoned the *Press*, "is that it was won on Pennsylvania soil, by a Pennsylvania general, and, in a great degree, by Pennsylvania soldiers." The paper credited the victory to "General Meade, whom we are proud to claim as a fellow-citizen . . . the gallant General [John] REYNOLDS, a Pennsylvania solider" and "General [Winfield Scott] Hancock, a Pennsylvanian, who so nobly bore the brunt of the battle on Cemetery Hill." The *Press* concluded for its predominantly Keystone State audience: "In this crisis of the nation's fate, it was Pennsylvania that came to the rescue."[43]

The decisive repulse of Lee's invasion in southern Pennsylvania, purchased in part by that state's soldiers, revealed the partisanship by region that so often characterized the Civil War press. Printers betrayed this bias, as historian James McPherson writes, by "exaggerating the fighting prowess of troops from one state or denigrating the cowardice of those from another."[44] Forney proved guilty of the former. After Gettysburg he accentuated the fighting prowess of Pennsylvanians, particularly Philadelphians. After the battle a soldier in the 29th Pennsylvania wrote Forney a letter requesting he publish that the 29th and 109th Pennsylvania Regiments, both of which came from Philadelphia, clinched the Friday victory by repulsing Ewell that same morning on the Union right. The soldier fulminated, "[It is] too steep to be robbed of our credit." Like Raymond, Forney jumped at the chance to foreground his own. On July 11, he granted the soldier's request with flash. Headlined "Justice to Philadelphia Soldiers," the man's letter landed on the *Press*'s front page next to a story about the contributions of two other Pennsylvania regiments at Gettysburg.[45]

The victory on Pennsylvania soil exposed not only the home state and home city biases of Pennsylvania printers but also their disdain for the influential New York City press. Bolstered by his Pennsylvania "to the rescue" narrative, Forney demanded that New York City printers "cease to sneer and cavil at everything Pennsylvanian" with their "constant superciliousness" and "air of affected superiority." New York City newspapers irritated pressmen from other states for catering to New York readers' tastes while circulating nationally. As Forney put it, "They misrepresent the action and sentiments of our people."[46] The victory at Gettysburg offered him and other Keystone State printers a unique opportunity to vent their antipathy for New York, which continued to flare on and off and to varying degrees for the rest of the war.

Chicago's main pro-Lincoln printer, Joseph Medill, walked shoulder to shoulder with his peers in New York and Pennsylvania. Medill's *Chicago*

Tribune, which planted a solo reporter on the ground at Gettysburg, slanted the Wednesday battle in a way that would make any reader doubt that a Union rout had taken place. The newspaper insisted that, without losing any cohesion, Union troops simply "retire[d]" to the commanding heights south of Gettysburg. Like *Times* correspondent Lorenzo Crounse, Medill gave cause to view this as a success by misrepresenting the combatants' relative strength. The *Tribune* promised, "There was no discouragement over the results. It is the inevitable consequence of the fact of the rebel [force] being nearly double the number of our own." In case this numerical stunt failed to satisfy his readers, Medill offered another. The *Tribune* vouched that on July 1 the Union army netted as many prisoners as did the Confederate army. "We have taken so many [rebel] prisoners," gasconaded the paper, "that the account is fully balanced."[47]

Medill's coverage of July 2 and 3 proved just as dishonest. The doubtful Thursday firefight became an undoubtable Union victory. Rather than acknowledge the ground gained by Ewell and Longstreet, for example, the *Chicago Tribune* confirmed success across the entire battlefront, with all enemy attacks rebuffed.[48] Friday's "complete victory" and "glorious triumph" became a springboard to overstate the Union army's overall success.[49] The *Tribune* estimated that, when combined with the previous two days, July 3 resulted in a total Union loss of between five thousand and seven thousand—approximately sixteen thousand less than the actual figure.[50] But Medill's meddling with the numbers did not stop there. While he cut Union losses, he also cut Meade's army strength while inflating Lee's like a balloon. The *Tribune* contended, "Meade led into the battle . . . less than half what it [the Army of the Potomac] contained four months ago," while Lee had invaded Pennsylvania with a Mongol-sized horde of 109,000 gray-clad warriors.[51] This number ought to have beggared belief. Four months earlier, just before its debacle at Chancellorsville, the Army of the Potomac had bristled with 120,000 men. If the *Tribune* were correct, the manpower-deprived Confederates would have outnumbered the federals at Gettysburg by 109,000 to no more than 60,000.

Pro-administration printers on both sides bent the numbers to their will. The most popular misuse involved casualties. By overestimating Confederate casualties and underestimating those for the Union, pro-Lincoln printers could make any victory seem more impressive and any defeat seem less concerning. Ten months before Gettysburg—on September 17, 1862—the Army of the Potomac purchased a costly victory at Antietam Creek in Maryland. When the accounting finished, 12,400 Union soldiers wound up missing, wounded, or buried in early graves.[52] On September 20, however, a *New-York Tribune* reporter cited Union losses at 5,000 to 6,000, even when he knew that an army staff officer had estimated the total at 10,000—much closer to the true figure.[53] Greeley cared not that a reliable source contradicted his reporter's low casualty count. He tossed aside his journalistic scruples like disposable gloves and did the unconscionable: he published the reporter's estimate anyway. The news titan once wryly remarked, "My readers can select which set of figures they will believe in."[54] Plainly put, the North's pro-administration newspapermen ran casualty figures that drove the most encouraging war narrative. For these indefatigable advocates of Lincoln's war effort, maintaining morale through uplifting war coverage functioned as a means that more than justified the political and military ends they sought.

But slanting casualties proved just one path toward those ends. As noted, pro-Lincoln printers also played the numbers by misrepresenting the strength of both armies. As with casualties, cratering the Union army's strength while raising it for the Confederate army helped amplify victories and minimize defeats. By undercutting Meade's strength and overstating Lee's, Medill transformed the Union victory at Gettysburg into one that also defied the odds. Of course, he multiplied this effect by throwing casualties into the equation. By skewing casualties as well as the combatants' relative strength, Medill turned a magnificent victory at Gettysburg into something bordering miraculous. Meade not only defeated an army that dwarfed his own, but he did so while sustaining only five to seven thousand casualties.[55] Ultimately, the number gymnastics performed by pro-Lincoln printers—whether twisting casualties, contorting army strength, or both—made the Union victory at Gettysburg seem even more striking than it actually was.

Pro-Lincoln printers nationwide locked arms with their colleagues in New York, Pennsylvania, and Chicago. The Wednesday battle drew the same misleading spin. New Englander Charles O. Rogers, the wizard behind the *Boston Daily Journal*'s wartime success, denied that the Confederates had routed federal forces. Using the report of his ace correspondent, Charles Carleton Coffin, Rogers told readers that the federals resisted the enemy until 4:00 p.m., when they—adhering to orders—withdrew beyond Gettysburg.[56] Native Ohioan Edwin W. Cowles and William J. Murtagh in D.C., both of whom championed the abolitionist cause, sanitized the July 1 battle for their respective readers. Cowles's *Cleveland Leader*, the most circulated Ohio paper outside Cincinnati, posited that only the enemy's strength compelled Union troops to retreat to the heights beyond Gettysburg.[57] And Murtagh's *National Republican*, the sole Lincoln backer in Washington at war's start, vowed, "[Union forces] withstood on Wednesday the shock of Lee's best and freshest troops, superior in numbers to ours, and entirely defeated their attempt to . . . drive us."[58] By underscoring the Confederates' numerical superiority and refusing to honestly cover the Union rout, the pro-Lincoln press packaged the Wednesday battle in a way that, at the very least, refuted a Confederate victory.

Coverage of the Thursday battle rarely revealed a close contest. Cowles's *Leader* summarized, "The enemy at length fell back after fearful slaughter, Meade remaining victor of the field."[59] Sickles, as elsewhere, received a pass. Leaning again on Coffin's report, Rogers's *Journal* excused the general from any fault, misreporting, "The 3d corps was ordered to advance across the fields and reconnoiter the enemy on the left."[60] If this failed to enrage Meade, then Murtagh's flattering portrayal of Sickles almost certainly did. Rather than blame Sickles for inviting a Union disaster, the *National Republican* claimed Sickles had "saved the army from disaster that day."[61] Of course, numerical acrobatics tumbled into the picture and made the Army of the Potomac shine brighter. According to Coffin, Sickles and his lone Union corps stood like a dam, holding back a flood of thirty thousand to forty thousand Longstreet-commanded rebels.[62] By ignoring Confederate successes, denying Union mistakes, and favorably tweaking the numbers, the pro-Lincoln press converted the uncertain Thursday battle into an undisputed Union victory.

In case the July 2 battle left readers craving more heartening news, the pro-Lincoln press dished up coverage of July 3 to satisfy any appetite. Murtagh's *National Republican* cheered the "invincible" Union troops, who "hurled back broken, discomfited, and clearly whipped" Lee's "whole army."[63] Arithmetic malfeasance ran rampant. While the Kentucky-born printer of the *Baltimore Clipper*, L. A. Whiteley, calculated Union losses at no more than fourteen thousand, Murtagh surmised, "twelve thousand . . . will fully cover them."[64] Of course pro-Lincoln printers not only trimmed Union losses but also spiked those suffered by the Confederates. Whiteley assessed overall rebel casualties at forty thousand, over half of Lee's army.[65] Meanwhile, Minnesotan William Bell Mitchell and his *St. Cloud Democrat*, a misleadingly named Republican and abolitionist tract, projected Lee's losses at thirty-five thousand and a whopping 118 guns.[66] When overestimating Lee's artillery losses, however, Cowles shamelessly took the crown. The *Cleveland Leader* credited Meade with capturing 168 enemy cannons, which if true would have reduced Lee's artillery by 60 percent.[67]

These overstated results encouraged pro-Lincoln printers to absolve the Union army of its past sins. Excepting Antietam, the Army of the Potomac spent the war's first two years wandering in the desert of defeat. George Templeton Strong regretted "its long disheartening list of hard-fought failures."[68] But Gettysburg ripped that list to shreds. The Union army "gloriously vindicated its own honor and that of the nation," lauded Forney's Philadelphia *Press*.[69] Bryant's *New-York Evening Post* raved, "[The] noble Army of the Potomac . . . has revenged itself for all past reverses."[70] The past was erased. The days of wandering in the desert were over. Gettysburg, in one redemptive fell swoop, washed clean the Union army's blotted history. Rather than furthering its "history of misfortune," opined Raymond's *New York Times*, the Army of the Potomac saved the Union in its darkest hour and "triumphantly vindicated its claim to be classed with the veteran and heroic armies that history delights to honor."[71]

The trumped-up Friday results also prompted pro-Lincoln printers to revive one of the war's ongoing sideshows. Ever since Fort Sumter, when Presidents Lincoln and Jefferson Davis first issued their opposing calls for troops, Northerners and Southerners boasted superior fighting men. Since nothing proved soldierly superiority like victory, the debate swung back and forth like a pendulum based on the outcome of every passing battle. Gettysburg, the North's great victory over the South's greatest army, handed pro-Lincoln printers fresh ammunition to charge that Billy Yank outshined Johnny Reb in every way that mattered. "The vigor of manhood, and of endurance, and of indomitable perseverance, belongs to the North," crowed Whiteley's *Baltimore Clipper* after Gettysburg.[72] The Army of the Potomac proved "more than a match for any army that the South could pitch against it . . . man to man . . . we never had a doubt of the superiority of the Northerner."[73]

Harrisburg's George Bergner also believed Gettysburg settled the debate in Northern favor. "[The Gettysburg victory] has proven to the world the superiority of the northern over the southern soldier when fairly pitted against each other in an open field," touted Bergner's *Evening Telegraph*. "Until the battles fought in Pennsylvania, the Army of the Potomac has never been able to meet the army commanded by Lee on equal ground."[74] Although some past battle terrains had benefited Lee's army, namely Fredericksburg in December 1862, the ground at Gettysburg manifestly advantaged the Army of the Potomac. That Bergner dismissed this inconvenient fact is unsurprising. Admitting that Gettysburg's topography favored federal forces would have diminished their fighting ability while undermining their supposed superiority.

Extolling one's own soldiers usually came with disparaging the enemy's. Indeed, while pro-Lincoln printers praised Billy Yank during the Gettysburg campaign, they also pilloried Johnny Reb. Whiteley maligned Lee's soldiers as nothing more than "marauders" let loose like bloodthirsty hounds for "plunder and devastation."[75] For requisitioning Northern property, something federal troops did on Southern soil, Forney scorned Lee's Confederates as "covetous rascals."[76] Pro-Lincoln printers often paired Southern scorn with Northern praise. In late June, as Lee's men scoured Maryland and Pennsylvania for supplies, Forney admonished them for "wonton acts of barbarity" while admiring Northern soldiers hastening to intercept them for being "temperately conducted."[77] Ultimately, in an othering attempt to sustain Northern support for the war, pro-Lincoln printers seized on the Gettysburg campaign to glorify Billy Yank and vilify Johnny Reb. The day the Battle of Gettysburg erupted, Forney's *Press* decided, "[The] rebels do not make war a sentimentalism."[78]

The press, however, thrived on sentimentalizing the war, and the pro-Lincoln press did its fair share of sentimentalizing the Battle of Gettysburg. When Major General John Sedgwick's men helped blunt Longstreet's final July 2 thrust, the Philadelphia *Press* hymned, "They went down upon the haughty foe like an avalanche."[79] The pro-Lincoln press romanticized the July 3 defense of Cemetery Ridge almost as much as the pro-Davis press romanticized the charge against it. The *Press* melodramatized, "The National troops stood like a wall of fire whose flaming tongues enwrapped in death whatever came near. . . . Our men fought like tigers."[80] After Crounse led him to the battlefield, reporter Whitelaw Reid gave *Cincinnati Daily Gazette* readers a gripping description of the July 3 stand. "From thrice six thousand guns there came a sheet of smoky flame, a crash of leaden death. The [rebel] line literally melted away."[81] Historical allusions added more flare to these flashy takes. Sam Wilkeson, the *Times* reporter who tragically lost his son Bayard on the battle's inaugural day, jotted, "There never was better fighting since Thermopylae than was done . . . by our infantry and artillery."[82]

Pro-Lincoln press correspondents proved up to the challenge of artfully grappling with Gettysburg's significance, but three of Byington's peers—Wilkeson, Reid, and Coffin—went above and beyond. Wilkeson's glorification of the Gettysburg dead, who "baptized with . . . blood the second birth of Freedom in America," added much-needed gravitas to the battle's unbelievable bloodletting.[83] "Patriot blood," according to the surreal imagery offered by Reid, "watered the roots" of flowers along Cemetery Ridge and rendered "them doubly sacred."[84] Coffin's account, meanwhile, approached Homeric profundity. His full *Boston Daily Journal* report captured, better than any Northern correspondent, the battle's deeper meaning for the Union. As he beheld the carnage left after Pickett's Charge, Coffin penned, "The invasion of the North was over, the power of the Southern Confederacy broken. There at that sunset hour I could discern the future—no longer an overcast sky, but a clear unclouded starlight—a country redeemed, saved, baptized, consecrated anew to the coming ages."[85]

In all likelihood Lincoln, a ravenous news consumer, read these well-known accounts before drafting the Gettysburg Address.[86] Historian Harold Holzer believes they "certainly won enough acclaim to have invited the president's attention."[87] Although scholars hesitated to say so until recently, these accounts also likely influenced the Gettysburg Address. The president's "this nation . . . shall have a new birth of freedom" mirrored Wilkeson's "second birth of Freedom in America." The idea of the Gettysburg battlefield being "consecrated" by "the brave men, living and dead, who struggled" there echoed Wilkeson's "baptized with . . . blood," Reid's making "sacred" with blood, and the use of both "baptized" and "consecrated" in Coffin's account.[88] As much influence as Lincoln exercised over his press supporters, those supporters exerted at least some measure of influence over him as well.

If the address-inspiring victory at Gettysburg failed to please, on its heels came the only war news that summer capable of rivaling it. On July 4, just one day after the battle, Union general Ulysses S. Grant complemented Meade's victory in the Northeast by conquering Vicksburg a thousand miles to the southwest. Unlike Gettysburg, however, news of Grant's war-truncating achievement wallowed in limbo for several days before finally bursting onto front pages of newspapers. Medill and Greeley, both of whom covered the Gettysburg battle before it even ended, did not headline Vicksburg's capture until a much-belated July 8. The story languished in this purgatory for at least two reasons.

First, with no wired nexus that far south, much of the distance between Vicksburg and the North's press offices needed to be physically traversed, which delayed the story's debut. The nearest Union wirehead lay at Memphis and, due to Confederate cavalry slashing about outside the city, its wires were in shambles. To forward the news, the federals relied on the fastest pre-telegraphic method for delivering information: steam power. Union admiral David Porter, whose brown-water fleet proved crucial to Grant's Vicksburg campaign, dispatched his swiftest steamboat up the Mississippi with word that the citadel had capitulated. That steamboat chugged several hundred river miles north to the federal base at Cairo, Illinois. From there the story unburdened itself from the need to be physically transported and was wired to Washington, where Lincoln learned the good news just before the whole nation did.

Second, an uncharacteristic spate of journalistic skepticism slowed Vicksburg's passage from purgatory to publication. Like Constantinople to the Ottomans, Vicksburg long scoffed at Union efforts to vanquish it. Beginning in October 1862, Grant undertook several attempts to subdue the fortress, all of which ended in failure. Meanwhile, the Northern press enflamed matters by trotting out story after story prematurely predicting Vicksburg's downfall. As a result, Northern readers became increasingly cynical toward Vicksburg news and Northern printers progressively cautious in their Vicksburg coverage. When Grant finally felled the rebel colossus, many printers initially vacillated between airing the story and sitting on it until official government confirmation for fear they might be crying wolf and further disillusioning the public. But on July 7 the U.S. government stepped in. The War Department released Grant's official dispatches to the press, which helped free the story from its stasis. Thereafter Northern printers announced with conviction that the long defiant Confederate Gibraltar could, at long last, defy the Union no more.

With Grant's victory verified, pro-Lincoln printers could not help but compare the Union's twin triumphs. Several embraced them on equal terms. When news of Vicksburg reached the *Philadelphia Inquirer*, Harding emblazoned the headlines "Gettysburg!—Vicksburg!" and "Great Victories" as though they needed no differentiating.[89] He also gave equal attention to Gettysburg and Vicksburg pictorially, each with its own massive front-page map. Raymond's *New York Times* also showed no reason to privilege one victory over the other. When he received confirmation that Grant had captured Vicksburg, Raymond fired off the headline "Great Jubilation" and added: "The fall of Vicksburgh, conjointly with the Gettysburg successes, is regarded as the turning point in the war."[90]

Most pro-Lincoln printers who disagreed with the Harding-Raymond view emphasized Gettysburg over Vicksburg. Out of fifteen headlines on his July 10 front page, Forney devoted twelve to Gettysburg and Meade's post-battle pursuit of Lee. Only two mentioned Vicksburg, one of which casually stated "Congratulations on the Fall of Vicksburg."[91] Bergner kept an eagle-eyed focus on Gettysburg as much as Forney. On July 7, the first day it published news of Vicksburg's fall, the Harrisburg *Evening Telegraph* ran just one paragraph on the story. The paper explained that Vicksburg "did not create any very great sensation. . . . Its reduction was a mere question of time." It added that the news "was received gratefully, but not enthusiastically." In case this failed to convey which victory mattered more, Bergner ended his terse Vicksburg coverage by pivoting back to Gettysburg. The *Telegraph* chuffed,

"The fall of Vicksburg will not be pleasing news to the rebels . . . seeking to escape the hosts under Meade."[92] Like Bergner, Cowles encapsulated the dominant pro-Lincoln press view toward Gettysburg. Before obtaining definitive word of Vicksburg's capture, the *Cleveland Leader* chalked up Gettysburg alone as "the turning point of the rebellion."[93]

Occasionally the pro-Lincoln press stressed Vicksburg as the greater triumph. Whiteley's *Baltimore Clipper*, for example, concluded, "No event of the war, not even the glorious victory of Meade over the renowned favorite general of the rebels, has given as much cause for congratulation, as has the fall of Vicksburg."[94] But the *Clipper* sailed against a Northern wind. Ultimately, the prevailing opinion held that Meade's victory not only eclipsed that of Wellington's at Waterloo but also either matched or eclipsed that of Grant's at Vicksburg.

Meade's towering triumph convinced pro-Lincoln printers to shower him with praise immediately following the battle. Greeley became an instant fan. The *New-York Tribune* commended Meade for fighting "as no one ever fought the Potomac army before."[95] Few printers fawned over Meade's generalship as much as Forney. The Philadelphia *Press* vaunted, "[Meade] was possessed with a degree of calm deliberation truly wonderful, and seemed intuitively to know what was necessary to be done, and to be endowed with a superior genius in the . . . handling of his forces."[96] As if this inadequately expressed his awe of Meade, Forney promoted the general to the uppermost echelons of military history. The *Press* swooned like a Victorian, "The military annals of the great Napoleon present nothing at all approaching Meade's Three Glorious Days of July."[97]

Praise for Meade's generalship became ubiquitous. Ingratiating biographical sketches and editorials proved commonplace. Cowles's *Cleveland Leader* and Medill's *Chicago Tribune* both declared that Lee had finally met more than his match in George Meade.[98] Bryant's *New-York Evening Post* proclaimed the Union general "equal to the almost unexampled difficulties of his position . . . and the real hero of the day," while Whiteley's *Baltimore Clipper* extended "all honor to the gallant Meade."[99] The catalyst of the penny paper revolution also hitched itself to the bandwagon of veneration. "When we consider the circumstances under which GEN. MEADE assumed the command of the Army of the Potomac," clucked the New York *Sun*, "it must be conceded that the new commander looms up as the ablest leader of the war."[100]

Meade's reputation underwent a swift and seismic transformation. He left the Virginia front for Gettysburg a relatively unrecognized corps commander. Those few who knew him found his temper combustible and his appearance uninspiring. Behind Meade's back they prattled like schoolkids. "Damned old goggle-eyed snapping turtle," they called him.[101] With his triumph on July 3, however, Meade rocketed from ill-treated obscurity to national celebrity. *Times* reporter Sam Wilkeson, before burying his son, told Meade on July 3, "You're in very great danger of being President of the United States."[102] Setting aside the fact that Meade's Spanish birth disqualified him from the presidency, the spirit behind Wilkeson's comment felt as true as gravity. Meade instantly won the love and admiration of the press, which just as quickly rebranded him a national savior endowed with supreme military genius. His meteoric rise drove the press to expect further feats of greatness from him.

Indeed, Meade's genius, the reported extent of his victory at Gettysburg, and nature's intervening hand—heavy rains that flooded the Potomac—led many pro-administration printers to expect him to finish what he started. After pronouncing the rebel retreat to have been blocked by Potomac floodwaters, Cowles anticipated "the complete destruction or capture of the invading horde" by Meade.[103] Murtagh and Forney published almost identical forecasts. The *National Republican* plastered the headline "Lee's Army Almost Certain to be Annihilated," while the Philadelphia *Press* chimed "We may predict his [Lee's] final and utter discomfiture [thanks to the] master of the situation [Meade]."[104] One of Byington's colleagues forwarded a similar divination, which Greeley slapped on the *New-York Tribune*'s July 10 front page: "Gen. Meade will force him [Lee] to a final engagement before he can possibly escape."[105]

These predictions launched the hopes of the nation skyward. "[Everywhere] strong hopes are entertained that LEE will not be able to escape," puffed the *Wisconsin State Journal*.[106] George Burmeister, an Iowa soldier and diarist fighting and writing in the Western Theater, recorded his press-fueled excitement in a mid-July entry: "Received some good news. . . . The report says Lee's army will be annihilated. Glory and Honor to God in the Highest!"[107] The pro-Lincoln press put Northern newsreaders in a state of suspense. The Gettysburg victor seemed poised to corner Lee's beleaguered army against a wall of water, where it, and the Confederacy with it, would be utterly destroyed.

Lincoln himself hoped that Meade would destroy Lee's army before it could lick its wounds in Virginia. "If General Meade can complete his work . . . by the literal or substantial destruction of Lee's army," commented Lincoln just four days after Gettysburg, "the rebellion will be over." But when Lincoln learned that Lee had safely forded the Potomac on the night of July 13 without Meade giving battle, he exploded like a geyser. "Great God!" steamed

Lincoln. "Our Army held the war in the hollow of their hand & they would not close it."[108] Lincoln blamed none other than the "master of the situation" for gravely mismanaging it.[109] The president sat at his desk, wetted his quill in ink, and proceeded to write Meade what one historian called "one of the harshest passages Lincoln ever penned."[110] "I do not believe you appreciate the magnitude of the misfortune involved in Lee's escape," read the president's critique. "Your golden opportunity is gone, and I am distressed immeasurably by it."[111] Lincoln's better angels eventually prevailed, and he never sent Meade the letter. But his frustration with Meade's failure to strike a war-ending blow quickly became known to both Meade and the Northern press.

Meade reacted like a spoiled child. Rather than attempt to remedy the situation, he sulked in self-pity and offered Lincoln his resignation. When apprised of the president's displeasure by General-in-Chief Henry Halleck, Meade replied, "the censure of the President . . . is, in my judgment, so undeserved, that I feel compelled . . . to ask to be immediately relieved from the command of this Army."[112] The president declined Meade's request. Lincoln knew better than to remove the victor of Gettysburg from command, even if that victor had allowed a golden opportunity to slip between his fingers. Lincoln seemed to think that Meade got the message. And if, for whatever reason, Meade failed to comprehend his commander-in-chief's disappointment, Lincoln's supporters in the press made certain that the general understood.[113]

Whether due to their sincere outrage at Lee's escape or their loyalty to the president (or likely both), pro-Lincoln printers fell in line and Meade fell from favor. Because he "hesitated" to strike an early killing blow, griped Harding, Meade missed a prime opportunity to bag Lee's retreating army.[114] Greeley groused that Meade "hesitated to give the order, and the Rebel army was allowed to make its escape."[115] As if in coordination with Harding and Greeley, Whiteley voiced the same complaint. The *Baltimore Clipper* wished Meade had attacked Lee because it "would most probably have finished the war in the space of 30 days." Instead, Meade "hesitated" and the "rebel army was allowed to make its escape."[116]

Meade enjoyed but a short-lived honeymoon with the press. His "hesitation" to crush Lee triggered a barrage of criticism from the very newspapers that just two weeks before had canonized him. Meade's sudden fall from grace swelled his distrust for newsmen and sent him spiraling down a path of worsening press relations. By the summer of 1864, when the ill-fated episode with reporter Edward Cropsey took place, Meade had soured what little good graces remained between him and the correspondents assigned to cover his army. He became persona non grata—a Union commander at war with rebels to his front and pressmen to his rear. Few Civil War generals, especially victorious ones, treated correspondents more poorly or received more poor treatment from those correspondents in kind. Meade's metamorphosis from press golden child to black sheep in part prompted his woeful comment, "I suppose after awhile it will be discovered I was not at Gettysburg at all."[117]

If history buried Meade's Gettysburg legacy, the man who promoted his own supplied the shovel. Major General Dan Sickles put Meade in his Gettysburg crosshairs for two reasons. First, Meade's official Gettysburg report, submitted in October, told the truth: on July 2 Sickles unilaterally, and by inference perilously, unlinked himself from the Union army's defensive chain. Second, when the one-legged Sickles attempted to resume his corps command in late October, Meade cited Dan's still incomplete recovery and denied his return. These two strikes, combined with word that Meade had contemplated court-martialing him, put the image-obsessed Sickles on the warpath. Meade threatened his Gettysburg hero persona. To keep himself raised high, Sickles tore Meade down. In early 1864 he testified against Meade at congressional committee hearings on Gettysburg and, writing under the pseudonym "Historicus," published letters in the *New York Herald* making himself the hero of Gettysburg at Meade's expense.[118] Having burned his bridges with the press, Meade failed to mount an effective defense. Ironically, the man who nearly lost Gettysburg for the Union, elevated himself at the expense of the man who actually won it.

Pro-Lincoln printers' fascination with the Gettysburg victory waned about as quickly as their admiration for Meade. By mid-July, interest in Gettysburg among pro-Lincoln printers began to plummet, whereas pro-Davis printers, the Southern corollary, kept Gettysburg in the limelight through much of the summer. This seems counterintuitive. One might expect the opposite: that the North would have basked in its moment of glory while the South shifted attention away from its point of dejection. But the reverse proved true due to a torrent of newsworthy events that both pushed and pulled pro-Lincoln press attention away from Gettysburg.

Lee's escape provided the strongest push. The rebel army's evasion of Meade and successful retreat into Virginia siphoned oxygen from the Gettysburg story. Rather than leading to Lee's destruction and war's end, as so many pro-Lincoln printers predicted, the Gettysburg campaign resulted in Lee's escape and Lincoln's prediction that the war would be "prolonged indefinitely."[119] This proved a profound disappointment—one amplified by the hollow promises made by so many pro-Lincoln printers. Thanks to their optimistic conjectures, Burmeister had spent an entire day in bed poring over newspapers, giddy with anticipation of Lee's destruction. When he learned that Lee had escaped, however, his heart sank into his stomach. "Lee got away safe," he despaired.[120] Lincoln found this press-induced whiplash inexcusable. He once cautioned printers against getting "ahead of the hounds, outrunning events, and exciting expectations to be later dashed into disappointment."[121] Yet his press supporters did exactly that after Gettysburg.

Lincoln's comment, while applicable to the Gettysburg campaign, had come after the first Union army defeat at Bull Run in July 1861. The buildup to that war-christening clash saw the Northern press repeat the battle cry, "On to Richmond!"[122] The mantra encouraged the public to expect a hasty end to the war and pressured the Union army to hastily plunge into battle. When First Bull Run ended in a Union defeat that "dashed" public "expectations . . . into disappointment," Lincoln blamed the press for getting "ahead of the hounds."[123] In the wake of Gettysburg it seemed even Lincoln's devotees in the press did not learn their Bull Run lesson. At least one Southern newspaper noticed. Due to the pro-Lincoln press ginning up post-Gettysburg anticipation of Lee's demise, the *Chattanooga Daily Rebel* snidely called this "another 'On to Richmond.'"[124]

Some pro-administration printers attempted to manage the disappointment they helped sow by suggesting that nothing had changed after Lee's escape. Cowles, for example, claimed that things remained just as promising even after Lee reached Southern soil. The *Cleveland Leader* reassured readers on July 17, "In [Lee's] weakened and crippled condition he may yet be gobbled up by Meade's pursuing columns. Altogether, the general aspect is encouraging and full of hope."[125] But most pro-Lincoln printers mitigated the letdown they helped manufacture by first turning on Meade and then turning their attention to more uplifting news.

Fortunately, they needed not look far, for the positive pulls that summer proved legion. Indeed, the momentous summer of 1863 offered no shortage of encouraging military events toward which pro-Lincoln printers could pivot their coverage. Of course, on July 4 Grant captured Vicksburg, along with its ragged thirty-thousand-man rebel garrison. That domino helped topple the last Confederate bastion disputing Union control of the Mississippi, Port Hudson and its seven thousand gaunt defenders, just five days later. As if these events were not monumental stories in their own right, Confederate general Braxton Bragg's Army of Tennessee retreated from Tennessee, and on July 10 Union forces launched a promising new campaign to avenge Fort

Sumter by wrestling Charleston, a major blockade-running port and the Cradle of Secession, from the clutches of the Confederacy. Forney summarized the summer in three words: "Victory is everywhere."[126]

These victories demanded press attention regardless of the Gettysburg campaign outcome. But many pro-Lincoln printers spotlighted these encouraging war developments when Lee escaped and the Gettysburg story lost its luster. "We may regret that LEE escaped annihilation," admitted Forney's Philadelphia *Press* in mid-July, "[but] the Confederacy has been rent in twain and the Mississippi is ours. . . . BRAGG is retreating into Georgia." As for "the forts in Charleston harbor," the *Press* asserted: "The day of their doom is at hand."[127] This clever pivoting helped sustain the summer surge in morale despite the disappointing end to the Gettysburg campaign.

The pulls that wrenched the focus of the pro-Lincoln press from Gettysburg worked in reverse in the South. The summer's "immense" and "decisive gains over the rebellion," as the *Chicago Tribune* described them, all came at the South's expense.[128] The Confederacy's pro-administration printers simply could not pivot toward less discouraging war news. Events in the Southwest proved disastrous, and developments in Tennessee and South Carolina looked bleak at best. Louisianan Sarah Morgan Dawson saw it as a nadir for the Confederate cause. "It is so hard!" she pined. "How the mighty are fallen! . . . I cry hourly."[129]

This partially explains why the pro-Davis press kept its gaze on Gettysburg longer than its Northern counterpart did. Rebeldom's unholy trinity—Gettysburg, Vicksburg, and Port Hudson—fused with Bragg's backpedaling and Charleston's siege to form a dark cloud that loomed over the Confederacy that summer. But Gettysburg offered a silver lining that made it less difficult to spin favorably. Even if pro-Davis printers acknowledged Gettysburg as a defeat—which they seldom did—that defeat unleashed war on the North, ceded no additional Southern territory, spared Virginia from another summer of war, starred the South's most successful general and army, and scored that army desperately needed supplies. As historian Gary W. Gallagher explains, "In a season marked by . . . loss . . . Lee's operations in Pennsylvania did not stand out as especially harmful to the Confederate cause."[130] With nowhere else to look to buoy Southern morale, pro-Davis printers stayed glued to Gettysburg to convince Southerners that all was not lost.

Although the pro-Lincoln press enjoyed many positive pulls, one negative pull wrested its attention from Gettysburg like nothing else. Beginning on July 13, just ten days after the Union victory at Gettysburg, one of the worst riots in American history consumed New York City in a four-day-long "Reign of Terror."[131] The start of the Union's first draft—something Alexis de Tocqueville thought a generation earlier would be opposed ("so opposed . . . that I do not imagine it can ever be sanctioned by the laws")—sparked a powder keg of racial, class, and political animosities.[132] Greeley called it "the torch that lit the flame."[133] That flame began engulfing New York City in mayhem. Rioters assailed the city's blacks, wealthy, and anyone or anything supportive of the Republican Party and Lincoln's war. Greeley and Raymond, whose offices nearly fell prey, fended off the mob by arming their staffs and barricading their buildings with stacks of newsprint.[134] Raymond even lined the *Times* building with three quickly purchased Gatling guns, weapons yet unused in battle.[135]

The situation grew so anarchic that it required the Union army to quell it. On July 16, several regiments of Gettysburg veterans, hurriedly transferred from Pennsylvania, stormed the streets with bayonets fixed and brought the chaos to an abrupt end. A grim scene emerged when the dust settled. The New York City draft riots left numerous buildings vandalized or destroyed, thousands injured, and 105 people dead—including eleven black men who were lynched.[136] Abolitionists cried foul. William Lloyd Garrison blamed Copperhead leader Clement Vallandigham for inciting lawless violence and hatred against black folks.[137] Meanwhile, the nation's foremost black printer, Frederick Douglass, decried the racist mobs in New York and their "malice towards colored men."[138] But perhaps no black newspaperman better articulated the justification for indignation than Pennsylvanian Elisha Weaver, the printer of Philadelphia's *Christian Recorder*. Weaver reprimanded the rioters as "a most stubborn, insolent, malicious, concocted, rum-headed, pro-slavery, copper-headed, mob of negro-haters, and negro-murders, who violently resisted the authorities of the law for drafting men to aid in putting down this rebellion."[139]

The draft riots gave the New York City press tunnel vision. Not only were the riots newsworthy, they also dragged Greeley and Raymond into the news as direct participants. The business of covering the war could not continue as usual. Gettysburg fell to the wayside, and the riots took center stage. On July 14, the day after Lee's escape across the Potomac, Greeley devoted his entire front page to the riots. Raymond, who personally manned one of the Gatling guns guarding his office, committed his columns to covering the riots intently as well.

This sent shock waves across Northern newsdom. Greeley and Raymond, two of the most influential printers, helped set the pro-Lincoln news agenda.

That the draft riots occupied their attention necessarily meant that they captured pro-Lincoln printers' attention nationwide. Major pro-administration newspapers across the country, from the *Chicago Tribune* to the *Boston Daily Journal*, recycled the draft riot coverage of Greeley and Raymond, which, after Lee's escape, further loosened their grip on the Gettysburg story. The novel news obsession with the riots attracted the ire of at least one pro-Lincoln newspaperman. After copying several New York City press accounts, Medill damned the riots as "the all absorbing topic."[140]

The push of Lee's escape and the pull of the riots proved insurmountable. In press terms these events dealt a two-punch knockout to the Gettysburg story. Neither the campaign generally nor the battle specifically ever truly recaptured the spotlight. In fact, by the time the Northern press jettisoned the riots and restored the war to the forefront, Gettysburg had been all but displaced by other war fronts. The Union campaign to cleave Charleston from the Confederacy and the pursuit of Bragg's army into northern Georgia, both of which remained active and highly encouraging, diverted pro-Lincoln printers' attention like dogs picking up a new scent. By the fourth week of July, the Gettysburg campaign had all but faded from the pages of the pro-Lincoln press and begun its transition into the pages of history.

The pro-Lincoln press spun the Gettysburg campaign favorably. It polished off the victory by mischaracterizing casualties, army strength, and the enemy himself. It also filed down the battle's rough edges by falsely reporting an orderly "withdrawal" on Wednesday and a "complete success" on Thursday, engendered in part by an undeserving Sickles. The pro-Lincoln press even overhauled the remarkable Friday triumph, steeping it in exaggeration and slathering it in sentimentalism. The overstated victory led many pro-Lincoln printers to stress Gettysburg over Vicksburg and to all but guarantee that Meade, the nation's new star, would end both Lee and the war itself. For failing to deliver this result, Meade's brief honeymoon with the press came to a screeching halt, and pro-Lincoln printers pivoted their coverage from Gettysburg to brighter theaters of the war.

Pro-Lincoln printers approached the Civil War with a blatant bias. As cheerleaders of the Union cause, motivated to sustain Lincoln's administration and its war effort, they covered major battles in the most auspicious manner possible. This bias generally did not discriminate between victories and defeats. Indeed, both often drew the same overly favorable spin throughout the war in order to boost public support for it and lift public confidence in Lincoln's leadership. Remarkably, it also rarely discriminated based on the severity of a defeat or the extent of a victory. Even the decisive Battle of Gettysburg—which Reid called the Army of the Potomac's "clean, honest, and acknowledged victory" and after which historian Allen Guelzo says, "the sun never shone for the South again"—required a biased refining from Lincoln's press supporters.[141] It seems that partiality so permeated the North's pro-administration press that even the great Union victory at Gettysburg needed to be repackaged as a "Waterloo Eclipsed!!"[142]

CHAPTER SIX

Ronin of the South

The anti-Davis *Savannah Republican*, helmed by Georgians James R. Sneed and Frederick W. Sims, placed three knights of the quill at Gettysburg, more than any other Confederate newspaper. The three made an odd team. One marched to Gettysburg in tattered gray. As a veteran soldier-reporter, his brothers-in-arms and readers at home knew him as Captain Virgil A. S. Parks—D Company, Seventeenth Georgia, Henry Benning's Brigade, John Bell Hood's Division, First Corps, Army of Northern Virginia. A second trotted in on horseback wearing civilian attire and, though a freelancer, was amicably described by the *Republican* as Parks's "co adjutor in the same army."[1] While the captain initialed his accounts "V.A.S.P.," the second reporter jealously guarded his identity behind a pen name, "Tout-le-Monde," a French phrase meaning "Everybody" or "All the World." The third man also rode on horseback and sported civilian garb, but, by initialing his accounts "P.W.A.," Peter Wellington Alexander was identifiable and often identified as correspondent royalty in the South. The only threat to his journalistic throne came from the South's adopted son, Felix Gregory De Fontaine, and De Fontaine's own adoptive publication, the *Charleston Courier*, esteemed Alexander with the lofty title "The Prince of Correspondents."[2]

One of the three never finished his report. When he earned his captaincy in early 1863, Parks had survived every battle fought by the Army of Northern Virginia without suffering a scratch.[3] But on July 2 his luck ended along with his life. After Parks bravely stormed the Gettysburg battlefield at the head of his company, a Yankee rifleman defending Devil's Den shot the twenty-six-year-old soldier-reporter through the skull, killing him instantly.[4] While Parks's men mourned their captain, Parks's *Republican* colleagues honored his sacrifice with two remarkable accounts of the Gettysburg campaign—both of which refused to hide its uncomfortable truths behind the usual pro-Southern veneer.

According to Alexander, Wednesday, July 1, left the Confederate army holding a hollow prize.[5] After routing the Yankees through Gettysburg, "the enemy was not pressed after dark, after the fashion of [Stonewall] Jackson," he rued. Had Lieutenant General Richard Ewell showed his predecessor's resolve, argued Alexander, the federals would have been chucked like birds from their nest and the heights south of Gettysburg seized by Confederate general Robert E. Lee rather than by Union general George Meade.[6]

The price of not consummating the July 1 victory was paid for in rebel blood the next day. "Everywhere, horror had a great feast that day," shuddered Tout-le-Monde as he witnessed Lieutenant General James Longstreet's First Corps bludgeon itself against the Union left. In boulder-strewn Devil's Den, where Parks's company broke like a wave against a breaker, so many soldiers fell, observed Tout-le-Monde, that the nearby stream Plum Run ran red with blood. Meanwhile, Alexander leveled another critical finger at Ewell, this time for mismanaging the Confederate Second Corps against the Union right. Ewell's tardiness in commencing his attack and sloppiness in executing it, needled the reporter, put victory beyond Confederate reach. Because the rebel left hand knew not what its right hand was doing, the disjointed July 2 blows against the enemy's flanks resulted in the numbing repulse of both.[7]

The reporters' criticism mounted with the Confederate death toll. The folly of Pickett's Charge on July 3 drove Tout-le-Monde to discard the South's unwritten commandment against taking Lee's name in vain. "For some reason or other the strength of the Southern army was hurled against a position almost as impregnable as Vicksburg or Gibralter, and wasted away as if a perfect infatuation had possessed our commander." But this stab proved just the tip of a sword that Tout-le-Monde boldly plunged in to its hilt. The reporter claimed Lee's "usual sagacity deserted him" and called his repeated attacks "perfect madness." He concluded, as the threadbare Army of Northern Virginia tottered homeward like the South's prodigal son, "This invasion has been of very little profit to the Confederacy so far."[8]

Alexander and Tout-le-Monde ventured where few in the Southern press dared. From blasting the unconsummated Wednesday victory and the uncoordinated Thursday attacks to questioning Lee's mental fitness and whether his invasion lost more than it gained, the *Republican*'s correspondents told a sobering Gettysburg story, one printers supporting Confederate president Jefferson Davis were loath to tell. The *Republican*'s anti-Davis printers were not only willing to tell it, they were eager to do so. Back at their Savannah office, Sneed and Sims anticipated their correspondents' reports with glee. They announced on July 12, "The present campaign of Lee . . . is one of the most remarkable and sanguinary in the history of the world." And they falsely claimed, "'P.W.A.' . . . is the only regular reporter with the army during these mighty events, and hence the record, true, faithful and graphic in all its parts, is only to be found in the *Savannah Republican*." They even sought to profit from their celebrity correspondent's critical account. With Alexander's frontline dispatches imminent, Sneed and Sims leaned on readers as brazenly as New York City newsies: "*Now* is the most favorable time to send on their subscriptions to the *Republican*." They vowed, "Not a letter should be lost."[9]

"Confederate reaction to Gettysburg," writes historian Gary W. Gallagher, "covered a wider spectrum than is commonly supposed."[10] Indeed it did, especially when it came to the South's anti-administration press. With neither party machinery nor presidential fealty to channel their dissent, anti-Davis printers found themselves beholden to no one but themselves. They functioned as the press equivalent of masterless samurai: ronin bound by no man and no party. As a result, printers Robert Barnwell Rhett, John M. Daniel, James McDonald, William Woods Holden, J. Henley Smith, and James R. Sneed and Frederick W. Sims—the core of the anti-Davis press after two whittling years of war—carved their own Gettysburg paths. At times some covered the campaign in a manner similar to their pro-Davis peers, burnishing its roughness into a smoother finish. Often, however, they blazed a different course. Rather than buff smooth the campaign's rough edges, they depicted Gettysburg mostly as history has long regarded it: a Confederate defeat with potentially disastrous implications.

On June 3, Lee began disengaging from the Rappahannock front in northern Virginia. Just six days later came the Gettysburg campaign's opening act: the Battle of Brandy Station. Federal cavalry, eager to track Lee's movements, swashed over the Rappahannock River and tore into the rebel horsemen screening his march. The gray troopers, commanded by Major General J. E. B. Stuart, retreated in confusion, and although Stuart eventually hurled the bluecoats back, both the pro- and anti-Davis presses reported on the unpleasant but universally attested to fact: like an unseen crocodile watching its watering prey, the Yankees caught Jeb with pants down. While the anti-Davis *Savannah Republican* regretted that the attack had been "unexpected," the pro-Davis *Richmond Enquirer* upbraided Stuart for being "totally unprepared."[11]

But Lee's thrust north soon wore triumph's crown. On June 14, Ewell's Second Corps shattered and then scattered the Union garrison at Winchester in what one historian called, "one of the most swift, total, and bloodless Confederate victories of the war."[12] The false start at Brandy Station fell from mind as Southern printers turned to cover the exciting news. The Winchester triumph, like a trail forked at its start, gave anti-Davis printers a choice early on in the Gettysburg campaign. They could either join their pro-Davis counterparts and applaud the unequivocal victory or distinguish themselves by sitting on their hands.

They stood and applauded. Georgian native J. Henley Smith, whose Atlanta *Southern Confederacy* proved as anti-Davis as any remaining in Rebeldom, praised Ewell's "complete success" and cheered the vast quantities of prisoners and supplies captured.[13] Virginian James McDonald, whose *Richmond Whig* unremittingly savaged the Confederate president, expressed even more enthusiasm.[14] "Glorious deeds have been done at Winchester," cheered the *Whig*, "and one of the most complete victories of the war has been achieved. . . . All honor to Ewell." McDonald went on to pay further tribute to the newly christened Second Corps commander. In a column straightforwardly titled "General Ewell," the *Whig* recounted his wartime laurels and intimated that, with his victory at Winchester, Ewell became to Stonewall Jackson what Pyrrhus became to the slain hero Achilles: a worthy successor.[15] The comparison, considering that Jackson towered over the South despite lying in his grave, spoke volumes about the new Second Corps commander.

The sentiment of North Carolinian William Woods Holden, the *North Carolina Standard*'s printer, also spoke volumes. Holden proved an unusual case. During the early secession crisis he counseled moderation, urging Tar Heels after Abraham Lincoln's election to "watch and wait" rather than follow Deep South Fire-Eaters out of the Union.[16] But the fireworks over Fort Sumter and Lincoln's call for troops changed his tune. On May 20, 1861, Holden joined his fellow state delegates in unanimously approving North Carolina's departure from the Union. Yet the struggle that followed changed his tune again. By 1862, Holden perceived the war as unwinnable and implored the South to negotiate a peace before the North pummeled it into submission. Ironically, Holden's peace embraced a restoration of the Union he once voted to dissolve.[17] His willingness to extend the olive branch short of Confederate independence made him a lightning rod for abuse across Southern newsdom. The pro-Davis Richmond *Sentinel* tarred Holden as "a tory and traitor" for favoring "reunion with our enemies."[18] As an anti-administration and antiwar printer, Holden emerged as a rare bird in the Southern flock—one almost always flying against the prevailing wind.[19]

But not when it came to Winchester. The *Standard* described the triumph as an uplifting and stunning accomplishment, commending "the gallant Gen. Ewell—the 'right arm' of the lamented Stonewall." Apparently, Holden's peace at the cost of Confederate nationhood did not preclude celebrating an unmistakable and virtually bloodless Confederate victory—especially when, with four Tar Heel brigades in Ewell's corps, his fellow North Carolinians disproportionately helped fashion it. The rare bird could fly with others when conditions permitted. But the Confederate war effort seldom saw Winchester-like conditions, and even when it did Holden remained resolute in his commitment to peace. Holden professed, in the same issue he extolled the victory, "The people of both sections are tired of the war, and desire peace . . . both sections should give utterance to their views, and should pave the way for negotiations."[20]

The wave of confidence that swept up pro-Davis printers after Winchester also swept up their anti-Davis counterparts. Winchester proved satisfying, but it remained only the appetizer. Soon Lee would deliver a far more substantial victory as the entrée. "The army is in fine spirits and confident of victory," wrote "Georgian"—the *Southern Confederacy*'s lone reporter with Lee's army—after Winchester. "When I next write I hope to be able to give you particulars of a great victory."[21] The *Southern Confederacy*'s Richmond correspondent, writing like his colleague "Georgian" under a pseudonym—in this case "Cherokee," felt no less hopeful. "Be not surprised, should you learn, in a week or less time, that Washington City looms up prominently in the programme of offensive operations," reported Cherokee.[22] Back at the home office in the Confederate news hub of Atlanta, Smith caught his correspondents' excitement as if it were infectious. In fact, he defied both the Sabbath and the South's stifling printing supply shortage to convey his enthusiasm in a novel Sunday issue. "It is evident that we are on the eve of the most important events of the war," raved the *Southern Confederacy*. "Every heart throbs with anxious hope for the army of General Lee in their new enterprise."[23]

While every Southern heart throbbed with hope, not everyone saw it as a prudential move. Holden harbored two reservations, both of which pointed back to his polestar. "We doubt the present policy of invading the enemy's territory, simply because we are deficient in power to conquer a peace in that way," objected the *Standard*. "In addition to this, an aggressive movement by us will certainly unite the North more thorough than ever, and hush at once all clamors for peace in that quarter."[24]

Holden invoked recent history to thicken his argument. In September 1862, Lee had crossed the Potomac hoping to rally sympathetic Marylanders to his banners and win a decisive battle for the Confederate cause. He obtained neither. Instead, the Old Line State gave Lee the cold shoulder and then, on September 17, gave him the costliest single day of the war: the Battle of Antietam. Although both sides claimed victory, Antietam provided a Northern morale surge that temporarily hushed any talk of peace with the South (and provided the impetus for Lincoln's preliminary Emancipation Proclamation).[25] Now, as Lee stood poised to cross the Potomac again in late June 1863, Holden remembered this lesson and wanted his readers to as well.

"The former invasion of Maryland by our main army was not productive of beneficial results. We gained nothing by it."[26]

Although few anti-Davis printers sided with Holden and distrusted the wisdom of Lee's invasion, many opposed his invasion policy. On June 21, as Ewell's corps slipped over the Potomac draped in its Winchester laurels, Lee issued one of his most famous decrees, General Order 72. "While in the enemy's country," stipulated Lee, "no private property shall be injured or destroyed by any person belonging to or connected with the army, or taken, except by the officers . . . designated." The order even promised Yankees compensation for requisitioned property, albeit in either inflated Confederate currency or worthless IOU receipts.[27] Lee's directive largely bridled his invasion army. By prohibiting the indiscriminate plunder of Northern property, he aimed, as historian James McPherson explains, "to show the world that southern soldiers were superior to the Yankee vandals who had ravaged the South."[28]

But the order's rationale went unappreciated by many anti-Davis printers. Few opposed the policy as vehemently as John M. Daniel, the irascible Virginian behind the *Richmond Examiner*.[29] Daniel asked his readers, "Where in history or in ethics does it occur that a barbarous and brutal enemy entitles himself to the refinements of war, the protection of private property, and the restraint of every thing like revenge?" He condemned the policy as "the philosophy of milk-sops in war"; said of Davis, who heartily endorsed the order, "he is gentle as the sucking dove"; and demanded eye for an eye retribution against Yankeedom.[30] Daniel ignored the fact that Lee's own men sometimes failed to live up to his wishes. On June 28, in his last letter to the *Savannah Republican*, Parks reported Virginian and Alabaman soldiers taking revenge in Pennsylvania for wrongs perpetrated against their homes.[31] But like a fixed weathervane, Daniel remained adamant. "Few are satisfied with [Lee's] determination to inflict no retaliatory punishment on the nation that has desolated the Southern country."[32]

Daniel stood on solid ground. Even influential newspapermen in the pro-Davis press longed for Lee to don the mailed gauntlets of retaliation rather than what seemed to them the white gloves of conciliation. Nathaniel Tyler of the pro-Davis *Richmond Enquirer* echoed Daniel's demand for Old Testament justice. Believing Yankeedom unworthy of Southern hospitality, the *Enquirer* snarled, "To leave it all one waste like the Stony. Arabia would be only fitting retribution."[33] But, as often proved the case with pro-Davis printers, Tyler refused to strike the same irreverent tone as the notoriously anti-Davis Daniel. In a much humbler note of dissent, the *Enquirer* later commented,

"We only desire respectfully to protest against the principle laid down in General Lee's order, namely, that 'Christianity and civilization' require us to suffer national outrage and wrong without exacting national retribution."[34]

This rare press bipartisanship stemmed from a reality that neither the pro- nor anti-administration faction could completely ignore: the majority mood in the South. The war's hard turn by 1863 left Southerners acrimonious. In late June, Catherine Edmondston bitterly diarized about how Yankees rendered Southern women and children homeless, hungry, and altogether destitute.[35] Edmondston, alongside many war-embittered Southerners, saw Lee's invasion as a chance for the South to finally give Yankeedom its own hard-war medicine. In mid-July, as she fled her war-torn home in northeastern Louisiana for refuge in Texas, Kate Stone hoped, "If only the Pennsylvanians may feel some of the horrors of war and know the bitterness of defeat."[36] But General Order 72 dashed both women's hopes just as they appeared on the cusp of fulfillment. When Edmondston learned that Lee's men showed restraint on Northern soil, rather than the unfettered wrath craved, she despaired. "Grant me patience whilst I write this!" she cried. "Well may [the Yankees] tremble for fear that a just retribution will be meeted out to them."[37]

The press remained subject to public opinion. Regardless of the ideological bank on which Southern printers stood, the popular current flowing between them could never entirely be ignored. And when that popular current surged with Mississippi-like strength in one direction, as with General Order 72, printers on both banks often did the logical thing: rather than resist the current, they swam with it—even if doing so meant swimming in the same direction as their political opponents. Alexis de Tocqueville's prewar observation rang no less true in 1863 than it did in 1831. Even amid a great civil war, "the power of the periodical press" stood "only second to that of the people."[38] Ultimately, Southern coverage of General Order 72 showed that the seemingly indomitable power of ideological division could, at least on occasion, be overcome by the omnipresent power of public opinion.

When the rest of Lee's army splashed over the Potomac River behind Ewell on June 25, Southern printers found themselves left out to dry. On the eve of the war's most momentous events, contact became severed. And to further frustrate matters, the more distance Lee put between the telegraph station at Martinsburg, the northernmost tip of the South's telegraphic spear, the less likely that it would be restored. Tempers ran short. Holden griped, "The farther Northward our army moves, the more difficult communication becomes and the rapid transmission of authentic news almost impossible. Gen. Lee's forward movement this year is veiled in mystery." It may have been veiled in mystery, but the implications were clear as crystal. "The first intelligence of his whereabouts will be through Yankee sources," predicted Holden, "and the battle will be fought and won before our people know it."[39]

Of course, Holden predicted correctly. Southerners did first learn about Gettysburg from Northern newspapers, which began arriving in the Confederate capital on July 4. Those papers warranted Southerners' alarm. Yankee printers claimed a complete federal triumph at Gettysburg, one wholly at odds with the confident, post-Winchester forecasts made by most pro- and anti-Davis newsmen. That incongruity, however, could not go unchallenged, and anti-Davis printers attempted to discredit those Northern reports by playing on the same theme used by their pro-Davis peers: Yankee deceit. "There is a great straining [in the Northern press] to produce the impression that they were not beaten, but the fact is pretty evident notwithstanding," averred McDonald's *Richmond Whig* on July 6. "When we remember how uniformly and how egregiously they have lied in their accounts of former battles, especially in the first bulletins from the field . . . we may readily infer . . . that they were seriously worsted."[40]

Faith in the triumph of Lee, a man worshipped by pro- and anti-Davis printers alike, remained unshaken by Northern victory claims. Like a true believer, McDonald reasserted his faith that Marse Robert would prevail in the same July 6 issue. After inferring that Lee had "seriously worsted" his adversary, the *Whig* barked, "We have not the slightest doubt that Gen. Lee's despatch, when it comes, will confirm this conclusion. All hail, then, to our first victory on the soil of the enemy."[41]

As if right on cue, word of a Southern victory came clacking in the dots and dashes of Morse Code to the Richmond telegraph office from Martinsburg. The news, forwarded by Confederate Military Telegraph superintendent Major J. T. Coldwell just after the July 6 morning newspaper run, more than confirmed the expectations of anti-Davis printers like McDonald. Lee purportedly gutted the Union army. In what amounted to a modern-day Cannae, Lee not only secured a victory on enemy soil, as McDonald anticipated. According to Coldwell's cables Lee also captured forty thousand Yankees—nearly halving the Army of the Potomac in prisoners alone.

The news caused handwringing among anti-Davis printers, who generally believed in its veracity as much as their pro-Davis peers. On July 7 the *Whig* roared, "It has come! . . . the despatch from Martinsburg that informs us that Gen. Lee defeated the enemy . . . that they are retreating towards Baltimore and Lee pursuing. This is great news! What may it not lead to!"[42] Sneed and Sims thought they knew exactly where it led. "The Yankee army of the

Potomac is either in our hands or *hors du combat*," beamed the *Savannah Republican* on July 7. "Thus opens up to us the way to Washington."[43]

But the way to Washington remained shut. The information relayed by Coldwell proved erroneous, and on July 8 he amended his originally exultant telegrams with the heart-palpitating truth: rather than advancing on Washington after a signal victory, Lee retreated on Hagerstown following a costly repulse; and rather than hauling in forty thousand prisoners at Gettysburg, he netted only four thousand. The sudden swing in fortune stupefied anti-Davis printers no less than their counterparts. McDonald groaned on July 9, "The intelligence from Gen. Lee falls short of the promise of the despatches published yesterday, and will prove grievous disappointment to the high wrought hopes of the public."[44] The Gettysburg coverage of anti-Davis printers following the July 8 revelation took many paths. While at times some tracked the pro-Davis press, casting the campaign favorably to avoid the morale-plunging effects of admitting defeat, often times they carved their own unique trails and, unencumbered by the conforming restraints of party loyalty and presidential fealty, represented Gettysburg much closer to the Confederate reverse it truly was.

Coverage of the Wednesday battle showed their willingness to trailblaze. Unlike his pro-administration counterparts, McDonald presented July 1 about as straightforwardly as any Southern newspaperman. Using the report of Richard J. Yarington—a correspondent who missed Gettysburg but raced to Winchester afterward to piece it together—the *Whig* admitted that, after suffering a rout, the Yankees assumed and strengthened a commanding position south of town.[45] Sneed and Sims ventured further. By foregrounding Alexander's critical report, which stressed the Confederate failure to press the victory in Jackson-like fashion by seizing Cemetery Hill, the printers may have actually undercut the Southern army's impressive July 1 performance. The *Republican* regretted that "the enemy was not pressed after dark, after the fashion of Jackson." Had the Confederates pressed their advantage full tilt on July 1, charged the paper, "the advantageous position subsequently taken by Meade would have been secured for [themselves]."[46]

Coverage of Thursday took many forms. Some anti-Davis printers described that inconclusive melee as just that. Sneed and Sims, for example, used Alexander's report to offer among the more honest summaries published by a Southern source. "The Confederates inflicted a tremendous loss upon the enemy, drove him . . . and won the ground on which the conflict for the most part had been waged," explained the *Republican*. But three things kept total victory from Southern grasp: the enemy's advantageous position, his effective artillery fire, and "the want of previous knowledge on our part of the precise nature of the ground" (a subtle jab at Stuart's absence). Consequently, acknowledged the *Republican*, the rebels failed to hold the ground they gained, and the butcher took more than his pound of flesh. "Our own loss was very heavy, especially in Hood's and [Lafayette] Mc'Laws' divisions," conceded the paper.[47]

While Sneed and Sims refused to sugarcoat July 2, other anti-Davis printers sweetened it into yet another Confederate triumph. This they accomplished using the same misleading tactic as their pro-administration counterparts: conflating Thursday and Wednesday into one homogeneous thrashing. Daniel made it seem as though the two fights produced the same one-sided results when the *Richmond Examiner* chimed, "[Gettysburg] was a battle in which the Confederates had their own way during [the first] two days."[48] Even Holden, the unswaying patron of peace, positively spun the July 2 battle by fusing it with the July 1 success. The *North Carolina Standard* remarked, "It seems that General Lee was successful at all points until Friday."[49]

Friday proved its own leviathan. The unambiguous July 3 disaster, made so by Lee's vain bid to take Cemetery Ridge in Pickett's Charge, could not be easily manipulated like the more ambiguous July 2 result. And the even starker contrast between Friday and Wednesday made conflating those two days too heavy a lift for even the most tendentious Southern printers. Conjuring up excuses, however, offered a way to shrug off the failure without blaming Lee, and some in the anti-Davis press offered them as readily as those in the pro-Davis ranks. McDonald's *Whig* attributed the Confederate repulse not to Lee's poor judgement but instead to Meade's "almost impregnable position on the mountain near Gettysburg."[50] Daniel ate from the same reassuring plate. The *Examiner* maintained, "The Confederates had their own way during two days, and were repulsed in an attack made during the third day on certain powerful positions." Daniel added, his confidence in the Southern performance swelling as he wrote, "So far as the fighting went, all that the federal army did was prevent its own annihilation. The Confederates were repulsed, but cannot, at present, with justice or candor be said to have suffered defeat."[51]

Some anti-administration printers refused to make excuses for the Friday repulse. Rather than lick Lee's boots, they laid blame at his feet. No Southern printers platformed this view quite like Sneed and Sims when they published Tout-le-Monde's account in the *Republican* on July 25. The account proved so biting that at times it made the sharp analysis of X, the unidentified correspondent of the pro-Davis *Richmond Enquirer*, appear toothless.[52]

Tout-le-Monde—who dispatched his account from Hagerstown, Maryland, on July 13—complained that Lee unthinkingly threw his army at Cemetery Ridge, a position he deemed as unassailable as the fortifications ringing Vicksburg. He asked, "Why could not the army have been withdrawn when the strength of the position was discovered? . . . Was that the only way to Baltimore, or was there no other battle field on the wide extent of Pennsylvania? . . . Was Gen. Lee's military lore wanting, to discover what was next to be done?" After loosing this audacious volley of questions, Tout-le-Monde arrived at his even more audacious conclusion: "Gen. Lee's usual sagacity deserted him on this occasion at Gettysburg."[53]

Tout-le-Monde's report turned the Marble Man into a paper tiger. As a Confederate correspondent, he knew that criticizing Lee's generalship would provoke a backlash from Lee's many sycophants in the press. But Tout-le-Monde refused to sacrifice truth on Lee's altar. "Probably this may cause other correspondents and venerators of the General to annihilate this exposition," he anticipated in his report, "but it may go forth in defiance, for our convictions are honest."[54] Steeled by the belief that he gave Lee an honest accounting, stripped of the idolatry exhibited so often by other newsmen, Tout-le-Monde stood his ground. As a result, his account ought to stand with X's as one of the finest Southern analyses of Lee's generalship at Gettysburg.

Yet in all likelihood honest conviction alone did not steel Tout-le-Monde. Southern correspondents, more than their Northern counterparts, used pseudonyms when writing Civil War battle accounts. Of the thirty-six Northern reporters at Gettysburg, only "Bonaparte" from the infamously anti-Lincoln New York *World* curtained his identity behind a pen name—a rate of just 3 percent. But of the nine Southern reporters at the battle, no less than five—or at least 55 percent—cloaked their identities in aliases.[55] The disparity stemmed from an order issued by Meade's predecessor, Joseph Hooker, requiring that correspondents with the Army of the Potomac "publish their communications over their own signatures."[56] The order, which sought to curb the publication of sensitive military information by holding reporters accountable, gave birth to the byline in Northern newspapers, and once born it lived on. Even after Meade assumed command and Hooker's order lost sway, Northern correspondents overwhelmingly continued to authenticate their dispatches using their real names. But in the South, where no equivalent order emerged to help launch the byline into journalistic orbit, Confederate newsmen disproportionally used pseudonyms until war's end.

In all likelihood, Tout-le-Monde's pseudonym helped steel his criticism of Lee. By early 1863 Marse Robert had ensorcelled the South's anti-administration printers almost as much as their counterparts. After Chancellorsville, Robert Barnwell Rhett's ultracritical *Charleston Mercury* hailed Lee as "the central figure of the war . . . beyond all question."[57] With that centrality came a new journalistic reality. As the editor of the *Southern Literary Messenger*, Frank H. Alfriend, put it, "The South regards Lee as beyond all criticism."[58] By the Gettysburg campaign, Lee was sacrosanct. Full-throated criticism of his generalship became blasphemous. The offending reporter, whether or not truth backed his case, faced nearly universal condemnation from Lee's army of disciples in the press. Only by using a pseudonym, as if donning armor, could Southern correspondents cover Lee candidly without risking reputational ruin. Ultimately, the fact that the two Southern correspondents most critical of Lee's generalship at Gettysburg, X and Tout-le-Monde, used pseudonyms in their reports, proved no coincidence.[59] As *New York Times* reporter Sam Wilkeson put it, "The anonymous greatly favors freedom and boldness in newspaper correspondence."[60]

One might assume that the byline only positively affected Civil War journalism. After all, if forcing correspondents to take public credit for their work deterred the publication of sensitive military information, it ought to also deter them from furnishing sloppy reports, thereby raising the bar of journalistic professionalism. While, broadly speaking, the byline helped produce this effect, when it came to the unique situation of covering Lee in the South the opposite resulted.[61] The byline fostered a fawning conformity around Lee. In the case of Gettysburg, identifiable Southern correspondents proved far likelier to handle Marse Robert with velvet gloves. This was doubtless due to the perceived impact on Southern morale but also to the perceived impact on their own professional reputations. In contrast, unidentifiable Southern correspondents proved far more willing to do their journalistic due diligence and scrutinize his fraught performance at Gettysburg. At least when it came to Lee in the South, these correspondents reinforced Wilkeson's point: anonymity promoted honest and courageous reporting.[62]

Only one identifiable Southern correspondent furnished a critical report of Lee. That man was none other than the South's "Prince of Correspondents," Peter Wellington Alexander.[63] Tout-le-Monde's illustrious *Savannah Republican* colleague saw Friday as a missed opportunity. In a report dispatched on July 4 and published in the same July 25 issue as Tout-le-Monde's, Alexander wished Lee had postponed Friday's assault until the Confederates thoroughly scouted the surrounding terrain. Like they had on Thursday, the Confederates put the cart before the horse. Had they first meticulously reconnoitered Meade's position, rather than heedlessly thundering forth on

July 3, Lee could have positioned his forces for "a systematic, combined and simultaneous attack from all points of the lines." This, maintained Alexander, would have wrenched the federals from Cemetery Ridge like a door from its hinges and sent them fleeing in panic all the way to Washington.[64]

Setting aside the merits of his argument, Alexander faulted Lee for the oversight. "Gen. Lee's desire . . . to fall upon his adversary before he could get into position, confident that his troops were equal to any demand," prompted the premature attack. But unlike Tout-le-Monde, Alexander refused to go for Lee's jugular. Instead, he followed X's example and offered a bit of self-serving equipoise regarding Lee's decision to charge Cemetery Ridge. "No person, much less one who, like myself, is unskilled in military affairs, can safely criticize the operations of such a commander as Lee and I forbear, not for his sake, but my own."[65]

Despite this prevarication, Alexander won himself high marks. He furnished the Southern press with not only its most reprinted Gettysburg campaign account but also one of its best. Historian J. Cutler Andrews judged Alexander's account among the South's finest, and historian Carol Reardon calls it "the most factual Southern newspaper report on the Gettysburg campaign."[66] Considering the reports of their two surviving correspondents in tandem, Sneed and Sims gave voice to more criticism of Lee's crowning failure on July 3 than any other printers in the Confederacy.

While anti-Davis printers showed a greater inclination to criticize Pickett's Charge, they simultaneously showed a disinclination to romanticize it. In fact, the anti-Davis press largely refused to soothe grief-stricken Southerners by waxing poetic in that idealistic prose Reardon calls "the real soul of this journalistic era's craft."[67] In what amounted to a unanimous protest vote, Rhett, Daniel, McDonald, Holden, Smith, and Sneed and Sims all abstained from romanticizing the climactic conclusion to the Battle of Gettysburg.

Anti-Davis printers also proved less likely to engage in something else widely practiced by their complements: dehumanizing the enemy. Unsurprisingly, a war brought on by the verbal flame-fanning of Fire-Eaters lost none of its heat once the shooting started. From Fort Sumter through to Appomattox, Southern pressmen regularly and zealously demonized Billy Yank, fueling the South's superiority complex and helping immunize it against surrender.[68] No Southern printers sullied Yankees quite like those in the pro-Davis press. The Gettysburg campaign proved no exception. Before the battle, just after Ewell had seized Winchester along with its prisoners, James Cowardin's Richmond *Dispatch* snubbed Union soldiers as "wretches" and "arrant cowards."[69] And after Gettysburg, John McClanahan and Benjamin

Dill's *Memphis Daily Appeal* scorned federal troops as a "barbarous and relentless foe."[70]

But most anti-Davis printers shrank from this sort of mudslinging. With the notable exception of the sharp-tongued Daniel—who slandered Yankees after Gettysburg as "barbarous, bloodthirsty, and devilish"—most engaged in name-calling with less zeal than their counterparts during the Gettysburg campaign.[71] Some even did the opposite. Using Tout-le-Monde's report, Sneed and Sims actually gave Billy Yank his Gettysburg respects. "The enemy showed examples of bravery in that battle that they never exhibited to such an extent in any fight before," admitted the *Savannah Republican*.[72] Holden also cited Gettysburg as proof of Billy Yank's ability. "They fought at Sharpsburg [Antietam] and at Gettysburg, and they worsted us at the latter place," conceded the *North Carolina Standard*. "Northern troops are not cowards."[73]

The day after Lee ordered his army to charge Cemetery Ridge, he ordered it to retreat to Virginia. Like a wounded beast, the rebel host then slogged southward, slowed and then stalled by an untimely rain that flooded the Potomac River beyond fording. When Lee reached the river's north bank at Williamsport, Maryland, his army appeared trapped between the flooded Potomac's anvil and the Army of the Potomac's hammer, which if swung with vigor might finish the work begun at Gettysburg. The pro-Davis press conveniently glossed over this precarious situation. But some in the anti-Davis press expressed the requisite consternation. "The Potomac . . . has been and is now so much swollen at Williamsport ford as to render it impassable to man or horse," fretted Alexander. "This is indeed vexatious . . . [and] would render escape impossible in the event of a disaster to our arms."[74]

Of course, that disaster never came. On the night of July 13, after the river receded, the Army of Northern Virginia returned to its namesake before the Union hammer came crashing down. Some anti-Davis printers seconded their parallels by giving Lee and his decision to retreat the benefit of the doubt. Smith assured *Southern Confederacy* readers, "Gen. Lee's movement to Hagerstown was so deliberately executed . . . that it was the result of a plan matured before the battles were fought."[75] If Lee preordained his return, he also prepared its way by crippling Meade beyond all capacity for serious pursuit. Holden informed his readers, "Gen. Meade was too much crippled [after Gettysburg] to be able to pursue him [Lee] in force."[76]

Just like their counterparts, some in the anti-Davis press refused to read the disturbing signs. Lee's hasty retreat following a bloody, three-day battle ought to have sounded disaster's alarm. But for McDonald, Lee's successful retreat confirmed the opposite. "Instead of the complete rout and wild and disorderly retreat, with the hot pursuit of Meade's army," explained the *Richmond Whig*, "Lee withdrew his forces leisurely and in perfect order, with no attempt at concealment." What permitted this unhindered retreat? According to McDonald, only one answer made sense: the rough handling Lee gave the Yankees at the Battle of Gettysburg, "in which their position alone saved them from a disastrous defeat."[77]

Lee's return to Virginia in mid-July marked the end of the Gettysburg campaign and the beginning of a period of introspection among Southern printers. The time had come to reflect on the campaign's results. Casualties offered one metric by which to score the campaign. And just like the pro-administration press, the South's anti-administration printers more often than not undercut Lee's losses and overshot those suffered by Meade. Daniel's *Richmond Examiner* reported, "The Confederacy has lost several thousand able officers and brave soldiers; but war cannot be made without such losses. The enemy have lost more, and the comparative strength of the parties is unchanged."[78] Even Alexander's more factual report got facts wrong. While underestimating Confederate losses at between twelve thousand and sixteen thousand, he overestimated the federal toll at twenty-five thousand killed and wounded and six thousand prisoners. Thanks to Alexander's misreporting, Sneed and Sims felt free to editorialize, "The enemy's loss is evidently far greater than our own, if not double."[79]

But casualties, even if skewed favorably, only told part of the Gettysburg story. While pro-Davis printers believed that the Gettysburg campaign yielded worthwhile fruit, many anti-Davis printers glanced back and saw a mostly rotten harvest. Daniel complained that the campaign ended prematurely with "an unsuccessful battle . . . fought in a position which rendered success impossible."[80] McDonald, meanwhile, regretted how "so much valuable life came to be lost, and nothing gained, in the assault at Gettysburg."[81] Some conceded that Lee's invasion brought beneficial results. By temporarily driving out the bluecoats from northern Virginia and the Shenandoah, explained Smith's *Southern Confederacy*, the campaign guaranteed the wheat harvest from those regions for the Confederate cause. But this meager gain failed to offset the campaign's immense losses. Smith told his readers, "We . . . hope [Lee] will never attempt to go beyond the Confederate lines again."[82]

Few came down as hard as Holden against the campaign. With Antietam in his rearview mirror, the South's spokesman for peace had opposed the invasion from the jump. The outcome—which produced a disproportionate, 45 percent casualty rate among soldiers from Holden's home state (the highest of any Confederate state)—offered nothing to change his mind.[83] "No substantial victory has crowned [Lee's] arms," gnarred the *Standard*. "We are weaker today than when he crossed the Potomac into Maryland." Just as Holden feared, Lee's invasion doomed the possibility of an immediate peace with the North. "The movement on Pennsylvania by Gen. Lee [and other Confederate reverses] have hushed all clamors for peace in the North." The Army of Northern Virginia's 1863 invasion, like that of the previous year, guaranteed only one thing in Holden's mind: "The war, then, will go on."[84]

Criticism like this brought the hot water in which Holden swam to a boil. Soon he found himself in his fellow printers' crosshairs and also in the crosshairs of the army he implicitly rebuked for a failed campaign. Seven weeks after the Army of Northern Virginia returned to northern Virginia, Longstreet took two divisions (his third, George Pickett's, remained too weakened) to reinforce the Army of Tennessee, which retreated from its namesake into northern Georgia. In early September, Longstreet, Lee's "Old War Horse," crisscrossed the Carolinas on railroads as run down by war as were his own men. While transferring trains in Raleigh on September 9, Benning's Georgian brigade—a command that scarcely fared better than Georgia's own Captain Parks at Gettysburg—marched directly past the office of the reviled *North Carolina Standard*. The temptation proved too much for these coarsened Gettysburg veterans. In retaliation for Holden's war coverage, the Peach Staters bashed in the *Standard*'s front doors, smashed its press and type, and festooned its office walls in a farrago of precious printing ink.[85]

The incident temporarily convulsed the Southern press. Holden's many press critics eschewed the law and excused what happened as a lesson in reaping what you sow. The South's rare bird, meanwhile, exposed his talons and clawed back, blaming his detractors for having long urged "the government, the people and the soldiers to suppress the paper by force."[86] Although Holden repaired the damage, the incident left the *Standard* inoperable for nearly a month.[87]

Perhaps no Southern printer denounced the Gettysburg campaign more harshly than Rhett. The South's Father of Secession initially characterized the campaign positively. On July 18, the *Charleston Mercury* claimed Lee gave better than he got at Gettysburg, which enabled his army to withdraw "at its own time and pleasure, in broad daylight, over the open country, carrying all its prisoners, with every troop and company marching in place."[88] But on July 20 Rhett abruptly reversed course. Through the mail came word from Virginia native George W. Bagby, the *Mercury*'s Richmond correspondent. Bagby confirmed the distasteful rumors about Gettysburg that Rhett, until then, had refused to seriously entertain. Suddenly Rhett turned angrier than Lincoln after Lee's escape. From then on, the South Carolinian mixed his ink with malevolence, railing against the campaign with a vituperation rivaled only by his secession-inspiring days as a Fire-Eater. It was "impossible for an invasion to have been more foolish and disastrous," simmered the *Mercury* on July 30. "It was opportune neither in time nor circumstances . . . [and now] we must pay the penalty and redeem our errors like men."[89]

The Gettysburg campaign looked especially inopportune in light of developments out west. When Lee and Meade began grappling at Gettysburg on July 1, Union general Ulysses S. Grant had already invested Vicksburg and subjected its thirty-thousand-man garrison to a forty-four-day siege. Disaster circled like a vulture. As resources dwindled and empty stomachs gnawed at men's spines, Vicksburg printers turned to wallpaper for newsprint, and Vicksburg defenders turned to local dogs and cats for food. While pro-Davis printers offered false hopes, including that Confederate general Joseph E. Johnston would soon compel Grant to raise the siege, anti-Davis printers often refused to sugarcoat the situation. "Vicksburg is in a critical condition," warned Smith's *Southern Confederacy* on June 27. "We shall not be surprised if we hear of its fall. . . . Let us all therefore be prepared for the worst."[90]

The worst came on July 4. Confederate general John C. Pemberton, after forty-seven days under siege, lowered the stars and bars and hoisted the white flag of surrender. With Vicksburg went thirty thousand rebels, 172 cannons, sixty thousand rifles, and, thanks to the subsequent surrender of Port Hudson and its seven-thousand-man garrison, all Confederate control of the Mississippi River.[91] The loss proved a grave blow to the Confederate cause. And the hollow promises made by so many pro-administration printers only added insult to injury. Sneed and Sims fumed. The *Savannah Republican* complained about the "systematic lying that has been put upon the public regarding the ability of this place [Vicksburg] to hold out."[92] Some anti-Davis printers joined their counterparts and spun the situation optimistically by downplaying the loss. After warning Southerners that Vicksburg would fall, Smith promised, "This victory will be empty and barren as all others it will bring the Yankees no fruit."[93] But anti-Davis printers proved likelier to give the hard truth about Vicksburg's loss, rather than more false hope. Holden soberly told his audience, "The valley of the Mississippi has in all probability passed permanently into the hands of the enemy."[94]

The fall of Vicksburg directly after Gettysburg cried out for a comparison of the two. While pro-Davis printers drew a sharp line between Gettysburg and Vicksburg, anti-Davis printers often either blurred that line or erased it. Daniel viewed them as dual defeats, equally damaging to the Confederate cause. The *Examiner* admitted, "The Confederacy has lately received two 'facers.' It has a bloody nose and a black eye [from Vicksburg and Gettysburg]."[95] Of course, Holden believed that the South's two facers bore equal blame for torpedoing the possibility of peace. "The movement on Pennsylvania by Gen. Lee, and the fall of Vicksburg and Port Hudson," carped the *Standard*, "have hushed all clamors for peace in the North, and have banded the people there as one man for the prosecution of the war."[96] Meanwhile, Rhett's ink remained boiling hot. On July 22, Charleston's firebrand went so far as to fault the Gettysburg campaign for Vicksburg's demise. The *Mercury* damned Lee's invasion as an "ill-timed Northern campaign" that cost the Confederacy "Vicksburg, with the States of Mississippi and Tennessee, and endangered Charleston," by concentrating Confederate troops in the less-threatened Eastern Theater.[97]

Rhett's criticism did the impossible: it got under the Marble Man's skin. On July 27, Davis sent Lee a letter and enclosed an article from the *Mercury*. The article, which came from Rhett's incendiary July 22 issue, blasted Lee and his army's performance at Gettysburg. Seeking succor in a trying season of war, Davis invited Lee's comment. "The remarks fall harmless," replied Lee on July 31, "the object of the writer & publisher is evidently to cast discredit upon the operations of the Government & those connected with it & thus gratify feelings more to be pitied than envied." But the remarks did not fall harmless. Rather than leave it there, the old man went on to address specific accusations, including the decision to attack Cemetery Ridge on July 3, the focus of the *Mercury*'s core censure. "Could I have foreseen that the attack on the last day would have failed . . . I should certainly have tried some other course," explained Lee. "But with the knowledge I then had, & in the circumstances I was then placed, I do not know what better course I could have pursued."[98]

Over the next week Lee ruminated on the Gettysburg criticism of anti-Davis printers like Rhett and fell into an uncharacteristic spell of self-pity. "I have seen and heard of expressions of discontent in the public journals at the result of the expedition," Lee wrote Davis on August 8. "I do not know how far this feeling extends in the army." It did not extend far in the army, nor for that matter did it extend far in the Confederate press. But fearing that his own soldiers might harbor the same discontent as a minority of Southern printers, Lee proceeded to do the unthinkable. "I have been prompted by these reflections more than once since my return from Pennsylvania to propose to your excellency the propriety of selecting another commander for this army."[99]

Lee's resignation offer chilled the marrow in Davis's bones. It was not he who most needed succor but rather his most beloved general. After regaining his composure, the Confederate president crafted a carefully worded reply—one aimed at lifting his unusually brittle commander from his press-induced, post-Gettysburg slump. “Expressions of discontent in the public journals furnish but little evidence of the sentiment of an army,” reassured Davis on August 11. “I wish it were otherwise, even tho'all the abuse of myself should be accepted as the results of honest observation.” He added, “I wish I could feel that the public journals were not generally partisan nor venal.” After consoling Lee by dismissing the press's partisan censures, Davis turned to the subject of his shock. “To ask me to substitute you by some one in my judgement more fit to command . . . is to demand for me an impossibility.”[100] Davis's adroit letter slew two birds with one stone. It gently closed the door on Lee's resignation and also snapped Lee out of his press-inspired, post-battle spell. Going forward, neither rare censures in the press nor setbacks in the war provoked Lee to again tender his resignation.

Despite Lee's apparent lack of self-confidence, the South remained confident in his ability after Gettysburg. In fact, anti-administration printers remained no less certain in Lee's capacity to lead the South's principal army to victory than pro-administration printers. In mid-July, for example, McDonald's *Richmond Whig* tipped its hat to “General Lee, in whom [they had] the fullest confidence.”[101] Lee remained, despite one's Gettysburg interpretation, Rebeldom's central figure and its beacon of hope in dark times. When in midsummer Confederate reverses seemed more the norm than the exception, the anti-Davis press eagerly spotlighted Lee to buoy the Confederate people. As late as early August, the *Whig* kept focused on Lee. “[It is Lee in whom] the main hope of the Confederacy now rests.”[102]

Of course, light soon pierced the darkness. War's shifting fortunes—from General P. G. T. Beauregard's defense of Charleston to Clement Vallandigham's Copperhead comeback and the deadly New York City draft riots—handed Southern printers more uplifting stories to highlight rather than only holding up the shiny object of Lee. Many anti-Davis printers pivoted to these positive developments with as much ardor as their counterparts. In the same July 25 issue in which they published their correspondents' critical Gettysburg accounts, Sneed and Sims celebrated the New York City draft riots with the headline “The Day of Retribution Has Come!”[103]

But some in the anti-Davis press remained sour amid war's sweeter turns. When it came to the draft riots, Daniel saw more reason for dismay than celebration. “These disturbances do but hasten and precipitate [the Yankees'] leading object,” charged the *Examiner*. “It gives them an excuse for inaugurating a reign of terror at home in order the better to prosecute their truculent designs upon the South."[104] Daniel enjoyed company in this austere assessment. "[Because] it affords Lincoln at once a pretext and satisfactory excuse for the exercise of dictatorial powers," argued McDonald's *Whig*, "the first effect of the New York riot will be disadvantageous to the Confederate cause."[105] Regardless of how the anti-Davis press interpreted these stories, their sudden influx helped push Gettysburg from newspapers' front pages toward, as Reardon puts it, "the entryway of Clio's gates."[106]

On several occasions, anti-Davis printers joined their parallels to refurbish the Gettysburg campaign. Before the battle itself, they readily turned from J. E. B. Stuart's Brandy Station surprise to overstate Ewell's already impressive Winchester victory, which they saw as the prelude to an even greater triumph on Northern soil. But, of course, that triumph never came. And once the Southern press recovered from the letdown of Coldwell's telegrams, some of its anti-Davis printers went on to echo their counterparts by painting the Gettysburg battle and Lee's retreat in favorable hues. These anti-administration printers demonstrated that a denunciation of the Confederate president did not necessarily translate into less positive military coverage. Indeed, one could oppose Davis and remain a patriotic cheerleader for the Confederate war effort.

But others blazed their own paths. Unmoored by the conforming restraints of party politics and presidential loyalty, these anti-administration printers characterized the campaign in ways that no pro-Davis printers dared. With the helpful hand of their reporters, they questioned Lee's generalship, doubted whether the campaign's gains offset its losses, and refused to comfort grieving families back home by coating those losses in romanticism's glossy polish. Their sharp criticism cut so deep that it even cut the Marble Man himself, prodding Lee into tendering his resignation. While a denunciation of Davis did not necessarily mean less positive military coverage, it certainly increased its likelihood. Ultimately, as Gary W. Gallagher writes, "Confederate reaction to Gettysburg covered a wider spectrum than is commonly supposed."[107] And nowhere is that more manifest than among the Confederacy's anti-administration printers—the ronin of the Southern press.

CHAPTER SEVEN

Divided Opposition

The *New York Herald*'s corps of correspondents descended on Gettysburg like a swarm of locusts. George W. Hosmer, Charles H. Graffan, George H. Hart, L. A. Hendrick, Thomas N. Cook, Galen H. Osborne, J. H. Vosburg, Nathaniel Davidson, and "heaven knows how many others from the *Herald*" trekked by train, horse, and foot to report on the fighting for the nation's most-read daily.[1] Yet some never made it. In fact, J. E. B. Stuart's Confederate cavalry captured two hapless *Herald* men en route to the battlefield. Others, whether due to misinformation or train delays caused by Stuart's sideshow of destruction through Maryland and Pennsylvania, never reached Gettysburg in time to witness the battle. But several *Herald* correspondents, with some luck and much determination, tramped with the Union Army of the Potomac or exhaustedly into its arms while the battle still raged. These Northern knights of the quill played their parts well, writing several remarkable reports for a news-hungry nation.

On July 2, 1863, just before sunset, Hosmer observed Lieutenant General James Longstreet's Confederates crash like a freight train into the federal left.[2] The rebel divisions "came forward in their usual magnificent style," skirting boulders and trees as one dense mass, "until . . . they made a rush with all possible yells roared out in one."[3] Instantly, musket and cannon fire drowned out the bloodcurdling cry. A fellow *Herald* man, S. M. Carpenter, reported a deafening "roar like that of Niagara," with "the air . . . filled with fiends, contending with the fierceness of fallen angels." The battle's fate soon hung in the balance. Carpenter watched as "the lines swayed to and fro beneath a canopy of smoke, which gleamed in the setting sun like a fiery furnace." Both sides maintained a withering fire, pelting one another with sheets of angry lead, until suddenly and in one vast movement, the rebels broke in retreat all across the battlefront. Relieved and exhausted, the bluecoats threw themselves on the ground faster than their own haversacks after a draining march. The struggle for the Union left had ended. A relieved Carpenter wrote, "We are successful."[4]

The next day Cook beheld the battle's dramatic finale: Pickett's Charge. As three rebel divisions heaved themselves up the long, sloped face of Cemetery Ridge, a "storm of bullets and canister . . . fearfully thinned their ranks."

The Confederates floundered. "[Then] in wild disorder they fell back, first in one position and then in another, until they were everywhere repulsed." The battle was over. As the Southern attack receded like a spent wave, Cook noticed a dreadful scene surface in its wake. "It had been a terrible day. The ground all around was red with blood and covered with mangled bodies." Yet Cook understood what this grim sight meant. He concluded, "*The day is ours, the victory is won, the country is saved*."[5]

While most Northern correspondents took this as their cue to race off and submit their battle accounts before the competition, one *Herald* man stayed behind to explore the now abandoned battlefield itself. Thomas W. Knox gaped at a landscape transformed by war. Everything was "scarred by bullets" and "the ground . . . trodden smooth by the feet of the soldiers." Abandoned equipment and personal effects, from swords and rifles to photographs and Bibles, were strewn on the ground as thick as grass. But nothing drew Knox's gaze like the sea of corpses left to rot in the July sun. Some, reported Knox, remained intact, "with . . . hands thrown upward, in the position taken when the soldier received his fatal wound." Others were gorily "cut in two by a shot or shell," leaving the ground nearby so "drenched in . . . blood, that even the [post-battle] rain" had "not washed [it] away." Knox's solemn tour left him grateful for the sacrifice that made victory possible. He closed his report, "To those whose valor stood for the nation's defence we . . . render our heartfelt thanks."[6]

Like Felix Gregory De Fontaine's Fort Sumter account, the Gettysburg accounts of the *Herald*'s correspondent corps enthralled the nation. The paper sold out virtually everywhere. New Yorkers scarfed up copies "faster than the newsies could make change," as one historian liked to put it.[7] Meanwhile, Washingtonians turned Pavlovian for the *Herald*. Hundreds if not thousands converged on their train station, anticipating the latest *Herald* issue to arrive by rail from New York. When the iron horse whinnied into the Union capital on July 5, saddled with fresh, Gettysburg-themed *Heralds*, Washingtonians devoured them all in minutes.[8] Once again, "All newsdom was in ferment."[9] And once again the *New York Herald*, captained by the indomitable James Gordon Bennett—"the Napoleon of the American press," stood at the center of it all.[10]

When the North's correspondents proclaimed Gettysburg a victory, the North's anti-administration printers greeted the news with a mixture of open arms and cold shoulders. An ecstatic Bennett saluted Gettysburg as on par with Waterloo, while native Washingtonian William Douglas Wallach happily embraced the victory as "great and glorious news!"[11] But others saw little great and glorious about it. Samuel Medary viewed Gettysburg as nothing more than a war-unaltering holocaust, and one brash Kentuckian turned New York newsman emphatically agreed.[12] Sounding more like a rebel than a Yankee, Benjamin Wood bemoaned "the butcheries of Gettysburg . . . as the unimpeachable proofs of the utter hopelessness of a reconstruction by force of arms."[13]

When covering Gettysburg, the North's opposition printers revealed a rift in their ranks. On one side stood Democratic moderates like Bennett and Wallach, newspapermen who combated President Abraham Lincoln's policies—such as the Emancipation Proclamation—but backed his war to restore the Union. As anti-Lincoln but pro-war members of the Democratic press, the moderates clasped Gettysburg in open arms and often with the same exaggerated warmth that marked their pro-Lincoln peers. They demonstrated that dissent and patriotism could walk hand in hand. Indeed, their Gettysburg coverage showed that an opposition against Lincoln needed not entail an opposition against the war he prosecuted as commander-in-chief.

But on the other side stood peace Democrats like Medary and Wood. These printers not only opposed Lincoln's policies but also sympathized with the South and actively undermined his war to restore it to the Union. As anti-Lincoln and antiwar radicals in the Democratic press, denounced by detractors as Copperheads, they sank their venom deep into their Gettysburg coverage. Indeed, in a blatant attempt to undermine the war they opposed, the Copperheads downplayed the decisive Union victory at Gettysburg at almost every turn. Ultimately, the Civil War divided more than a nation. By 1863 the rift between Copperheads and moderates cut so deep that it cut the anti-Lincoln press coverage of the Gettysburg campaign in two.

As always, New York led the way. Anti-Lincoln moderates in the Empire City covered the Wednesday battle with a surprising degree of accuracy.[14] Rather than sugarcoat July 1, Bennett, Massachusetts native Manton Marble, and native Irishman Thomas Kinsella removed the favorable polish that defined pro-administration printers like Horace Greeley and Henry J. Raymond. With its nearly dozen Gettysburg correspondents, Bennett's *Herald* summarized, "Our right flank was completely turned and our left at the same time." As a result, the federals "retreated slowly . . . the rebels closely pursuing."[15] The lone Gettysburg reporter for Marble's New York *World,* a man who disguised his identity behind the pseudonym "Bonaparte," framed the fight similarly. Because two Union corps broke like a wishbone and fled the field, Bonaparte declared July 1 a Southern "success" and a Northern "reverse."[16] Kinsella's *Brooklyn Daily Eagle* flew away with the same take.

Boasting the country's largest afternoon circulation, the *Eagle* recapped Wednesday as "upon the whole unfavorable to the Union arms."[17]

But New York's moderates stressed a silver lining to Wednesday's dark cloud: the high ground gained south of Gettysburg. Kinsella's *Eagle* explained that the heavy losses suffered on July 1 bought the Army of the Potomac time to secure "a commanding position on the south of town."[18] *Herald* correspondent J. H. Vosburg agreed. Thanks to the defensive sacrifice made by the First and Eleventh Corps, argued Vosburg, the federal army won highly advantageous ground just beyond Gettysburg.[19] By emphasizing this key point while admitting to a Union reverse, New York's anti-Lincoln moderates covered the July 1 battle more honestly than the city's pro-Lincoln press.

They also covered the Thursday battle more honestly. Rather than turn July 2 into a decisive victory, Bennett portrayed the battle as the indecisive tug of war it was. Thursday "was desperate; but there was no decisive result," divulged the *Herald*. "The Union troops . . . lost some [ground] . . . and the enemy still held Gettysburg."[20] Like Bennett, Marble and Kinsella gave no reason to think Thursday had ended in a conclusive Union triumph. While the *World* labeled the battle "sufficiently terrible," the *Eagle* admitted that Longstreet threw Major General Dan Sickles and his entire corps through a Southern woodchipper.[21] The Union Third Corps, reported the *Eagle*, "was literally cut to pieces."[22]

Whether Sickles erred in the Thursday battle, however, proved a different matter. New York's anti-Lincoln printers whitewashed Sickles's Gettysburg contribution about as eagerly as their pro-Lincoln counterparts. Bennett led the charge with hussar-like zeal. Rather than ticket it as an unauthorized gamble, the *Herald* argued as early as July 4 that Sickles followed orders when he advanced his corps into the peach orchard.[23] If this angered Union general George Meade, then Cook's account for the *Herald* would have made his blood boil. Although Cook correctly laid the decision to reposition the Third Corps on Sickles's shoulders, he claimed the move did not endanger the Union army. To the contrary, asserted Cook, "Sickles . . . saved the army and day by assuming the responsibility of changing the front of his corps."[24]

Sickles enjoyed positive press on a bipartisan basis. While the loss of a limb and Lincoln's favor won him kudos with pro-administration printers, his Democratic politics and New York roots won him support with anti-administration printers, especially in Democrat-dominated New York City. Indeed, the nation's news mecca skewed heavily Democratic, with the majority of its seventeen dailies directing more routine antipathy against Lincoln than against Jefferson Davis.[25] While the *World*—which absorbed James Webb's *Courier and Enquirer* when the war erupted—joined the *Herald* in leading the city's moderate opposition, Benjamin Wood's *Daily News* led the city's sizeable den of snakes.[26] Fully five Copperhead dailies called the city home during the Civil War. When it came to Gettysburg, no one benefited more from New York's Democratic bend than Dan Sickles. Because the city's Democratic newsmen refused to throw their own to the wolves, the Gettysburg fool enjoyed positive press on both sides of the North's political divide.

While New York's moderates restrainedly covered the first two days, they tossed all restraint to the wind when covering the decisive Friday battle. Bennett's *Herald* raved, "The Rebel army [was] virtually annihilated . . . [and reduced to] a disorganized mob, calling upon the rocks and the mountains to hide them from the face of their pursuers."[27] Just like their pro-Lincoln foils, Marble and Bennett overstated the results won on July 3 by overstating rebel losses. Writing for Marble's *World*, Bonaparte announced overall Union losses, "compared with those of the enemy," were "like pebbles to grains of sand along the shore."[28] If figurative language failed to convey the damage Meade dealt at Gettysburg, literal figures hammered in the point. The *Herald* reported that Meade rounded up almost as many rebel prisoners at Gettysburg as General Ulysses S. Grant did at Vicksburg: twenty-eight thousand.[29] The figure proved so inflated that it actually matched the Gettysburg total in Southern killed, wounded, and prisoners combined. These sensational reports prompted Knox, the *Herald* man who surveyed the battle's harrowing aftermath, to reach the same conclusion as the pro-Lincoln press. Knox declared Gettysburg, "As great or greater than . . . Waterloo."[30]

Historians traditionally link sensationalism to the "yellow journalism" of the late 1800s. According to that tradition, New York printers Joseph Pulitzer and William Randolph Hearst launched a new and unethical age in American journalism by striving to outsell the competition through shocking stories that bore little to no resemblance to reality. But a generation earlier, Civil War printers waded deep into sensationalism's yellow waters. To lure readers from the competition, Civil War printers often ran extraordinary stories from the front without verifying the information beforehand. The Gettysburg campaign proved no exception.

On July 6, Frank Chapman, the wily *Herald* man who used the Bible to hog a Baltimore line, wired Bennett an electrifying follow-up story to the Battle of Gettysburg. Chapman claimed that Union general Darius Couch, commanding Pennsylvania's militia at Harrisburg, had sallied forth from the city in Meade's direction. Like heroes teaming up against the villain, the two commanders combined their forces and then turned their sights on Confederate general Robert E. Lee. They not only caught up to Lee's fleeing army after Gettysburg, reported Chapman, but also commenced "slaughtering and capturing the graybacks by regiments and brigades."[31] Chapman's story turned out to be totally fictional. Rather than wait to verify it, however, Bennett proved as willing as Greeley to toss aside his journalistic scruples if it meant giving his readers what they wanted. On July 7, just one day after Chapman telegraphed the story, Bennett published it in the *Herald*. Ever the capitalizing businessman, Bennett enlarged the issue into a titanic triple sheet (twelve pages rather than his usual eight) and generated the buzz he no doubt desired. Some New Yorkers snatched up copies before the ink fully dried.

The following day Bennett yellowed his Gettysburg coverage again. On July 8, one day after running Chapman's bogus piece, Bennett recounted in the *Herald* a July 7 battle at Williamsport, Maryland, involving Meade's forces.[32] But there was one major problem: the battle never happened. "At the time it was alleged to have occurred," wrote historian J. Cutler Andrews, "the Army of the Potomac was not within twenty miles of Williamsport!"[33] It did not take long for the sensational news coming from the post-Gettysburg front to get under Meade's thin skin. In a late July letter to General-in-Chief Henry Halleck, Meade wanted to "remove the impression which newspaper correspondents have given the public that it was only necessary to advance [after Gettysburg] to secure an easy victory."[34]

The moderate press generally avoided sensationalizing the Wednesday battle. In Washington, D.C., Wallach's *Evening Star* admitted the truth: Southerners broke the federals in retreat, chased them like hounds through Gettysburg, and gobbled up a good many prisoners in the process. But, like Bennett and Marble, Wallach brightened this dim picture by highlighting the high ground won south of Gettysburg. "At the end of the fight," beamed the *Evening Star*, "General Meade shifted his position to the heights [gained] above Gettysburg."[35] Ohio printer John Stephenson fell into the *Star*'s orbit. Stephenson's *Plain Dealer*, Cleveland's Democratic counterweight to the Republican *Leader*, summarized the fight, "On Wednesday we were out-flanked and overpowered, with heavy loss, but secured a position in the rear of Gettysburg and held it."[36] By stressing the losses suffered alongside the ground gained, the nation's moderate opposition painted a far fairer picture of the July 1 battle than their pro-administration rivals.

Anti-Lincoln moderates also gave a fairer take of the Thursday battle. Stephenson's *Plain Dealer* reminded readers that, thanks to the day before, "On Thursday . . . we had the advantage of ground."[37] But even with this advantage anti-Lincoln moderates acknowledged that both sides fought staunchly and suffered dearly. Stephenson conceded that "the rebels fought with the utmost desperation," while Wallach acknowledged that both sides endured "heavy losses." Although most moderates refused to follow the pro-Lincoln press by styling Thursday as an unambiguous triumph, they also refused to call it a draw. Instead, most gave the Union army the edge. Stephenson's *Plain Dealer* informed readers that Thursday resulted in the rebels being "terribly cut up, and repulsed," while Wallach's *Evening Star* overshot the result with its headline "The Enemy Repulsed at All Points."[38] Despite Wallach's overstatement, the moderate anti-Lincoln press showed more restraint in covering the July 2 battle than their pro-Lincoln counterparts.

One might conclude that the moderates' "for the war but against Lincoln" stance helped stay their hand or that their unique pro-war and anti-Lincoln biases—the former more patriotic, the latter more critical—proved the best combination for more measured Gettysburg coverage. After all, the moderates generally avoided giving the battle's first two days the pro-Northern polish that characterized the pro-Lincoln press. But this conclusion should be taken with a mountain of salt. Whatever credit the moderate press earned for restrainedly covering the Wednesday and Thursday battles, their unbridled coverage of Friday more than negated.

Unionwide, moderate printers smothered the already decisive July 3 battle with the same gloss that marked Lincoln's toadies in the press. Native Keystone Stater James P. Barr, a printer who transformed the *Pittsburgh Post* into western Pennsylvania's principal Democratic organ, revved like an engine freed from its governor.[39] The *Post* hailed Friday's magnificent news: the Confederate Army of Northern Virginia having been left "entirely demoralized, and scattered promiscuously in every direction."[40] Michigan printer William E. Quinby parroted the view. Running the state's first daily, the *Detroit Free Press,* Quinby fired off a war extra packed with more triumphant articles than students in a New England schoolhouse.[41] Above them he plastered the hyperventilating headline, "Lee's Army Demoralized and Flying to the Mountains."[42]

Quantitative overstatements accompanied the qualitative. Stephenson's *Plain Dealer* claimed that Friday saw Meade haul in a corps-sized catch of fifteen thousand to twenty thousand gray prisoners.[43] Quinby also inflated Confederate losses to augment the victory, but he saw no need for Stephenson's generous range. The *Detroit Free Press* contended that Meade had bagged twenty thousand Confederate prisoners.[44]

These trumped-up results pushed moderates everywhere to trumpet Meade's greatness immediately after the battle. Bennett sang the general's praises as loud as any Northern newspaperman. "Praises of General Meade are on the tongue of every officer and soldier," roared a correspondent in the *Herald*'s July 7 issue. "He has shown masterly generalship. . . . Lee has found his match at last."[45]

Meade worship went hand in hand with cutting Lee down to size. In fact, what made idolizing Meade so deserved hinged less on how Meade won at Gettysburg and more on who he won against. Marse Robert, the South's supposedly invincible champion, had too often frustrated Northern hopes for victory. By lifting up Meade after Gettysburg, however, Northern printers could finally bring low the man who, by so often besting the North's largest army, complicated their positive framing of the war. By vanquishing "one of the greatest Captains of the age," relished Quinby's *Free Press*, "Gen. Meade has fully justified the high expectations of him."[46] Barr also lauded Meade for putting Lee in his place. The *Pittsburgh Post* cheered like a proud parent: "[Lee] was beaten by our glorious and modest Meade . . . [and now his] prestige is gone."[47]

While Gettysburg drove moderates to wrap Meade in victory's laurels, it also drove them to wash clean the Army of the Potomac's checkered history. Quinby's *Free Press* claimed, "The Army of the Potomac . . . redeemed its reputation . . . and thus gloriously vindicated the honor of the soldiers of the East."[48] Anti-Lincoln moderates, like their pro-Lincoln counterparts, heavily pushed the redemption narrative. Perhaps no Northern newspaperman, whether pro- or anti-administration, sermonized on the army's redemption better than Stephenson. "All [the Army of the Potomac's] accumulated disasters; all its wounds, and wrongs, and sufferings," ordained the Cleveland *Plain Dealer*, "are atoned for in the blaze of victories [at Gettysburg]."[49]

The Army of the Potomac's atonement at Gettysburg handed pro-war printers something they had longed for since Antietam: a chance to silence the army's many detractors. Stephenson targeted naysayers on both sides of the Mason-Dixon. "The sneers of the Richmond papers are answered; the vaunts of the rebel officers are answered; the scoffs of our own unjust press and people are answered," reveled the *Plain Dealer*. "[The Army of the Potomac] stands to-day the noblest gathering of brave and constant men who ever marched forth to battle."[50]

The Gettysburg victory especially exonerated the army's soldiers. According to many Northern newsmen, the eastern soldiers who overwhelmingly comprised the Army of the Potomac lagged behind their western comrades in the victory column not because they were inferior fighters but instead because they had been led by inferior commanders. However, under what Barr called Meade's "genius and celerity," the army's men in blue finally showed disparagers everywhere that they bore no blame for the blunders of the past.[51] Stephenson's *Plain Dealer* chortled, "Who will now sneer at those soldiers, who . . . through the blunders of incompetent Generals, have now shown to all the world that *the fault was not with them*."[52]

Meade's genius, his soldiers' overstated performance at Gettysburg, and torrential rains that flooded the Potomac convinced moderate printers that Lee's doom laid at hand. Cook reported for the *New York Herald* that, thanks to Meade's pursuit and heavy rains, the rebels were "completely vanquished . . . with no hopes of ever escaping to the South of the Potomac."[53] Chapman echoed his colleague. The *Herald* correspondent predicted that no more than 10 percent of the Army of Northern Virginia would return to its namesake.[54] Meanwhile, in the nation's capital, at the *Evening Star*'s office on Eleventh and Pennsylvania, Wallach studied the signs and saw the end as clearly as if it were a neon banner. Between Meade's victory and the Potomac's providential swelling, the stars had aligned. Wallach's headline on July 8: "The Annihilation of Lee's Army Reduced to a Certainty."[55]

Moderate printers beyond the New York City and Washington, D.C., press hubs saw the same auspicious signs and came to the same confident conclusion. Back in Cleveland, Stephenson read the tea leaves and then gleefully spilled the tea. The *Plain Dealer* promised that the flooded Potomac not only blocked Lee's escape but also forced Lee into one of two inescapable outcomes: surrender or battle.[56] Whichever option Lee chose, insinuated Stephenson, Lee's fate was sealed. After consulting his crystal ball back in Detroit, Quinby all but guaranteed the same outcome. "From present appearance there must be another great battle between Lee and Meade, and we believe another great and still more disastrous defeat," charged the *Free Press*. "Everything now indicates continued success."[57]

These hopeful predictions put anti-Lincoln moderates in the same boat as their pro-Lincoln counterparts. Although opposed politically, the anti-Lincoln moderate and pro-Lincoln presses shared a pro-war bias that often manifested itself in the same encouraging war coverage. After Gettysburg, both pro-war presses set aside their political differences and peddled the same triumphant predictions, swelling Yankeedom with confident anticipation. Northerners held their breath awaiting news not just of Lee's end but also of war's end itself. The *Herald* confessed, "The nation, with breathless suspense, is watching the termination of this campaign, to see whether it will virtually end the war or protract the struggle."[58]

But when the North's pro-war presses learned that Lee escaped on July 13, the bipartisanship collapsed. While pro-Lincoln printers turned on Meade faster than news readers from an ad page, anti-Lincoln moderates raced to the general's defense (likely because Meade shared their pro-war and Democratic biases). Kinsella swiftly swooped in to support the Gettysburg victor. On July 15 the *Brooklyn Daily Eagle* warned readers that blaming Meade for Lee's escape "would be ungenerous in the extreme."[59] Bennett also rushed to Meade's aid. After reporting that Lee could never escape thanks to the heavy rains flooding the Potomac, the *Herald* tried to have it both ways by claiming those same rains "impeded the concentration of our army."[60] In case this explanation did not wash, however, Bennett offered another. The *Herald* commended Meade as "not a man to hazard the sacrifice of a portion of his forces in a doubtful attack [at Williamsport, Maryland,] upon the concentrated columns in a strong defensive position."[61] Apparently by not attacking Lee in retreat, Meade exhibited his genius once more.

Whether or not Meade should have struck Lee's defenses at Williamsport north of the Potomac was, and remains in historical circles, highly controversial. Of course, Lincoln and his allies assumed Meade dropped the ball by not doing so. Edwin Stanton, Lincoln's war secretary, fumed even hotter than the president. "No man ever missed so great an opportunity of serving his country as [Meade] lost by his neglecting to strike his adversary at Williamsport," vented Stanton to a friend.[62] But Meade, alongside many anti-Lincoln printers, saw the matter differently. When Meade caught up to Lee at Williamsport, he refused to put the cart before the horse by striking Lee's entrenched position without first reconnoitering it. While in hindsight this gave Lee time to make his escape, at the time Meade believed it necessary to avoid a Yankee bloodbath.[63] Despite attempts by the *Herald* to carry Meade's water on the subject, the general never shook himself free of the controversy. When Congress's Joint Committee on the Conduct of the War examined the matter several months later it determined that "the battle of Gettysburg . . . was not followed by such active measures as . . . were necessary and practicable to enable us to reap the full fruits of the victory there gained."[64] According to one scholar, "Williamsport . . . became the one criticism that was hardest for Meade to live down."[65]

Lee's escape on July 13 sent the moderate press into damage control. Just like their pro-Lincoln analogues, the moderates forgot Lincoln's Bull Run warning and fanned hopes later snuffed out.[66] Several moderates tried to manage the disappointment they fueled by pretending nothing had changed with Lee's escape. After the Confederates slipped into Virginia unmolested,

Stephenson continued to push the same high hopes that Meade would finish the job. "A Gloomy Feeling in Washington is said to exist owing to the escape of Lee," conceded the *Plain Dealer* on July 17, "[but] this feeling is not shared . . . [and we] are waiting hopefully for that glorious result."[67] Bennett also reassured readers that the status quo remained unchanged. On July 18 the *New York Herald* promised, "It is not yet too late to pursue and intercept the army of Lee. . . . Let him be vigorously followed up, and let the victory of Gettysburg be crowned by the destruction . . . of the whole rebel army."[68]

Like the pro-Lincoln press, most moderates tended to the fire they fueled by simply diverting attention elsewhere. Fortunately, the momentous summer of 1863 afforded a veritable buffet of uplifting war news to draw from while drawing the nation's gaze away from the disappointing end to the Gettysburg campaign. As Stephenson put it, the summer air was "charged with the electricity of success."[69] Barr swung the spotlight from Lee's escape to brighter military theaters as skillfully as any printer. "The escape of Lee . . . and the . . . rioters and ruffians of New York, materially obscure the glorious news which has been crowding in upon us from other important directions," remarked the *Pittsburgh Post*. The paper demanded that Northerners take stock: "Vicksburg . . . has fallen . . . the ball was opened again against Charleston . . . [and] Port Hudson has surrendered, which places the Mississippi in possession of the Union forces."[70]

The North's pro-war printers viewed themselves as stewards of Northern morale. To sustain the summer spike, anti-Lincoln moderates—like their pro-Lincoln rivals—shifted the nation's attention from the dim end of the Gettysburg campaign to brighter theaters of the war. This effort faced a major challenge, however, from a newsworthy event engulfing the heart of newsdom itself. The "rioters and ruffians of New York" obscuring the "glorious news" of the war, simply could not be ignored.[71] In fact, the New York City draft riots effectively hijacked the press's war focus by sparking one of the great political firestorms of the American Civil War.

The Northern press responded to the New York City draft riots by circling the partisan wagons. Anti-Lincoln printers, moderates and Copperheads alike, closed ranks and exchanged fire with their common political foe: the pro-administration press. Both the anti- and pro-Lincoln presses, galvanized by their support for or opposition against Lincoln and his controversial draft, blamed the other side for the riots. One pro-Lincoln paper slammed the unrest as "The Copperhead Riot" while another accused "the New York *World*, *Herald*, and similar rebel sheets" of laying its violent groundwork.[72] The moderates and Copperheads gave no quarter either. The moderate *Detroit*

Free Press claimed the administration was "nearly as much to blame as the rioters," while the Copperhead *New York Daily News* blamed the riots on the "Black Republican party . . . the Abolition journals . . . [and] their violent advocacy of the illegal and odious conscription."[73]

The partisan firestorm sparked by the riots sidelined news of the war in the nation's news hub. In mid-July, just after Lee recrossed the Potomac, Bennett ran multiple issues obsessively centered on the chaos consuming New York City. His Democratic colleagues followed suit. A riot on their doorstep, triggered in part by Lincoln's conscription policy, proved far too irresistible for these partisan newspapermen not to foreground. Wood's July 15 issue of the *Daily News* barely covered anything else. The war, especially Lee's escape, took on a peripheral role. Wood relegated the close of the Gettysburg campaign to page 4, where he paid little more attention to the story than "Lee has crossed the Potomac."[74]

The riot-obsessed coverage of New York's anti-Lincoln printers reverberated across Northern newsdom. Bennett, Marble, Kinsella, and Wood set the nation's anti-Lincoln news agenda at least as much as Greeley and Raymond set it for the pro-Lincoln press. Anti-administration printers across the North took their cues from New York and copied, often literally, their riot-intense coverage. The war eventually returned to the fore but not until July 18—after the riots had died down. Several newspapermen saw the mayhem in New York City as an untimely sideshow that yanked the nation's focus away from what mattered most: the extraordinary progress of the war. When the rioting ended, Stephenson expressed his relief in print. "Now that we have time to turn our gaze from the unwonted and offensive details of a great local disturbance," explained the Cleveland *Plain Dealer*, "we see that a wondrous 'change has come over the spirit' of that larger revolution which threatened, not the security of a single city, but the integrity of the whole nation."[75]

While the draft riots brought moderates and Copperheads together, almost every aspect of the Gettysburg campaign wrenched them apart. Nothing left them more riven than the battle itself. Unlike the moderates, the Copperheads cast the Wednesday fight in perhaps the worst possible light for the North. Few even stressed the high ground gained south of Gettysburg. Indiana's most venomous Copperhead, Joseph Bingham—a man arrested in 1864 on treason charges—ignored that key consolation prize altogether. In his Indianapolis-based paper, the *State Sentinel*, Bingham simply stated, "On Wednesday the Rebel army had the advantage."[76]

Bingham's terse take appeared generous when compared to his colleagues. Several Copperheads employed the word "disaster" to summarize the

Wednesday battle. The *Democratic Banner*—a rural tract published in Clearfield, Pennsylvania—described the July 1 battle as "decidedly disastrous to Federal arms."[77] Wood forcefully agreed. His *New York Daily News*, a Copperhead publication deemed so dangerous the U.S. government had suspended its mailing privileges in August 1861 to contain its venom, reported that on Wednesday "federal forces there were disastrously defeated."[78]

The U.S. government sometimes used the post to defang Copperheads. Since the mail remained unrivaled as the primary vehicle for news dissemination during the war, suspending a newspaper's postal privileges could effectively halt its circulation. The federal government's denial of access to the mail in 1861 so handicapped the *Daily News*, depriving subscribers of their issues and starving the paper of revenue, that Wood faced no choice but to shut down his press.[79] The New York Copperhead did not reopen his newspaper until May 1863, just one month before the Gettysburg campaign and only after the government restored his mailing privileges. Wood's hiatus did nothing to cool his fiery antiwar rhetoric. Just five days after Meade defeated Lee at Gettysburg, the *Daily News* denounced the war as "utter hopelessness" and called "for Peace to be most earnestly invoked."[80]

When the federal government declined to muzzle Copperheads using the post, postal workers sometimes did so on their own accord. Two weeks after Lee's escape, Medary learned that some postal workers had refused to deliver the Columbus *Crisis*, a paper that boasted the Ohio capital's largest circulation, to its subscribers.[81] For a Copperhead who had faced suppression from the military earlier that year, facing it from the comparatively innocuous post proved insufferable. On July 29 Medary seethed, "It is bad enough to submit to the petty despotism of brainless military upstarts, in preventing our circulation over whole districts. But when thieving Postmasters take it upon themselves to steal a paper from isolated subscribers . . . it is a nuisance beneath description."[82]

The Copperhead press continued to undermine the war by undercutting the Union army's performance on July 2. Many Copperheads refused to give federal forces the edge. The *Democratic Banner* spoke for its peers when it claimed "the result . . . of the second day [came] without much advantage to either side."[83] Sickles received an undeserved pass by receiving almost no press. In fact, most Copperheads refused to speak for or against the Union army's dullard at Gettysburg. Doing the former would have meant lionizing Sickles, giving teeth to the narrative that Thursday resulted in a Union success—a narrative most Copperheads disputed. Doing the latter would have required criticizing a prominent Democrat general, betraying the political bias of the entirely Democratic Copperhead press. As a result, most Copperheads—including Wood and Medary—stayed silent on the subject, and Sickles slipped through their columns unscathed.

The Copperheads poured cold water on the Friday triumph. Perhaps no Northern snake squelched the verve for victory more than Illinois transplant Wilbur Storey. His *Chicago Times*, a paper suppressed by the military a month before Gettysburg for subverting the Union cause, all but eviscerated that day's decisive result.[84] "The Federal army was on the defensive," snorted the *Times*, and, although it "succeeded after varying fortunes," it "suffered terribly" in the process.[85]

The heavy-handed suppression of his paper just before the Gettysburg victory likely made Storey more hostile toward it. General Ambrose Burnside sparked two civil liberties fires in as many months. Using his authority as commander in the federal Department of the Ohio, Burnside ignited one blaze on May 5 when he arrested Copperhead chieftain and soon-to-be Ohio Democratic gubernatorial candidate Clement Vallandigham. And less than a month later he lit another when he shut down Storey's *Times*. On June 1 Burnside issued General Order 84. "On account of the repeated expression of disloyal and incendiary sentiments," decreed Burnside, "the publication of the newspaper known as the Chicago *Times* is hereby suppressed."[86] At dawn on June 3, exactly one month before the Union victory at Gettysburg, federal soldiers seized possession of Storey's Chicago office, halted his press, and policed the surrounding streets outside.

The military takeover of the *Times* provoked a predictable backlash. Chicagoans cried foul. By midday on June 3 the city's Democrat mayor issued a request that Lincoln override Burnside's order. By nightfall twenty thousand Chicagoans, composed of as many Republicans as Democrats, amassed to protest Burnside's action as an affront to free expression and a free press. In Springfield, Illinois, state representatives echoed the sentiments conveyed in Chicago by passing resolutions condemning Burnside's order.[87] The "fire in the rear" grew so hot so quickly that it once again caught Lincoln's attention.[88] Just as he had in the Vallandigham case, the president intervened.

Lincoln saw two paths before him. He could either sustain or rescind Burnside's order. Sustaining the general's action might muzzle Storey, not to mention gratify Burnside, but it threatened to exacerbate the civil liberties inferno already raging in the Union rear. In contrast, rescinding Burnside's order might tame the flames by pacifying fears over civil liberties, but it would, apart from grating the general, reopen—not to mention reinvigorate—the *Times* as a Copperhead publication. Storey would return to his post a political martyr and, with the wind of public sympathy at his back, feel emboldened to ratchet up his antiwar and anti-Lincoln rhetoric. As one historian phrased it, the *Times* would, "put on fresh armor and return to the fray."[89]

Cognizant of the Vallandigham case, in which heavy-handedness yielded only heavier backlash, Lincoln pursued the latter course. After just one day he revoked Burnside's order. Lincoln explained himself through Secretary Stanton. Going forward, relayed Stanton to Burnside, civilian arrests and press censorship required Lincoln's prior approval because "the irritation produced by such acts is likely to do more harm than the publication would do."[90] In the long run Lincoln was doubtless proved right. But in the short run Storey reacted as expected. The Chicago printer, feeling embittered and empowered, restarted his press and redoubled his rancorous coverage just in time to unload on the Gettysburg triumph.

Storey's fellow Copperheads joined him in undermining that victory. Several did so by flipping an old trick on its head. The trick entailed reworking the overall Gettysburg casualty figures, but unlike the moderate press, which bent the numbers in federal favor, the Copperheads curved them against the Union army in a blatant bid to minimize the victory. According to Wood, the butcher demanded the same price from Johnny Reb as he did Billy Yank. Both armies, claimed the *Daily News*, suffered twenty-five thousand casualties.[91] The *Democratic Banner* also put rebel losses on par with those suffered by federal forces, but it set the figure much lower. The Pennsylvania paper estimated that both sides suffered between fifteen thousand and seventeen thousand casualties.[92] By both equalizing and underestimating Confederate casualties at Gettysburg, the Copperheads made the battle seem more like a draw than a definitive Union victory.

In case this glum Gettysburg narrative failed to stifle the country's triumphant mood, the Copperhead press attempted to discredit newspapers celebrating a mammoth victory. Medary effectively allied himself with the Southern press by accusing his fellow Northern printers of lying about Gettysburg. In a rare break from promoting Vallandigham's campaign in absentia for Ohio governor, Medary asked Columbus *Crisis* readers, "What is expected to be gained by the system of lying adopted after every battle. . . . It is a disgrace to all engaged in it."[93] Bingham more or less agreed with his forked tongue neighbor. The Indiana *State Sentinel* discounted the tidings of victory as "the grossest exaggerations" and like Lincoln berated the press for hyping "the hopes of the country, only to be disappointed."[94]

Unsurprisingly, Wood joined his Copperhead colleagues in condemning the press for misleading the nation. The *Daily News* hissed:

> The telegraphic wires have . . . conveyed the impression that the Confederate army was annihilated. . . . [There is scarcely] a newspaper that has not entered into the lists as a candidate for an imaginary prize, to be bestowed on the most imaginative inventor of sensation headings. Newsboys have not exaggerated, in crying out extras which contained [coverage of] the total capture of General Lee's whole forces; of more cannon than he ever possessed; with a slaughter of half of his troops; and the surrender of an equal number. Amid the din of false rumors, however, those who have held fast to General Meade's authentic dispatches, have not been deceived. They have known that the triumph of the Northern army has consisted in not being defeated, and that . . . is the extent of our victory.[95]

The tenor of Meade's official dispatches did contrast the hyperbolic Gettysburg coverage of most pro-Lincoln and moderate anti-Lincoln printers. Late on July 2, for example, Meade cabled the War Department a brief summary of that day's bloody clash that lent little credibility to the conclusion that it had ended in an unambiguous Union victory. Meade described the battle as "one of the severest contests of the war," in which the Army of the Potomac "suffered considerably in killed and wounded."[96] The gap between Meade's dispatches and many Northern printers' overstated coverage encouraged Copperheads to uncoil and lash out. Storey lambasted the Northern press for straying from the marked path of Meade's dispatches and into the wilderness of hyperbole. "The country has been excited by reports . . . of a total rout of the rebel army and the capture of impossible numbers of prisoners, all of which are totally unreliable," ranted the *Chicago Times*. "It is evident from the tenor of General Meade's dispatches that no general rout of the enemy has taken place."[97]

But Meade's dispatches proved fallible. Like many Civil War generals, Meade shielded his command from scrutiny by submitting brief reports that presented his actions in a more favorable light. His Thursday battle summary also claimed that the enemy "was repulsed at all points," even though Longstreet overran Sickles's corps on the federal left and Confederate lieutenant general Richard Ewell pried loose at least some ground against the federal right.[98] Like Meade, Lee also sugarcoated his Gettysburg report. In his July 4 dispatch to President Davis, Lee conveniently spent more time describing the Southern success on July 1 than he did describing the other two days of the battle combined. Ultimately, like the press itself, the opposing commanders at Gettysburg demonstrated no immunity to bias.

Although Meade massaged his dispatches to his own advantage, this paled when compared to the ways many printers leveraged them to their own benefit. Northern pressmen understandably leaned on Meade's official dispatches to help make sense of the battle, but they often did so selectively in order to promote the version of victory that aligned with their bias for or against the war. Pro-war newsmen, whether pro-Lincoln or anti-Lincoln moderates, seized on lines like "repulsed at all points" to forward a more auspicious victory narrative. Conversely, antiwar Copperheads zeroed in on phrases such as "suffered considerably" to help downplay the triumph. In both cases the Northern press cherry-picked evidence from a seemingly reliable source to advance their own biased agendas.

Despite attempts to undermine the victory Meade won, the Copperhead press generally praised him after Gettysburg. Medary's *Crisis* applauded the commander for showing "great judgment, coolness, bravery and energy, and none of the ridiculous bravado" that defeated his predecessors.[99] Bingham admired Meade for outshining all of his predecessors save one, a man who won favor as the favorite son of the Democratic Party: George B. McClellan. Meade commanded the Army of the Potomac "more successfully and with more skill and energy than any of his predecessors except McClellan," remarked the Indiana *State Sentinel*.[100] Storey also saluted Meade, though not with the same convincing vigor of most Northern printers. "General Meade is successful in having repulsed an attack upon his position," admitted the *Chicago Times*, "but the more difficult task awaits him in assuming the offensive."[101]

That more difficult task required following up the Gettysburg victory by crushing Lee's retreating army. While the moderates all but guaranteed Meade would finish the job, especially given the Potomac's brimming banks, the Copperheads dismissed all such guarantees as drivel. "The sensation[alist] reports alleging that the rebel retreat is cut off are unworthy of notice," scoffed Storey's *Times*. "Lee can demolish any force sent in front of him."[102] Since most Copperheads viewed Gettysburg as more draw than victory, Lee's retreating army remained intact and formidable. Coverage to the contrary demanded repudiation. Wood rejected reports depicting Lee's army on the ropes gasping for air. The *New York Daily News* mocked, "The representations that [Lee's] troops are a disorganized mob, huddled together upon the banks of an impassable stream, and awaiting till leisure serves the foe to annihilate them . . . [are] the visions of brains . . . overheated by the fever of an unlooked for victory."[103]

When word that Lee had escaped reached their offices, most Copperheads did not express disappointment. Wood summed up most Copperheads' blasé attitude when the *Daily News* announced, "General Lee's army has escaped. This was expected."[104] Some even complimented Marse Robert for managing the rebels' retreat into Virginia successfully. The rural Pennsylvania *Democratic Banner* credited Lee when it conceded, "The escape of the rebels was managed with extraordinary success."[105] And Medary tipped his hat to the rebel commander when he called the most newsworthy story "Gen. Lee's successful recrossing of the Potomac into Virginia, with all his plunder and most of his men in good condition."[106] But Lee's successful escape did not warrant scapegoating Meade. In fact, in a rare show of solidarity, Copperheads marched in lockstep with moderates and refused to shun the Gettysburg victor. Bingham's *State Sentinel* explained, "It is not easy to 'bag' an army," and the paper declined "to blame a General who failed to do it."[107]

The moderate and Copperhead wings of the anti-Lincoln press united in Meade's defense for one simple reason: politics. Whether or not Meade, a Democrat general like McClellan, deserved blame for Lee's escape became a political fight the moment the Republican president weighed in on the matter. As soon as Lincoln expressed his dissatisfaction with Meade for fumbling a war-ending opportunity, the anti-Lincoln bias of the moderate and Copperhead presses kicked in and overrode their differing stances on the war. They rallied to defend their fellow Democrat against the slings and arrows of a Republican president and his lackeys in the press. In the partisan melee, Medary accused Lincoln's administration of blaming Meade to protect its own hide. "There are various . . . reasons given why Gen. Meade did not attack Lee before he got across the Potomac," said the Columbus *Crisis*, "and to get the Government out of the scrape Gen. Meade, like all his predecessors, is made to suffer."[108]

When politics did not reign supreme, the war continued to drive a wedge between moderates and Copperheads. One major point of divergence involved how the two wings of the anti-Lincoln press characterized the soldiers who fought at Gettysburg. Like the pro-Lincoln press, the anti-Lincoln moderates pounced on the campaign as an opportunity to extol Billy Yank and libel Johnny Reb. Marble's New York *World* described Meade's boys in blue as "noble" warriors who had proved their mettle at Gettysburg and won themselves acclaim as national "heroes."[109] Meanwhile, over a four-day span, Barr's *Pittsburgh Post* spurned Lee's Confederates as "fanatical scoundrels," "rascally rebels," and "hungry hordes of marauders."[110]

Most Copperheads refused to go along with the hero/villain dichotomy. As antiwar printers sympathetic to the South, they rarely exalted Billy Yank as some sort of protagonist, let alone castigated Johnny Reb as something akin to a villain. Medary, for example, eschewed the hero-versus-villain narrative by putting the opposing soldiers at Gettysburg on an equal plane. Ignoring that Johnny Reb viewed himself as a Confederate citizen, Medary barked, "They [the soldiers at Gettysburg] were all American citizens" and, showing his racist slip, lamented that "American[s] . . . of the white race . . . should be forced to destroy each other."[111] Ultimately, the antiwar bias and Southern sympathies of Copperheads like Medary dissuaded them from smearing an enemy they viewed almost as fondly as the soldiers on their own side.

Moderates and Copperheads also found themselves divided on whether or not to romanticize Gettysburg in their coverage. While Copperheads found nothing romantic about the regrettable "butcheries of Gettysburg," the moderates joined the pro-Lincoln press in glorifying the battle in compelling prose.[112] Bennett's knights of the quill excelled in this regard. Due to their many vantage points at Gettysburg and their open patriotism for the Union cause, the *Herald*'s correspondents romantically portrayed more aspects of the battle than any paper North or South. Cook, for example, rhapsodized about the "personal heroism . . . and noble Martyrdom" of Union troops in repelling Ewell's often overlooked Friday morning attack against the Union right. The day before and on the opposite end of the battlefield, L. A. Hendrick captured in riveting detail the heroics of Union soldiers, including Colonel Joshua Lawrence Chamberlain, as they desperately defended Little Round Top. When the fighters finally fatigued near sundown, Hendrick wrote, "thousands were *hors du combat,* upon whom that setting sun had shone when rising in the fullness and freshness of manly strength and beauty."[113]

The Union repulse of Pickett's Charge attracted the same romantic flair from the moderate press as it did the pro-Lincoln press. In his report for the New York *World,* the unidentified "Bonaparte" transformed the battle's climactic scene on Cemetery Ridge into an idealized epic. As the rebels poured forward "hooting, crowding, showing their very teeth in the venom of their rage," recounted Bonaparte, "not a man in the Federal ranks flinched from his position." Then came truth's moment. As the "turbulent mass of gray uniform . . . lifted itself in a last leap forward . . . a volley of shell, shrapnel and bullets went crashing through it . . . as a scythe."[114] The result shocked even the most stouthearted. The rebels "fell upon their knees and faces, holding forward their guns and begging for mercy, while their escaped comrades, panic-stricken and utterly routed, rushed [back toward Seminary Ridge]." At this ghastly yet fateful sight, Bonaparte concluded, "The triumph fought for during these three terrible days belonged at last to the noble Army of the Potomac."[115] Overall, Bonaparte produced one of the Northern press's finest Gettysburg accounts. Andrews rightly ranked its quality alongside the superb accounts furnished by three other Northern reporters: Sam Wilkeson, Whitelaw Reid, and Charles Carleton Coffin.[116]

Like a cleaver, war-related news continued to dissever moderates and Copperheads. And no war news competed with Gettysburg quite like Grant's capture of Vicksburg a thousand miles to the southwest. Unsurprisingly, Copperheads dumped the same cold water on Grant's victory as they did Meade's. According to Medary, Grant's capture of the rebel river fortress warranted little enthusiasm: "We considered it a mere matter of time."[117] Even when considered conjointly with Gettysburg, the Confederate Gibraltar's fall provoked the same icy response. An apathetic Wood dismissed both victories as inconsequential. "A battle has been fought; a stronghold has surrendered; but . . . neither . . . has one hope of [bringing] a reconciliation," reprobated the *Daily News*.[118] The *Democratic Watchman* of Bellefonte, Pennsylvania, also brushed off the combined importance of Gettysburg and Vicksburg for the Union. "The general impression among the war element is that the 'back bone' of the 'Rebellion,' is broken," gibed the paper, "but we entertain the idea that it will take considerable work yet before the job is accomplished." The *Watchman* proceeded to discount the wider press celebration over both victories as "all 'bosh.'"[119]

But the moderate press found nothing "bosh" about those victories.[120] Many moderate printers, like several in the pro-administration press, celebrated Gettysburg and Vicksburg as equally vital contributions to the Union war effort. Bennett's July 8 issue of the *New York Herald*, which teemed with Vicksburg-related maps and accounts from its correspondent corps, called the "splendid victory" of Meade and the "magnificent triumph" of Grant "two of the most remarkable . . . events [of the war]."[121] Kinsella and Wallach not only agreed with Bennett but also believed that the North's twin triumphs brought the end of the war within sight. The *Brooklyn Eagle* greeted both victories with "rejoicing": "They promise that the war . . . is likely to result in the achievement for which it was commenced."[122] Meanwhile, the *Evening Star* exulted, "The decisive victories gained at Gettysburg and Vicksburg, coming together must crush the last hope of rebeldom."[123] The victory tide ushered in by Gettysburg and Vicksburg also swept up Barr. The *Pittsburgh Post* judged both victories "equally gratifying" and believed they placed "the end of the rebellion . . . within . . . sight of the naked eye."[124]

Like the pro-Lincoln press, most moderates who disagreed with Barr's analysis ranked Gettysburg as the more significant victory. In a headline after news of Vicksburg arrived on the heels of Gettysburg, Quinby's *Detroit Free Press* shouted "Victory upon Victory," but it ranked Vicksburg "second . . . in importance to that [victory] gained in Pennsylvania."[125] To many moderates, the Gettysburg victory proved sufficient to bring the South to its knees. Even after Vicksburg's capture had been verified, Stephenson's Cleveland *Plain Dealer* dubbed Gettysburg alone "the death-knell of the Confederacy."[126]

Only a few anti-Lincoln printers agreed with the prognosis that Vicksburg outshined Gettysburg. Bingham's Copperhead paper, for example, slithered far from its snake den. The Indiana *State Sentinel* claimed, "The fall of Vicksburg and Port Hudson are the two most important events of the war and the most crushing blows that the rebellion has received."[127]

The Gettysburg coverage of the North's anti-Lincoln printers reflected their commitment, or lack thereof, to the Union. Democratic moderates like Bennett and Wallach supported the Union and Lincoln's war to restore it. Their pro-war bias translated into overly favorable Gettysburg coverage. In fact, on most aspects of the campaign, moderate printers applied the same pro-Northern spin as their pro-Lincoln counterparts. They infused the already decisive July 3 victory with the same wild overstatements and generous casualty figures. The augmented triumph convinced most moderates, like most pro-Lincoln printers, that Gettysburg matched if not exceeded Vicksburg in importance and that Meade, the nation's new military genius, would follow up his victory by swallowing up Lee's retreating army. But Lee's escape dashed these hopes into dust. And to maintain morale most moderates, like most pro-Lincoln printers, simply pivoted to brighter theaters of the war. Only when Lincoln himself blamed Meade for Lee's escape did the moderates show their anti-Lincoln bias and break from the same Gettysburg narrative advanced by the pro-Lincoln press. Thus, the anti-Lincoln bend of the moderate press yielded more often to its pro-war bias, proving that opposition to Lincoln needed not entail opposition to his war to restore the Union.

The Copperhead press proved a different matter. These "rear rebels," as the pro-Lincoln *Chicago Tribune* tarred them, pushed a Gettysburg narrative that matched their antipathy for the Union cause.[128] Almost every aspect of the campaign, from the battle itself to Lee's escape, became a repudiation of the pro-war narrative peddled by the pro-Lincoln and moderate anti-Lincoln presses. Less than two months before the battle began, the pro-Lincoln *New-York Evening Post* identified one of the main signs of a Copperhead paper: "to magnify Confederate victories and depreciate those of the Union arms."[129] The Copperhead press clearly did the latter with Gettysburg, which illustrated just how far most Copperheads would venture to undermine the war they so venomously opposed. The Gettysburg coverage of the Copperhead press lent credibility to Lincoln's concern: "The enemy behind us is more dangerous to the country than the enemy before us."[130]

CHAPTER EIGHT

The Press and Gettysburg

The news on July 8, 1863, sent a splintering shiver down the Confederacy's mainmast. The great Southern citadel on the Mississippi had fallen, and the previously wired news of war-ending victory at Gettysburg—which had triggered a state of jubilee in Richmond—proved little more than the siren's song. It was among the worst news days in Confederate history. Some Southerners knew it and despaired for the cause. "Yesterday we rode on the pinnacle of success—today absolute ruin seems to be our portion. The Confederacy totters to its destruction," mourned Confederate ordnance chief Josiah Gorgas.[1] But for the South's mothers the news hit differently. Rather than worrying first for the fate of the Confederacy, they worried first for the fate of loved ones fighting for its survival. With immense trepidation they kept glued to the only thing capable of answering their prayers or confirming their worst fears: the newspaper.

Rebeldom's news hub hosted a heartbreaking scene over the ensuing days. Desperate for further updates from Gettysburg, Virginia's mothers emptied their homes and flocked by the hundreds to Richmond's newspaper row. They came gray-skinned, sullen, and gaunt—aged beyond years thanks to meal-less days and sleepless nights—and a deathful shadow lay over them, as if they already believed in their hearts that their prayers would go unanswered. But clinging to hope's fraying thread, they threw themselves like beggars against the *Whig, Dispatch, Examiner,* and *Sentinel* buildings and, in a chorus agonizing enough to turn the most callous soldier tearful, pleaded for information from the dazed newsmen inside.

"Are there any names of the killed and wounded given?" they shrieked from hoarse throats. "I heard that he was killed, but have not seen the name in the list published."[2] Violently clutching one another, the mothers squeezed their ration-frail bodies through the front doors and into the cramped news offices. Hooped dresses bowed inward, bonnets tore loose from heads, and the doleful, agonizing chorus grew all the louder and all the more unbearable.

Flustered newsmen flopped about, frantically searching for anything in their files that might ease the women's pain. But apart from telegrams revising down the once great victory at Gettysburg, information remained scant, and when answers came too slowly the mothers made a request to test the courage of the stoutest soldier: to scan the news files themselves. Panning the pressmen with red eyes, the mothers cried out, "[Let us] see if the names of a darling boy is amoung the list of casualties."[3]

Many, after failing to learn their sons' fates, abandoned all hope and ventured back to "their darkened homes in the distant country."[4] Others stayed in Richmond with family or friends, hoping to try again with better luck another day. Some, unwilling to trek home and with nowhere else to turn, remained outside the newspaper offices. Drunk with exhaustion and palled by death, they haunted the bulletin boards like specters—waiting, longing, and praying for "the lightning" to finally strike again. While early July proved a harrowing time in the Confederate capital, it spoke to the wartime experience of Southerners and Northerners alike. As historian George H. Douglas puts it, "the people lived by and through the newspaper during the four dreadful years of war."[5]

The late antebellum era saw the American newspaper ascend to new heights. Demand skyrocketed and—thanks to the post office as well as concurrent revolutions in printing, transportation, and communication—printers met that demand while recalibrating their papers to accrue a mass audience. Increasing press diversification and politicization further enlarged that audience, which helped transform the newspaper into a central component in the lives of nearly all Americans. By 1860 no other nation in the world valued, created, and consumed newspapers more than did the United States.

The Civil War accelerated the newspaper's ascent by intensifying the trends that preceded it. Demand spiked with the war's inauguration at Fort Sumter, and printers leaned on the lessons they learned from the antebellum era in order to meet it. Reliance on technology grew, edition frequency increased (particularly in the North), dependence on the mail deepened, and press hubs and associations developed at an even faster rate. Most importantly, printers radically expanded their news-gathering operations. To cover the action on the war front while promptly reaching readers on the home front, printers hired hundreds of correspondents and devoted more resources than ever to exploiting telegraphy's punctual power. The increased use of the wire and the reporter ensured that the Civil War enjoyed more extensive, detailed, and timely coverage than any war waged before it.

While the war intensified the use of correspondents and telegraphy, it also intensified press partisanship. Before the war Alexis de Tocqueville observed, "All the political journals of the United States are . . . arrayed on the side of the administration or against it."[6] The war reinforced Tocqueville's point by sharpening that partisan divide. The Northern press either threw its ink behind or against U.S. president Abraham Lincoln, while the Southern press either backed or combated Confederate president Jefferson Davis. The printers of the North and South by and large filtered their coverage through these pro- and anti-administration lenses.

As the war wore on, the North and South's anti-administration presses further bifurcated. The North's anti-Lincoln press, dominated by printers beholden to the Democratic Party, splintered into two separate branches: pro-war moderates and antiwar Copperheads. As one historian explained, "The Democratic press split between [pro-war] Unionists and [antiwar] peace Democrats, who favored compromise and even coexistence [with an independent South]."[7] As with their anti-Lincoln bias, the pro-war bias of moderate Democratic printers and the antiwar bias of Democratic Copperheads colored their Civil War coverage.

Meanwhile, a different dynamic emerged in the South. Without an opposition party to channel their dissent, the South's anti-Davis printers operated independently and clashed with Davis for an array of reasons. Some, such as the *Charleston Mercury*'s Robert Barnwell Rhett, censured Davis out of sheer spite, while at least one Confederate printer, the *North Carolina Standard*'s William Woods Holden, opposed Davis out of an opposition to the war itself. But unlike the North, where the anti-Lincoln and antiwar Copperheads held considerable sway, the South's anti-Davis and antiwar press remained small and never coalesced into a nationwide peace movement. Ultimately, the scattered state of the South's anti-Davis press translated into a more fragmented opposition than its Northern equivalent.

By the Battle of Gettysburg these conditions largely characterized the Northern and Southern presses. And so, in the summer of 1863, as two colossal armies and their corresponding armies of correspondents converged on Gettysburg, two nations' pressmen stood ready to interpret the ensuing battle through their respective biases. Although the initial wired wave of misinformation threw their earliest coverage awry, Northern and Southern newsmen eventually assembled the particulars of the Gettysburg campaign while interjecting their biases in an attempt to push the narratives they wanted. Their coverage yields several insights.

Although Northern and Southern pro-administration printers stood on opposite ends of the war's political spectrum, both reported the Gettysburg campaign in a strikingly similar fashion. For one, both skewed casualty figures to benefit their cause. While pro-Davis printers underestimated Confederate losses and overshot those absorbed by the Union army, pro-Lincoln printers softened Union losses and overestimated those suffered by the Confederate army. Second, both presses demonized the enemy's soldiers. Whereas pro-Davis printers traduced Billy Yank, pro-Lincoln printers smeared Johnny Reb—transforming the campaign into a grander struggle of good versus evil. Third, both presses seized on the inconclusive fighting of Thursday, July 2, claiming it as an unambiguous victory for their respective army. Fourth, both pro-administration presses downplayed any lack of success throughout the three days of battle while attributing letdowns to uncontrollable variables. The pro-Lincoln press, for example, revamped the Wednesday, July 1, battle—the worst day at Gettysburg for federal forces—as the inexorable consequence of engaging overwhelming rebel numbers. Similarly, the pro-Davis press repackaged the battle of Friday, July 3, the Confederate army's day of disaster, as the unfortunate and inevitable result of the federal army's elevated position and numerical advantage.

This latter point helped sow the seeds of a potent and long-lasting myth sold after the war: the Lost Cause. The Lost Cause myth arose out of a need among Southerners to provide a palatable rationale for their defeat. Its exponents excused that defeat by arguing, at least in part, that Southerners had conducted themselves more honorably and courageously than the Yankees but eventually succumbed—not because the Yankees possessed superior leaders and soldiers but rather because they ruthlessly wielded superior numbers and resources.[8] While this rationale budded after the war, pro-Davis printers helped plant its seeds after Gettysburg. They repeatedly stressed the Confederate army's numerical disadvantage (except on July 1) as a way to excuse failure. Many, for example, blamed the failure of Pickett's Charge not on Robert E. Lee—the general who ordered it—but instead on the Army of the Potomac's numerical superiority. Ultimately, in their race to excuse the Gettysburg outcome by emphasizing the Union's superior numbers, pro-Davis printers began laying the groundwork for an important piece of the Lost Cause rationale nearly two years before the war ended.

They also breathed life into the Lost Cause myth of Lee. After the war, Southern apologists transformed Marse Robert into, as historian Thomas L. Connelly wrote, "a virtual demigod."[9] To provide Southerners "a balm to sooth defeat," Lee became the "South's invincible general" and the virtuous "embodiment of the Confederate cause."[10] But Lee's transformation into the South's undefeated hero began well before the war ended as evidenced by the pro-Davis press whitewashing his Gettysburg performance. In addition to their general refusal to admit defeat at Gettysburg, the South's pro-administration printers claimed that Lee's military record remained as spotless as an alb. A week and a half after his devastating July 3 repulse, the *Charleston Daily Courier* praised Lee as "invincible," while the *Fayetteville Observer* thundered, "Lee neither has been nor will he be whipped."[11] Although Lee's metamorphosis into the South's undefeated hero blossomed decades after the war with the Lost Cause myth, pro-Davis printers also planted its seeds in their coverage of Gettysburg.[12]

The war's pro-administration presses mirrored one another in at least one more important aspect. Even though press admiration for Union general George Meade plunged after Lee's escape, both Northern and Southern pro-administration printers heaped praise on their top commanders immediately following Gettysburg because both sides claimed some kind of success. The pro-Lincoln press extolled Meade as a "superior genius," whose generalship at Gettysburg eclipsed "the military annals of the great Napoleon."[13] Similarly, praise for and faith in Lee remained remarkably high, despite his bloody repulse at Gettysburg. The pro-Davis press saluted the old man as the South's "great captain" and like some unblemished trophy continued to hold him and his army up as "unbeatable."[14] As both pro-administration presses claimed a version of success for their side at Gettysburg, it became necessary to exalt the general who achieved it.[15]

It is certainly remarkable that printers supporting opposing causes produced such comparable coverage. But it is directly due to their opposing positions on the war's political spectrum that made such analogous coverage possible. Casting Gettysburg in the most favorable light helped reinforce the ultimate objectives of both the pro-Davis and pro-Lincoln presses. On one side, the North's pro-administration press threw its efforts behind Lincoln's administration and his war to suppress the rebellion and restore the Union. On the other end of the spectrum, the South's pro-administration press placed its support behind Davis's administration and his war to achieve Southern independence. As patriotic cheerleaders of these opposing causes, both presses favorably reinterpreted the Gettysburg campaign in order to help achieve those opposing ends. And because the pro-administration presses of the North and South spun the campaign in manners congruent with their opposing political aims, they produced coverage that reflected one another.

Ultimately, the pro-administration printers of the North and South transformed Gettysburg into what they needed it to be, rather than what it truly was. Pro-Lincoln printers refused to report Gettysburg accurately. As indefatigable champions of the Union cause, conscious of the North's hunger for an eastern victory over Lee, pro-Lincoln printers felt the need to recast the already decisive Union victory at Gettysburg into an even greater, more satisfying triumph. The exaggerated coverage of the pro-Lincoln press would later help designate Gettysburg, whether deservingly or not, as the single turning point of the Civil War.[16] Meanwhile, pro-Davis printers refused to give the hard truths of a costly defeat, especially when Southerners had attached "magnificent expectations" to Lee and his "undefeated" Army of Northern Virginia.[17] For these Confederate mouthpieces, the Battle of Gettysburg did not foretell the South's eventual demise but rather brought the South one step closer to the final goal of Confederate independence. In the end, the pro-Lincoln press renovated Gettysburg into a Waterloo while the pro-Davis press denied defeat, claimed success, and directed Southerners to "look to glorious Lee" for hope that the war remained winnable.[18]

The Gettysburg coverage of the Northern and Southern anti-administration presses varied considerably more than their respective pro-administration counterparts. While the pro-Lincoln press produced a more monolithic Gettysburg narrative, the anti-Lincoln press produced two distinct narratives that largely reflected printers' biases for or against the war. The moderate, pro-war printers of the anti-Lincoln press spun Gettysburg similar to their pro-Lincoln peers by—among other things—overstating the triumph, skewing casualties in the Union army's favor, and participating in what could easily qualify as Meade worship. This proves that, when it came to covering Gettysburg, moderate printers' pro-war bias played a more significant role than their bias against President Lincoln. It also proves that a printer's stance against Lincoln need not entail negative coverage of the war he prosecuted as commander-in-chief. Clearly antipathy for Lincoln and a pro-war sense of Union patriotism were not mutually exclusive.

Of course, the Copperhead printers slithered down a different path. Although they were part of the anti-Lincoln press, it was their bias against the war, not necessarily their blatant and blanket bias against Lincoln, that played the greater role in influencing their Gettysburg coverage. The antiwar Copperheads attempted to undermine the war they opposed by painting the Gettysburg campaign in a manifestly negative light. The Wednesday battle became a "disaster," Thursday achieved nothing, and any newspapers heralding Friday as a decisive Union victory faced the venom of Copperhead condemnation. On July 11, for example, the *New York Daily News* dismissed Northern victory reports as "intensely sensational" and argued that it was highly probable, given many Southern printers claiming victory, that the North had "sustained a defeat, and a very bloody one."[19] The Copperheads' gloomy view of Gettysburg sharply contrasted the favorable take of most moderates, whose coverage closely matched the pro-Lincoln press thanks to a shared pro-war bias.

The bleak view of many Copperheads partially functioned as a reaction to the suppression they had faced before Gettysburg. Samuel Medary, Benjamin Wood, and Wilbur Storey all faced some degree of suppression before Lee launched his invasion in June 1863. To muzzle these vindictive printers without them retaliating in print would be like rocking a hornet's nest without getting stung. Put simply, the suppression of Copperheads before the Gettysburg campaign only increased their aversion toward it.

The Copperheads' bleak view also functioned as a reaction to the threat that Gettysburg posed to their cause. Before July 1863, the Copperhead movement had been riding high thanks to the prospect of Union victory sinking low. In June, General Braxton Bragg's rebels still disputed Union control of central Tennessee, Vicksburg still defied Union general Ulysses S. Grant, and Lee's reinforced army—fresh off its stunning triumph at Chancellorsville—blazed a trail unopposed into Pennsylvania. By souring Northerners' taste for war, these setbacks drew new recruits to the Copperhead cause of peace, even if at the price of reunion. During the Gettysburg campaign, Southern printers took great pleasure in the Copperheads' rising stock and took pains to point out the inverse relationship between Union defeats and Northern support for the Copperhead cause. The Atlanta *Southern Confederacy* wrote in early July, "The 'Copperheads' are pretty strong . . . and their strength is continually augmenting. Every failure of Northern arms . . . gives them more vitality and renewed impetus."[20]

The Gettysburg victory, however, dealt Copperheads their first major blow of the summer. Support for peace plummeted as Northern morale spiked. In a desperate bid to keep the cause alive, Copperheads lashed out by undermining the Gettysburg victory. On July 14, for example, Wood's *Daily News* went so far as to decry reports of a great triumph as "simply absurd."[21] Despite these flailing efforts to retain support, Gettysburg helped hurl Copperheads into a yearlong hibernation. Not until the summer of 1864, when Union victory again looked uncertain, did the Copperhead cause experience a resurgence in support that rivaled its pre-Gettysburg high.

Whereas a divided opposition characterized the Gettysburg coverage of the North's anti-Lincoln press, a dispersed opposition described that of the South's anti-Davis press. Occasionally anti-Davis printers sided with their pro-Davis counterparts by reporting Gettysburg in a manner far more favorable than reality. Some, for example, mischaracterized the campaign as another hard-fought Confederate success by, among other things, conflating

Wednesday's victory with Thursday's draw or offering a brighter portrait of Confederate and Union casualties. These printers, like the North's anti-Lincoln moderates, often held a pro-war stance. Because they put the Confederate cause first, they gave the Gettysburg campaign a flattering spin, showing again that printers' bias for or against the war often overrode their bias for or against their administration.

But several anti-Davis printers, some pro-war and some antiwar, burned a less auspicious path by characterizing Gettysburg as a costly draw, a disastrous defeat, or something in between. Some covered Gettysburg stripped of the over-the-top spin that characterized most pro-Davis, and many anti-Davis, printers. Rhett, for example, regarded the victory mostly as it was: an unsustainable defeat eventually dooming the Confederate cause. Others, such as Holden—the South's patron of peace—seesawed between a negative and positive portrayal of the campaign but more often leaned against it. Ultimately, the lack of cohesion among anti-Davis printers made it difficult for any coalesced narratives to emerge around Gettysburg. Instead, the anti-Davis press reflected its lack of party affiliation, and printers assumed positions that ranged from the highly favorable pro-Davis interpretation to the negative but brutally honest interpretation of printers like Rhett, sometimes landing in between.

That many anti-administration printers covered Gettysburg similarly to their respective pro-administration counterparts should not be overlooked. Their unlikely union resulted in the presses of the North and South overwhelmingly overhauling Gettysburg in a manner far more favorable for their side than reality. The "Waterloo eclipsed" and "Look to glorious Lee" interpretations predominated. Whereas the majority of Southern printers put a positive face on Gettysburg, which breathed life into the postwar image of Lee as the undefeated Marble Man, the bulk of the Northern press spun Gettysburg into a victory greater than it was, which helped elevate its status as the watershed of the Civil War. As the *Cleveland Leader* confidently asserted, Gettysburg alone constituted "the turning point of the rebellion."[22]

The two prevailing versions of Gettysburg likely shaded how printers covered the other seismic military event of early July: the Union capture of Vicksburg. With the notable exception of the Copperhead press, which undermined both victories, the Northern press seldom characterized Gettysburg as the less significant of the North's twin triumphs. Instead, the victory that eclipsed Waterloo either matched Grant's achievement at Vicksburg or topped it. To today's Civil War students this should seem backwards. After all, the historical profession tends to emphasize Vicksburg—the Union triumph that dismembered the Confederacy and removed an entire rebel army from the military chessboard—as the more significant victory and a worthier single candidate than Gettysburg for designation as the turning point of the war. But the Northern press by and large disagreed with this assessment due to a number of factors then at play.

The first factor was the proximity of Gettysburg to the North's great news hubs. As the culmination of a Confederate invasion of the North, the Battle of Gettysburg took place nearer to almost every major Union news hub than the Vicksburg campaign. Some of those hubs, such as Washington, Baltimore, and even to an extent Philadelphia, fell within frightening reach of that invasion. Northern printers simply could not prioritize the distant siege at Vicksburg while a major battle raged so close to their own bases of operation. Moreover, Gettysburg's proximity to Northern news hubs made it easier to dispatch additional correspondents to the battlefield. Rather than rely solely on correspondents already assigned to the Army of the Potomac, printers employed and deployed additional reporters to the scene. Horace Greeley, for example, hired Homer Byington as the Gettysburg campaign unfolded and just in time to nab what historian J. Cutler Andrews described as "one of the biggest news scoops of the war."[23] Gettysburg's proximity to so many Northern news hubs ensured the presence of more Northern reporters there than at Vicksburg, which supplied more firsthand accounts of Gettysburg and helped prioritize its coverage.

Secondly, Northern printers perceived that the immediate stakes of failure were higher at Gettysburg than at Vicksburg, which contributed to their tendency to emphasize the former over the latter. Thomas W. Knox, the *Herald* man who stayed behind to cover Gettysburg's aftermath, explained: "As great or greater than Waterloo are the results of this battle of Gettysburg. Lee victorious, Baltimore, Washington and Philadelphia would have fallen before him. The rebel flag would have floated over the national capital. The nations of Europe would no longer withhold the recognition that the rebel leaders have for so many months been asking. The way would have been opened for a peace which should embrace the downfall of our government. Lee defeated, and driven again to Virginia, with our army in pursuit, the nation breathes in safety."[24]

Although Vicksburg's capture functioned as a strategic necessity for ultimate Union victory, a failure to wrangle loose Vicksburg in early July 1863 would not have—unlike a failure at Gettysburg—put any Northern territory at risk, compelled the North to consider peace, or renewed the possibility of foreign intervention on the side of the South. Northern newsmen recognized this immediate disparity in risk. While Vicksburg needed to be won in the long run, Gettysburg had to be won in the short run. The higher immediate cost of defeat at Gettysburg simply made it difficult for printers, in the moment, to prioritize Vicksburg as the more significant victory.

Thirdly, the regional biases of the Northern press advantaged the Army of the Potomac, which helped foreground Gettysburg. The Yankees who fought at Gettysburg overwhelming hailed from the states of New England and the Mid-Atlantic, whereas the men in blue at Vicksburg came almost exclusively from the Midwest.[25] The news hubs of the Midwest generally devoted more coverage to military affairs involving midwestern soldiers, which in turn highlighted events like Vicksburg in the Western Theater. Similarly, news hubs in New England and the Mid-Atlantic generally gave more coverage to military affairs involving soldiers from those areas, which in turn accentuated events like Gettysburg in the Eastern Theater.

While this partisanship by region broke both ways, it did not break evenly. Since New England and the Mid-Atlantic housed the nation's largest and most influential press hubs, regional partisanship tended to shine a brighter national spotlight on events in the Eastern Theater. The national papers of New York City and Philadelphia, which knew no equals in the Midwest (not even in up-and-coming Chicago), spotlighted the actions of local soldiers in the Army of the Potomac in the Union's most-read and most-reprinted newspapers. In effect, the Army of the Potomac benefited from the power of a home press with national reach, which helped to magnify its actions at Gettysburg over that of Grant's army at Vicksburg.

Lastly, Lee added a luster to Gettysburg that Vicksburg lacked. By the summer of 1863 Lee already cast a large shadow over the war. His successes in command made him a not only great hero in the South but also a highly respected and feared adversary in the North. While the Southern press dubbed Lee "as great a General as breathes the breath of life," the Northern press widely acknowledged him as the best general on the Southern side if not, as the *Detroit Free Press* believed, "one of the greatest Captains of the age."[26] The same simply could not be said of Confederate general John C. Pemberton, Grant's less-conspicuous opponent at Vicksburg. Before Vicksburg fell, the *Richmond Dispatch* believed Pemberton, in sharp contrast to Lee, "suffered more from traducers than any other in the Southern Confederacy," and the *Memphis Daily Appeal* carped a month after Vicksburg capitulated, "No general ever possessed so little confidence of either the army or the people as Gen. Pemberton."[27] Add that the Army of the Potomac had not won a major battle over Lee for nearly a year and one begins to glimpse the press appeal of a Gettysburg versus a Vicksburg. When the telegraph heralded news of Union victory at Gettysburg, the drought plaguing the Army of the Potomac had ended, and Lee had finally been brought to heel. The Northern press flaunted the satisfying dual narratives of Lee reduced to a "shorn Samson" and the Army of the Potomac "redeemed."[28] Put plainly, the Northern press capitalized on the aura of Lee in a way that uniquely sweetened the Gettysburg victory.

Of course, other factors worked to privilege Gettysburg over Vicksburg. The staleness of a protracted siege at Vicksburg following several months of the press promising imminent victory compared rather poorly to the fast-moving, hard-hitting excitement of Gettysburg. Moreover, whereas Vicksburg's drama ended with a clean finish on July 4, the high-drama, post-Gettysburg pursuit of Lee kept the Gettysburg story front and center until mid-July. Pile over this the fact that Northern printers exploited the sheer scale of Gettysburg, such as its unequaled overall casualties, while further capitalizing on its drama—such as the valorous Union defense of Little Round Top or the valiant Union repulse of Pickett's Charge—in a way that, at the very least, implied the battle held unmatched significance. But while it is important to understand why Northern printers ranked Gettysburg as at least as important as Vicksburg, the fact that they did is an important point in itself. Printers' prioritization of Gettysburg ensured that the victory captured the nation's fascination and helped it win a special designation, one that seems unlikely to be shaken loose despite attempts by the historical community to center Grant's conquest of Vicksburg.

When considering why Gettysburg earned acclaim as the single turning point of the war, one rejoinder usually follows: the Gettysburg Address. That treasured elegy certainly helped win Gettysburg sustained acclaim by hallmarking it in America's collective consciousness.[29] The battle became inextricably bound to one of the most cherished speeches in American history, and that marriage garnered Gettysburg a distinct renown, especially in the ensuing years as the nation revisited Lincoln's address, like priests consulting old scripture, in an attempt to distill meaning out of four blood-soaked years of civil war.

But the Gettysburg Address, which the battle precipitated and coverage of the battle likely inspired, was not delivered by Lincoln until November 19—over four months after the Northern press had proclaimed Gettysburg a "Waterloo eclipsed." Thus, the battle obtained designation in Northern newspapers as the turning point of the war (warranted or not) well before Lincoln's speech lent any weight to that conclusion. Although the Gettysburg

Address contributed to the battle's towering status in the hallowed halls of American history, it did not establish it. Credit for that belongs to the Northern press.

While the Northern press weighed the twin triumphs of Gettysburg and Vicksburg and tipped the scale in favor of the former, the Southern press weighed the dual defeats of Gettysburg and Vicksburg and skewed the scale lopsidedly against the latter, seeing it as the greater loss. This occurred for several reasons. Some factors that worked to emphasize Gettysburg as the equal or greater victory in the North worked in reverse in the South. Whereas Northern newsdom's heart pulsed nearer and dearer to the Army of the Potomac, the Southern heart, Richmond, beat nearer and dearer to the Army of Northern Virginia. The national newspapers of Richmond displayed their regional bias with a general disinclination to cover the actions of the Army of Northern Virginia, an army composed disproportionately of Virginians, in a negative light. Even the nightmare of Pickett's Charge, a failure that cost the Old Dominion dearly, was revamped by the Confederate capital's great papers as a heroic and noble sacrifice. In effect, the Army of Northern Virginia—like the Army of the Potomac—benefited from the power of a home press with unmatched nationwide influence.[30]

The aura of Lee seemed also to play a role but in reverse. Whereas the Northern press used Lee to amplify the Union victory, the Southern press used Lee to dispute claims of a Confederate defeat. The glow of Lee's reputation cast a blinding glare into Southern newspaper offices. Rather than wait to confirm the earliest telegraphic reports, Confederate printers, dazzled by Lee's reputation, assumed the best from their champion and his veteran army. Headlines like "Gen. Lee Again Victorious!" blazoned the front pages of Southern papers before the details of the battle had a chance to take shape (all but confirming the *New York Times*'s prewar fear that the wire was often "too fast for the truth").[31] And even after the fog of battle lifted, the Southern press generally denied that the Confederate army suffered a defeat, doing so by invoking Lee's name, as though the old man and failure were mutually exclusive. The *Fayetteville Observer* promised readers, "Lee neither has been nor will he be whipped," while the *Richmond Examiner* swore Lee could not "with justice or candor be said to have suffered a defeat."[32] Lee's reputation warped printers' coverage of the Gettysburg campaign and disinclined most from characterizing it in an honest let alone negative light.

Although regional bias and Lee's reputation played a role in Southern printers' more flattering portrayal of the rebels at Gettysburg, another key factor was at play: the cost of defeat at Gettysburg, albeit high, simply paled when compared to Vicksburg. Historian Michael B. Ballard explains the point well: "With the fall of Vicksburg, the Confederacy lost an army that never fought again . . . thousands of square miles of territory and suffered a permanent disruption in logistical support . . . that the Trans-Mississippi supplied to the rest of the Confederacy."[33]

Lee's beaten army, however, remained intact. Gettysburg forfeited no new Southern territory to the North, spared Virginia from another destructive summer of campaigning, and furnished Lee's army with the supplies needed to carry on the fight. While Northern printers saw a disparity between Gettysburg and Vicksburg in terms of the immediate risk of failure, Southern printers recognized an actual disparity in consequences between the two. On July 14 the *Mobile Daily Advertiser and Register* chafed at Vicksburg's loss. "Nothing has happened in the whole war . . . that appears to us so profoundly disgraceful, reprehensible and injurious as the fall of two such positions as Vicksburg and Port Hudson."[34] While statements like these toward Vicksburg abounded in Southern papers, similar comments toward Gettysburg proved few and far between. As historian Gary W. Gallagher writes, "[Confederates] drew a sharp distinction between Gettysburg and Vicksburg. The latter represented an unequivocal disaster . . . [while] Gettysburg presented a far more ambiguous result."[35] As damaging as Gettysburg was, Vicksburg wrought disaster on the Confederate cause, and Southern printers reflected this by showing a greater willingness to criticize it.

The press's various biases colored every aspect of its Civil War coverage. The Gettysburg campaign proved no exception. Whether biased regionally, for or against an administration, or for or against the war, the printers of the North and South bent their Gettysburg coverage to align with those biases. Their partiality casts significant doubt not just on the trustworthiness of the press and its Gettysburg coverage, but also on the press and its Civil War coverage more generally. It is almost taken for granted today that professional journalists ought to at least strive for an objective standard. But, as historian Michael Schudson notes, "Objectivity was not an issue. American newspapers were expected to present a partisan viewpoint, not a neutral one."[36] And as a result, printers warped news of the Civil War to fit their own partisan agendas, and their Gettysburg coverage not only misled the readers of two nations during the war but also helped mislead interpretations of Gettysburg for generations to come.[37] Twenty years after the battle, Union brigadier general Alexander Stewart Webb proclaimed, "Gettysburg . . . was, and is now throughout the world known to be the Waterloo of the Rebellion."[38]

Epilogue

August 27, 1883, proved a fine day to dedicate a Union monument at Gettysburg. The heat kept a respectable distance, and the sun shined proudly on a fair landscape made famous by battle.[1] Atop Cemetery Ridge, seventy yards east of the stone wall, a large crowd gathered to the sound of martial music. Like pilgrims on a historical haj, hundreds came—old veterans, parasol-toting ladies, lawmakers, journalists—to dedicate a well-deserved monument to the Seventy-Second Pennsylvania Volunteers. Twenty years earlier, the Seventy-Second charged like a pride of hungry lions from this exact spot to the stone wall, where it helped maul to pieces the final Confederate assault at Gettysburg, known as Pickett's Charge.

The dedication began promptly at 4:30 p.m. After the monument's unveiling and what one newspaper called "a fitting speech of acceptance," a retired forty-eight-year-old brigadier took the stage for the keynote address.[2] Alexander Stewart Webb still looked like a commander. He fit his uniform like a sword to its scabbard, and his faintly lined face and thick goatee lent the impression that time would have as much trouble conquering him after the war as the Confederate army had during it. By all rights, Webb deserved the keynote slot. On July 3, 1863, he took a bullet to the groin defending Cemetery Ridge, and when Brigadier General Lewis Armistead's rebels briefly overran the stone wall, it was Webb who gave the order for the Seventy-Second to make its monument-inspiring charge and throw them back.

Webb spoke elegantly. While centering the Seventy-Second, he recounted in sweeping style the war's first two years, the tsunami-drawing buildup to Gettysburg, and—of course—the battle itself. The crowd hung on every word. Heads nodded in agreement, faces glowed with pride, and even the toughest veterans struggled to hold back tears.

But to anyone who read a Northern newspaper in the immediate weeks after Gettysburg, Webb sounded like a musician covering an old song. He romanticized the Union defense of Cemetery Ridge as much as any Yankee reporter and inflated the battle's significance as much as any morale-obsessed Northern printer. Gettysburg "decided forever the Rebel claim to rule this country," asserted Webb. "The Rebel blow at our Unity, and the slave-holders' proud boast . . . found on this spot their death-knell."[3]

Webb not only parroted the dominant narrative pushed by the Northern press after Gettysburg but also insisted that it had become the sole and definitive Gettysburg narrative twenty years later. In a sixteen-page speech that mentioned Vicksburg only once, Webb told his audience that Gettysburg alone had earned itself "the well-deserved name of 'the turning point of the war.'" And he confidently pronounced, "Gettysburg . . . was, and is now throughout the world known to be the Waterloo of the Rebellion."[4]

Webb was not wrong. The press had announced, and by 1883 the nation largely agreed, that Gettysburg was America's Waterloo. Never mind that Napoleon's France collapsed just days after Waterloo, whereas Robert E. Lee and the Confederacy fought on for nearly two more years after Gettysburg. Never mind that Vicksburg wiped out an entire rebel army, halved the Confederacy, and launched Ulysses S. Grant into the Union star who beat Lee and won the war. Gettysburg, not Vicksburg, mortally wounded the rebel beast and marked the Civil War's turning point. Three years after the battle, Northerner George J. Gross called Gettysburg "the turning point of the grand drama."[5] Two years after the battle, John W. Forney's Philadelphia *Press* declared Gettysburg "the memorable turning-point of the war for the Union."[6] And just over a year after the battle, Massachusetts lawyer Richard Henry Dana went so far as to call Gettysburg "the turning-point in our history."[7] That Gettysburg became what it became so quickly, deserved or not, stands as high testament to the remarkable, narrative-establishing power of the nineteenth-century American press—the era's vanguards of history.

Notes

Introduction

1. See bibliography for full citations. A generation earlier F. Lauriston Bullard helped plant the seeds that sprouted into this new garden of research with his 1914 book *Famous War Correspondents*.

2. These works remain influential. In 2000, for example, James M. Perry published a nod to Starr not just in substance but also in name with *A Bohemian Brigade: The Civil War Correspondents, Mostly Rough, Sometimes Ready*.

3. McNeely, Van Tuyll, and Schulte, *Knights of the Quill*. Although the book spotlights Southern correspondents, the catchy title also applies to Northern reporters.

4. G. Gallagher, *Lee and His Army*, 86.

5. See bibliography for these authors' works.

6. Historians have held this view for some time. In 1929 military historian J. F. C. Fuller argued that "[because] the South had been cleft in twain; Vicksburg, and not Gettysburg, was the crisis of the Confederacy." See Fuller, *Generalship of Ulysses S. Grant*, 157.

Chapter One. The Antebellum News Revolution

1. Tocqueville, *Democracy in America*, 209.

2. Ibid., 211. Other foreign visitors made the same observation. "The influence and circulation of newspapers is great beyond anything ever known in Europe," wrote Scotsman Thomas Hamilton, who came to the United States in 1830. "Every village, nay, almost every Hamlet has its press, which issues second-hand news and serves as an arena in which the political gladiators of the neighborhood may exercise their power of use and abuse." See Hamilton, *Men and Manners in America*, 74.

3. Mott, *American Journalism, a History*, 303.

4. Ibid., 303–304.

5. McPherson, *Battle Cry of Freedom*, 9.

6. Ibid., 20.

7. Howe, *What Hath God Wrought*, 455.

8. Douglass, *Narrative of the Life of Frederick Douglass*, 64; McPherson, *Battle Cry of Freedom*, 20. For more on black literacy and the Southern laws forbidding it, see Span, "Learning in Spite of Opposition," 26–53.

9. Howe, *What Hath God Wrought*, 455.

10. Ibid., 447.

11. Boylan, *Sunday School*, 19.

12. Mott, *American Journalism, a History*, 304.

13. McPherson, *Battle Cry of Freedom*, 19–20.

14. Howe, *What Hath God Wrought*, 455.

15. The curriculum taught males to extoll the virtue of citizenship in public spaces and females to inscribe it into the next generation through virtuous motherhood. For more on the influence of common schools in antebellum America, see Kaestle, *Pillars of the Republic*. For more on the importance of women and education in antebellum America, see Kelley, *Learning to Stand and Speak*.

16. Quoted in Howe, *What Hath God Wrought*, 543.

17. Kaestle, *Pillars of the Republic*, 65. For more on the development of an informed citizenry, see R. Brown, *The Strength of a People*.

18. Tocqueville, *Democracy in America*, 585.

19. Mott, *American Journalism, a History*, 216.

20. Tocqueville, *Democracy in America*, 587–588.

21. For a thorough look at the expansion of political equality in Jackson's time, see Watson, *Liberty and Power*.

22. Mott, *American Journalism, a History*, 204.

23. Emery and Emery, *The Press and America*, 95.

24. Howe, *What Hath God Wrought*, 227.

25. Douglas, *The Golden Age of the Newspaper*, 14.

26. John, *Spreading the News*, 3, 5, 4.

27. Ibid., 17–18.

28. Quoted in ibid., 17.

29. Quoted in Mott, *American Journalism, a History*, 194.

30. Ibid., 193–194.

31. Henkin, *The Postal Age*, 21.

32. John, *Spreading the News*, 37.

33. Keilbowicz, *News in the Mail*, 149.

34. Tocqueville, *Democracy in America*, 453–454.

35. Henken, *The Postal Age*, 22.

36. For more on the post office in American history, see W. Gallagher, *How the Post Office Created America*.

37. Gordon, *An Empire of Wealth*, 109–110. For more on New York City's canal-inspired economic boom, see N. Miller, *The Enterprise of a Free People*.

38. Fox, "New York City Newspapers," 122–133.

39. Douglas, *The Golden Age of the Newspaper*, 50. For more on the prewar and wartime history of Medill's *Chicago Tribune*, see Kinsley, *The Chicago Tribune: Its First Hundred Years*.

40. Gordon, *An Empire of Wealth*, 137–138. For more on Lincoln's flatboat experiences and why they mattered, see Campanella, *Lincoln in New Orleans*.

41. Taylor, *The Transportation Revolution*, 60, 143.

42. Howe, *What Hath God Wrought*, 223. See also Pred, *Urban Growth and the Circulation of Information*.

43. Tocqueville, *Democracy in America*, 454. The world steamers wrought impressed other observers as well. "After seeing . . . the Steam-engine," remarked President John Quincy Adams, "it was scarcely possible to say what could not be effected by an application of mechanical powers." John Quincy Adams diary, October 3, 1816, Adams Family Archives, Massachusetts Historical Society, Boston.

44. Taylor, *The Transportation Revolution*, 120.

45. The first transatlantic cable, laid in 1858, remained in operation for just a few weeks. Only after the Civil War, when the cable was laid again, were telegraphic communications reliably established between America and Europe.

46. Taylor, *The Transportation Revolution*, 71.

47. Douglas, *The Golden Age of the Newspaper*, 45–46.

48. Quoted in Boorstin, *The Americans*, 125.

49. Tocqueville observed, "[The American] is a highly civilized being, who consents, for a time, to inhabit the backwoods, and who penetrates into the wilds of the New World with the Bible, the axe, and a file of newspapers." Newspapers, he said, maintained civilization. See Tocqueville, *Democracy in America*, 348, 585. Of course, in a cruel twist, white America's "twin heralds of civilization" exacerbated the uncivilized treatment of Native Americans. For how railroad expansion impacted Native Americans in the nineteenth century, see Karuka, *Empire's Tracks*. For more on the economic impact of railroads in the antebellum era, see Fishlow, *American Railroads and the Transformation of the Antebellum Economy*.

50. "The Midwest" here refers to the region west of the Appalachians and north of the Ohio and Missouri Rivers.

51. Binder, "The Transportation Revolution and Antebellum Sectional Disagreement," 20.

52. For more on Southern literary output, see McCardell, *The Idea of a Southern Nation*.

53. Nothing discouraged the growth of Southern manufacturing like the South's commitment to slavery. By mid-century, the slave states contained less than one-fifth of the nation's manufacturing sector, and a decade later eleven of those slave states became embroiled in a civil war with little industry to help wage it.

54. Mott, *American Journalism, a History*, 362–363.

55. Zboray, "The Transportation Revolution and Antebellum Book Distribution Reconsidered," 63.

56. Emery and Emery, *The Press and America*, 114.

57. Quoted in ibid.

58. Taylor, *The Transportation Revolution*, 151.

59. Howe, *What Hath God Wrought*, 696.

60. Mott, *American Journalism, a History*, 248–249.

61. DuBoff, "The Telegraph in Nineteenth-Century America," 573.

62. Hochfelder, *The Telegraph in America*, 74–75.

63. Quoted in ibid., 73.

64. Andrews, "The Southern Telegraph Company," 319, 336–337. Southern telegraphers often hailed from the North. When the Civil War began, many simply went home rather than aid Confederate communications.

65. Douglas, *The Golden Age of the Newspaper*, 3.

66. Scharf and Westcott, *History of Philadelphia*, vol. 3, 1959.

67. *Sun* (New York City), September 3, 1833.

68. Emery and Emery, *The Press and America*, 100.

69. Howe, *What Hath God Wrought*, 228.

70. Schudson, *Discovering the News*, 18.

71. *Millennial Harbinger* 5, no. 1 (January 1834), 3. George Washington allegedly inspired the nickname after visiting New York City and commenting, "Surely this is the seat of empire!"

72. Howe, *What Hath God Wrought*, 228–229.

73. Mott, *American Journalism, a History*, 224.

74. *Richmond Whig*, July 9, 1863.

75. Schudson, *Discovering the News*, 16.

76. Tocqueville, *Democracy in America*, 208.

77. Howe, *What Hath God Wrought*, 228.

78. Schudson, *Discovering the News*, 17.

79. *Sun* (New York City) September 3, 1833.

80. Crouthamel, "The Newspaper Revolution in New York," 96.

81. Douglas, *The Golden Age of the Newspaper*, 34.

82. Crouthamel, "The Newspaper Revolution in New York," 101.

83. McPherson, *This Mighty Scourge*, 176.

84. Douglas, *The Golden Age of the Newspaper*, 56–57.

85. Dill, "Growth of Newspapers in the United States," 11.

86. Tocqueville, *Democracy in America*, 209; Dill, "Growth of Newspapers in the United States," 11.

87. Risley, *Civil War Journalism*, xiii.

88. Schudson, *Discovering the News*, 16.

89. Washington, "George Washington's Farewell Address"; Wood, *Empire of Liberty*, 209.

90. J. Kennedy, *Catalogue of the Newspapers and Periodicals Published in the United States*, 53.

91. Quoted in Mott, *American Journalism, a History*, 216.

92. Tocqueville, *Democracy in America*, 210.

93. Quoted in Mott, *American Journalism, a History*, 216.

94. For more on journalism in the hyper-contentious 1850s, see Sachsman and Borchard, *The Antebellum Press*.

95. Quoted in Holt, *The Political Crisis of the 1850s*, 243, 236.

96. For more on the antebellum black press, see Hutton, *The Early Black Press in America*. While men still dominated the newspaper industry throughout the nineteenth century, more recent research indicates that women in the North and South played a greater role in periodical printing than previously supposed. This proved especially true in the Northern and Southern magazine scene. For more on this and related topics, see Endres, "The Women's Press in the Civil War," 31–53; Belford, *Brilliant Bylines*; Perry and Weaks, eds., *The History of Southern Women's Literature*; and Wells, *Women Writers and Journalists in the Nineteenth-Century South*.

97. Quoted in Scarborough, "Propagandists for Secession," 137.

98. *Charleston Mercury*, February 1, 1858.

99. Holmes, "Bread and the Newspaper," 114.

Chapter Two. "Bread and the Newspaper"

1. *New York Herald*, April 13, 1861.

2. De Fontaine, "The First Day of Real War," 77.

3. *New York Herald*, April 13, 1861. For a lively history on the buildup to and events of Fort Sumter, see Catton, *The Coming Fury*.

4. De Fontaine, "The First Day of Real War," 77; *New York Herald*, April 13, 1861.

5. McNeely, Van Tuyll, and Schulte, *Knights of the Quill*, 46.

6. Starr, *Bohemian Brigade*, 30.

7. MacKay, "Philadelphia During the Civil War," 4.

8. Starr, *Bohemian Brigade*, 30.

9. Schudson, *Discovering the News*, 66, 67.

10. Research by demographic historian J. David Hacker places the Civil War death toll closer to 750,000 by comparing 1860 and 1870 census data. The traditionally cited 620,000, perhaps the most recognizable Civil War statistic, is an underestimate based on partial records. See Hacker, "A Census-Based Count of the Civil War Dead," 307–348.

11. For more on the correspondence of soldiers in newspapers, see Styple, *Writing and Fighting the Civil War*.

12. Douglas, *The Golden Age of the Newspaper*, 56.

13. Holmes, "Bread and the Newspaper," 118, 116–117.

14. Starr, *Bohemian Brigade*, 56.

15. Soldiers craved papers no less than civilians. As one enlisted man remarked, "We devour papers with a rapidity that would astonish them that have less leisure time." See Norton, *Army Letters*, 51. For more on this, see also Quinn and Sachsman, *The Civil War Soldier and the Press*. Curiously, foreign observers were no less astonished by the soldierly obsession with newspapers. When the comte de Paris spent time with the Army of the Potomac, he noticed its soldiers were "fully acquainted with public affairs and could not dispense with newspapers. . . . In every tent the latest news brought by the *Herald* and *Tribune* was read in the evening and eagerly discussed, while the soldier on duty, if he thought himself unobserved, walked up and down with his musket in one hand and his newspaper in the other." Quoted in Friedman and Sideman, *Europe Looks at the Civil War*, 52–53.

16. Houghton and Houghton, *Two Boys in the Civil War and After*, 96.

17. Starr, *Bohemian Brigade*, 31.

18. Andrews, *The North Reports the Civil War*, 32–33, 428.

19. Exodus 20:8 (New International).

20. "Even the mail": John, "Taking Sabbatarianism Seriously," 519.

21. MacKay, "Philadelphia During the Civil War," 4.

22. Andrews, *The North Reports the Civil War*, 34.

23. Starr, *Bohemian Brigade*, 31.

24. Andrews, *The South Reports the Civil War*, 26; Harris, *War News*, 11.

25. Emery and Emery, *The Press and America*, 139.

26. Campion, "Wallpaper Newspapers of the American Civil War," 132.

27. De Bow, "The South and the Union," 152.

28. Andrews, *The South Reports the Civil War*, 42.

29. *Galveston Weekly News*, August 26, 1863.

30. *Charleston Mercury*, April 15, 1863. The wartime surge in letter writing only exacerbated the problem.

31. Quoted in Baker, "Refugee Newspaper," 330.

32. Andrews, *The South Reports the Civil War*, 43.

33. Campion, "Wallpaper Newspapers of the American Civil War," 132–133. For more on Confederates publishing on wallpaper during the Vicksburg siege, see Neiderheiser, "Some Civil War," 211–213.

34. Andrews, *The South Reports the Civil War*, 44.

35. *Memphis Daily Appeal*, April 29, 1862.

36. Baker, "Refugee Newspaper," 326.

37. *Charleston Mercury*, January 28, 1862; *Columbus (Ga.) Enquirer*, February 18, 1862. Originally published in the *San Antonio Herald* and later reprinted by the *Columbus Enquirer*.

38. Tunnell, "Confederate Newspapers in Virginia During the Civil War"; Andrews, *The South Reports the Civil War*, 44.

39. Andrews, *The South Reports the Civil War*, 44.

40. *Columbus (Ga.) Enquirer*, February 18, 1862. Originally published in the *San Antonio Herald*.

41. Although Northern printers did not suffer on the same scale as their Southern counterparts, several suffered to the same degree. Elements of the Army of Northern Virginia, for example, destroyed newspaper offices in Gettysburg after the battle began. As the war primarily raged in the South, however, incidents like these occurred far less often.

42. Baker, "Refugee Newspaper," 333. The *Appeal* picked up new subscribers wherever it called home and reached peak readership when it settled in Atlanta.

43. Sternhell, "Communicating War," 179.

44. McPherson, *Battle Cry of Freedom*, 418, 461.

45. Andrews, "The Press Reports the Battle of Gettysburg," 177. Andrews counted nine Southern correspondents at Gettysburg. Two of the three Richmond correspondents worked for the *Enquirer* while the third claimed employ with the newly minted *Sentinel*. Of the remaining six correspondents with Lee's army, three reported for the *Savannah Republican*, one for the Atlanta-based *Southern Confederacy*, one for the *Mobile Daily Tribune*, and one, a Francis E. Lawley, worked as the Southern correspondent for the London *Times*.

46. W. Reid, *A Southern Tour*, 319. For more on Reid, see Duncan, *Whitelaw Reid*.

47. Baker, "Refugee Newspaper," 329.

48. Quoted in Andrews, *The South Reports the Civil War*, 38. For more on the Confederate news hub of Atlanta, see Malone, "Atlanta Journalism During the Confederacy," 210–219.

49. Scarborough, "Propagandists for Secession," 138.

50. Andrews, "The Press Reports the Battle of Gettysburg," 177. According to Andrews, ten correspondents worked "for the *New York Herald*, nine for the *Tribune*, four for the *Times*, and one for the *World*." Of course, the presses of other Northern cities were represented at Gettysburg as well. Andrews counted "three *Philadelphia Inquirer* correspondents, three reporters accredited to John W. Forney's Philadelphia *Press*, a highly respected Boston *Journal* news scribe [Charles Carleton Coffin], the chief Washington correspondent of the Cincinnati *Gazette* [Whitelaw Reid], a *Chicago Tribune* reporter, and Theodore Barnard of the New York Associated Press." With two journalists from "small-town newspapers in Pennsylvania" added to the total, no less than thirty-six Northern correspondents covered the Gettysburg campaign firsthand.

51. Douglas, *The Golden Age of the Newspaper*, 57.

52. Quoted in Starr, *Bohemian Brigade*, 12.

53. Mott, *American Journalism, a History*, 347.

54. Andrews, "The Pennsylvania Press during the Civil War," 30. For more on the press hub of Philadelphia, see Robinson, "The Public Press of Philadelphia During the Civil War."

55. Andrews, *The North Reports the Civil War*, 33. If civilian papers failed to please, soldiers published their own. According to one scholar, "At least 108 different military units of the Civil War are known to have published newspapers." See Lutz, "Soldier Newspapers of the Civil War," 381. For more on this, see Wiley, "Camp Newspapers of the Confederacy," 327–335.

56. Mathews, *Reporting the Wars*, 80; Schudson, *Discovering the News*, 67.

57. *Sacramento Daily Union*, September 27, 1896.

58. *New York Herald*, June 24, 1863. See also Andrews, *The North Reports the Civil War*, 413.

59. *New York Herald*, June 24, 1863. With no means yet to reproduce photographs, printers hired sketch artists to depict the fighting firsthand. *Frank Leslie's Illustrated Newspaper* and *Harper's Weekly*, Yankeedom's two most successful illustrated papers, hired several artists to furnish sketches from the front. Meanwhile, the South lacked an illustrated counterpart until September 1862, when a pair of Richmond newspapermen launched the *Southern Illustrated News*. Like most Southern papers, however, the *Southern Illustrated News* did not survive the war. For much more on this, see Thompson, *The Image of War*.

60. Starr, *Bohemian Brigade*, 212; quotation: *New York Times*, July 6, 1863.

61. Quoted in Mathews, *Reporting the Wars*, 80.

62. Quoted in "Letter from General George Meade to Mrs. George Meade," June 9, 1864, George G. Meade Collection, Historical Society of Pennsylvania, Philadelphia.

63. Cadwallader, *Three Years with Grant*, 208–209. Perhaps only Sherman despised reporters more than Meade. He once fumed, "I hate newspapermen. They come into camp and pick up their camp rumors and print them as facts. I regard them as spies, which, in truth, they are. If I killed them all there would be news from Hell before breakfast." His indignation proved partially justified. Before the capture of Atlanta, a *New York Herald* correspondent leaked to the press that Sherman had deciphered the rebel signal system, a story that got back to the rebels themselves. Quoted in Isbell, *Shiloh and Corinth*, xiv. For more on the problem of newsmen publishing sensitive military information, see Randall, "The Newspaper Problem in Its Bearing upon Military Secrecy during the Civil War," 303–323.

64. Catton, *The Civil War*, 209.

65. Andrews, *The North Reports the Civil War*, 20.

66. Catton, *The Civil War*, 4; Mott, *American Journalism, a History*, 329.

67. Andrews, *The North Reports the Civil War*, 428–429.

68. Quoted in ibid., 429.

69. Quoted in Douglas, *The Golden Age of the Newspaper*, 60.

70. Dicken-Garcia, *Journalistic Standards in Nineteenth-Century America*, 56.

71. Andrews, *The South Reports the Civil War*, 44.

72. Dicken-Garcia, *Journalistic Standards in Nineteenth-Century America*, 55.

73. The AP fielded more war correspondents than any of its individual members, including the *Herald*.

74. Andrews, *The South Reports the Civil War*, 56–57.

75. Sternhell, "Communicating War," 196.

76. Holmes, "Bread and the Newspaper," 118.

77. Chesnut, *A Diary from Dixie*, 171.

78. Holmes, "Bread and the Newspaper," 116.

79. Andrews, "The Press Reports the Battle of Gettysburg," 197.

80. *Richmond Enquirer*, July 10, 1863. As early as July 15, 1861, the *Chicago Tribune* complained that telegraphy brought "unmitigated falsehoods" to the degree that people had "lost faith in electricity."

81. *New York Times*, August 19, 1858.

82. Confederate States of America, Post Office Department, *Instructions to Post Masters*, 9.

83. Quoted in Baker, "Refugee Newspaper," 334.

84. Andrews, *The South Reports the Civil War*, 480.

85. Quoted in Starr, *Bohemian Brigade*, 6.

86. Ibid.

87. "Pennsylvania Dutch Yankee" quoted in Trexler, "The Davis Administration and the Richmond Press," 184; "Mr. Davis alone" quoted in Sachsman, *A Press Divided*, 310.

88. Andrews, "The Confederate Press and Public Morale," 455.

89. Sachsman, *A Press Divided*, 310–311.

90. During the Civil War, press partisanship took on a larger scale in the North than in the South. As McPherson wrote, "The Copperhead press in the North was far more extensive and outspoken than the Tory press in the South." McPherson, *This Mighty Scourge*, 164.

91. Lincoln did face opposition from within his own party as radical Republicans hit him on his left flank. But unlike Democratic printers, these Republicans were not reliably anti-Lincoln. And when they did oppose the president, they represented only a tiny subset of the broader anti-Lincoln press, which remained overwhelmingly Democratic. For more, see Sachsman, *A Press Divided*.

92. For more on Bennett's pro-war conversion, see "Covering the Civil War," chapter 7 in Crouthamel, *Bennett's New York Herald and the Rise of the Popular Press*.

93. See De Fontaine, *Marginalia, or Gleanings from an Army Notebook*.

94. McNeely, Van Tuyll, and Schulte, *Knights of the Quill*.

95. Andrews, "The Press Reports the Battle of Gettysburg," 177.

96. *New-York Evening Post*, May 20, 1863.

97. Quoted in Sachsman, Rushing, and Van Tuyll, eds., *The Civil War and the Press*, 293.

98. U.S. Const., art. I, § 9.

99. Quoted in Sachsman, Rushing, and Van Tuyll, eds., *The Civil War and the Press*, 300.

100. Waugh, *Reelecting Lincoln*, 14.

101. Quoted in Pollard, *The Presidents and the Press*, 378. For more on Lincoln and press freedom, see Carrol, "Freedom of Speech and of the Press during the Civil War," 516–551.

102. Lincoln, "President Abraham Lincoln to General John M. Schofield," October 1, 1863, in *New York Times*, October 26, 1863. See also Foote, *The Civil War, a Narrative*, 635.

103. Sachsman, *A Press Divided*, 308.

104. Quoted in McPherson, *This Mighty Scourge*, 158.

105. *Philadelphia Inquirer*, July 6, 1863.

106. For more on this, see Reardon, *Pickett's Charge in History and Memory*.

107. *Press* (Philadelphia), July 7, 1863.

108. Tocqueville, *Democracy in America*, 209–210.

109. Schudson, *Discovering the News*, 66–67.

Chapter Three. The Blood That Dried in Ink

1. G. Gallagher, *Two Witnesses at Gettysburg*, 8. See also Reid's Gettysburg campaign report, *Cincinnati Gazette*, July 8, 1863. For a complete history of Reid's wartime reporting, see W. Reid, *A Radical View*.

2. Ibid., 7, 9, 5.

3. Ibid., 9, 3–4, 12, 5.

4. G. Gallagher, *Two Witnesses at Gettysburg*, 7.

5. Ibid., 9, 12.

6. Ibid., 9, 12, 14.

7. Ibid., 13.

8. Ibid., 16. Taneytown was actually named after Chief Justice Roger Taney's eighteenth-century relative Raphael Taney.

9. Ibid., 16–17.

10. Ibid., 16, 17. Crounse's Gettysburg-heralding report, published in the *Times* the next day, briefly summarized the first half of the July 1 battle. His dispatch read, "Near Gettysburg, July 1—A heavy engagement has been going on since nine o'clock this a.m. between the rebel forces of Longstreet and Hill and the First and Eleventh corps, under Gens. Reynolds and Meade. The locality of the fight is beyond Gettysburg, on the Chambersburg Pike. Portions of the fight have been very severe, and attended with heavy loss. Thus far the onset of the enemy has been successfully resisted, and the Third and Twelfth are now coming up. I regret to say that Major Gen. Reynolds was mortally wounded, and has since died." *New York Times*, July 2, 1863.

11. G. Gallagher, *Two Witnesses at Gettysburg*, 17, 21, 9.

12. *New York Times*, July 7, 1863.

13. Quoted in Glatthar, *General Lee's Army*, 149.

14. Andrews, *The South Reports the Civil War*, 319.

15. In his two official reports on the Gettysburg campaign—the first dated July 31, 1863, and the second January 20, 1864—Lee limited his objectives to shifting the war away from Virginia, seizing the initiative from the Army of the Potomac, clearing the Shenandoah, stripping Union troops from other fronts to the Potomac army's aid, and using Pennsylvania's abundance to resupply his own army. Yet, as historian James McPherson wrote, "there is a considerable amount of evidence that he had more sweeping goals for his invasion of Pennsylvania than he described." Indeed, Lee longed for a Napoleonic victory that might compel the North to make peace on Confederate terms. See McPherson, *This Mighty Scourge*, 77–86.

16. *Daily Dispatch* (Richmond), June 16, 1863.

17. Foote, *The Civil War, a Narrative*, 438.

18. *Daily Dispatch* (Richmond), June 11, 1863.

19. Lee, "Letter from Robert E. Lee to J. E. B. Stuart," June 23, 1863, Lee Family Digital Archive, Stratford Hall Historic Preserve, Stratford, Virginia.

20. G. Gallagher, *Two Witnesses at Gettysburg*, 12.

21. Quoted in Andrews, *The South Reports the Civil War*, 305.

22. G. Gallagher, *Two Witnesses at Gettysburg*, 13.

23. Quoted in G. Gallagher, *The Second Day at Gettysburg*, 2.

24. *Sentinel* (Richmond), June 18, 1863.

25. Mingus and Wittenberg, *The Second Battle of Winchester.*

26. *The War of the Rebellion,* series 1, vol. 27, pt. 2, 307.

27. Ibid., 246–247.

28. *Boston Daily Journal,* July 7, 1863. Apparently Coffin's cleverness extended into foresightedness. "If Lee advances with nearly all of his force into Pennsylvania," he penned on June 26, "there must be a collision of the two armies not many miles west of Gettysburg." Five days later he was proven right. *Boston Daily Journal,* June 29, 1863.

29. *The War of the Rebellion,* series 1, vol. 27, pt. 2, 638.

30. G. Gallagher, *Two Witnesses at Gettysburg,* 32.

31. *Daily Dispatch* (Richmond) July 10, 1863.

32. G. Gallagher, *Two Witnesses at Gettysburg,* 35.

33. *The War of the Rebellion,* series 1, vol. 27, pt. 2, 317–318.

34. Quoted in Casdorph, *Confederate General R. S. Ewell,* 254.

35. Rhodes, "The Battle of Gettysburg," 672.

36. McPherson, *Battle Cry of Freedom,* 654. Gettysburg alone contributed three of those thirteen bloodiest days. For what motivated Civil War soldiers to withstand such losses, see Linderman, *Embattled Courage.*

37. "Letter from Robert E. Lee to Jefferson Davis," July 4, 1863, in Lee, *The Wartime Papers of R. E. Lee,* 538.

38. G. Gallagher, *Two Witnesses at Gettysburg,* 21.

39. Longstreet, "James Longstreet's Account of the Campaign," 63.

40. Ibid., 60, 61. Given the post-battle tendency of officers to distance themselves from decisions later proven unwise, Longstreet's account of this exchange should be read with a grain of salt.

41. Freeman, *Lee's Lieutenants,* vol. 3, 109.

42. *Boston Daily Journal,* July 7, 1863.

43. Longstreet, "James Longstreet's Account of the Campaign," 62.

44. Ibid.

45. *Savannah Republican,* July 25, 1863.

46. After the war, ex-Confederates blamed Longstreet, not Lee, for the delay. Longstreet's critics argued that since he had called for a different attack plan, he never fully committed to executing Lee's. The argument, peddled by Lost Cause advocates eager to make Longstreet the South's scapegoat, proved groundless. Lee's orders caused the delay, not Longstreet's supposed lack of commitment. For more on the postwar damage done to Longstreet's reputation, see Piston, *Lee's Tarnished Lieutenant.*

47. *Boston Daily Journal,* July 7, 1863.

48. *The War of the Rebellion,* series 1, vol. 27, pt. 1, 592.

49. Longstreet, "James Longstreet's Account of the Campaign," 65.

50. *Boston Daily Journal,* July 7, 1863.

51. *Savannah Republican,* July 25, 1863.

52. No work brought Chamberlain's exploits to life like Michael Shaara's novel *The Killer Angels.*

53. *Boston Daily Journal,* July 7, 1863.

54. Alleman, *At Gettysburg,* 29.

55. *New-York Tribune*, July 6, 1863.

56. Ibid.

57. *New York Herald*, July 6, 1863.

58. *The War of the Rebellion*, series 1, vol. 27, pt. 2, 308.

59. Although General George Patton popularized it in the twentieth century, the phrase "Never take counsel of your fears" was likely coined by Stonewall Jackson during the Civil War. For the phrase's origin, see Krick, *Conquering the Valley*, 495.

60. For more on this decision, see K. Brown, *Meade at Gettysburg*.

61. *The War of the Rebellion*, series 1, vol. 27, pt. 2, 359.

62. Ibid.

63. Quoted in Trudeau, *Robert E. Lee*, 148, 150.

64. Leon, *The Diary of a Tar Heel Confederate Soldier*, 23.

65. *Boston Daily Journal*, July 7, 1863.

66. *The War of the Rebellion*, series 1, vol. 27, pt. 2, 448.

67. *Richmond Enquirer*, July 23, 1863. Also quoted in Andrews, *The South Reports the Civil War*, 312–313.

68. G. Gallagher, *Two Witnesses at Gettysburg*, 64.

69. *Boston Daily Journal*, July 7, 1863.

70. *The War of the Rebellion*, series 1, vol. 27, pt. 1, 117.

71. *New-York Tribune*, July 6, 1863.

72. *Richmond Enquirer*, July 23, 1863.

73. McPherson, *Battle Cry of Freedom*, 662.

74. Quoted in Emery and Emery, *The Press and America*, 137.

75. McPherson, *Battle Cry of Freedom*, 662.

76. G. Gallagher, *Two Witnesses at Gettysburg*, 68.

77. Quoted in McPherson, *Battle Cry of Freedom*, 663.

78. Quoted in Trudeau, *Robert E. Lee*, 154–155.

79. McPherson, *Battle Cry of Freedom*, 663.

80. *New York Times*, July 6, 1863.

81. McPherson, *Battle Cry of Freedom*, 663.

82. Quoted in ibid. Debate rages on whether or not Meade behaved judiciously by not counterattacking on July 3. Historian Warren W. Hassler Jr., for example, argued, "Meade was probably sagacious in not counterattacking—even if it could have been done—right after Pickett's repulse." See Hassler, "George G. Meade and His Role in the Gettysburg Campaign," 404.

83. *Richmond Enquirer*, July 21, 1863.

84. Broadwater, *Gettysburg as the Generals Remembered It*, 95.

85. McPherson, *Battle Cry of Freedom*, 664. For a foreigner's perspective see Fremantle, *The Fremantle Diary*.

86. Lincoln, "The Gettysburg Address."

87. Abraham Lincoln, "Letter to James C. Conkling," August 26, 1863, in *Speeches and Letters of Abraham Lincoln*, 210; *Daily Dispatch* (Richmond), July 10, 1863.

88. *Savannah Republican*, July 25, 1863.

89. "Letter from Robert E. Lee to Jefferson Davis," July 14, 1863, in Lee, *The Wartime Papers of R. E. Lee*, 550.

90. Abraham Lincoln, "Letter from President Abraham Lincoln to George G. Meade," July 14, 1863, Abraham Lincoln Papers, Library of Congress. Historian Bruce Catton once wrote, "Of all the country's armies, this was the one . . . that could most quickly and certainly lose the war: and so at times it was hard to see that this was the army, also, that could most quickly and certainly win it. A general who took the offensive with this army needed to be bold, determined, and uncommonly clear-minded." Meade lacked those qualities after Gettysburg, and President Lincoln knew it as well as anyone. See Catton, *Terrible Swift Sword*, 251. For an overview of Lincoln and his trials as commander-in-chief, see McPherson, *The War That Forged a Nation*, 123–143.

91. G. Gallagher, *Two Witnesses at Gettysburg*, 76.

92. *North Carolina Standard*, July 17, 1863.

93. *Richmond Enquirer*, July 15, 1863.

94. *New York Times*, July 7, 1863.

95. Guelzo, *Gettysburg*, 465.

Chapter Four. "Look to Glorious Lee"

1. Andrews, "The Press Reports the Battle of Gettysburg," 197.

2. With no identifier beyond the initial C, one cannot confirm with absolute certainty that Coldwell authored the Martinsburg telegrams. But given he was the superintendent of the Confederate Military Telegraph, supervised construction of the Martinsburg line, ran the Martinsburg telegraph station during the Gettysburg campaign, and his initial matched that on the telegram, it is a safe assumption. For more on this, see ibid.

3. *Savannah Republican*, July 7, 1863.

4. The resemblance between the victory relayed by Coldwell and Hannibal's at Cannae in 216 B.C. did not pass unnoticed. "It was a repetition of the narrative practiced by Hannibal at Cannae, which resulted in the slaughter of 70,000 Romans," observed Cowardin's *Dispatch*. "Hannibal killed the enveloped Romans. [But] Lee, according to this account, only took the Yankees prisoners." Just hours after publishing this observation, Cowardin learned the sobering truth about Coldwell's erroneous cables. See *Daily Dispatch* (Richmond), July 8, 1863.

5. *Savannah Republican*, July 7, 1863. The information contained a nugget of truth. Pickett's division did escort captured Yankees from Gettysburg. But it did so because July 3 wrecked it beyond the capacity to fight and because the prisoners numbered only four thousand, not forty thousand.

6. Jones, *A Rebel War Clerk's Diary*, vol. 1, 370–371.

7. *Savannah Republican*, July 7, 1863.

8. See *Richmond Enquirer*, July 7, 8, 1863.

9. *Savannah Republican*, July 7, 1863; *Daily Dispatch* (Richmond), July 8, 1863.

10. *Savannah Republican*, July 7, 1863.

11. *Daily Dispatch* (Richmond), July 9, 1863.

12. *Savannah Republican*, July 7, 1863.

13. Jones, *A Rebel War Clerk's Diary*, vol. 1, 374.

14. *Daily Dispatch* (Richmond), July 10, 1863.

15. Andrews, *The South Reports the Civil War*, 27.

16. *Richmond Enquirer,* July 10, 1863.

17. *New York Times,* August 19, 1858.

18. Andrews, *The South Reports the Civil War,* 319.

19. *Daily Dispatch* (Richmond), June 16, 1863. Like the *New York Herald* in the North, the *Dispatch* claimed to be nonpartisan, yet the general quality of its wartime coverage revealed it as a pro-Davis publication.

20. At war's start, Tyler co-owned and comanaged the *Enquirer* with W. B. Allegre and Obadiah Jennings Wise, the son of former Virginia governor Henry Alexander Wise. But Allegre proved more of a businessman than an editor and did not take an active role in the paper's content, while Wise lost his life fighting on Roanoke Island in early 1862. During most of the war, including the Gettysburg campaign, Tyler functioned as the paper's figurehead and its senior editor. For more, see Andrews, *The South Reports the Civil War,* 27. See also Tunnell, "Confederate Newspapers in Virginia During the Civil War."

21. *Richmond Enquirer,* June 26, 1863.

22. Andrews, *The South Reports the Civil War,* 33.

23. *Daily Dispatch* (Richmond), June 27, 1863, and July 2, 1863.

24. *Daily Dispatch* (Richmond), July 2, 1863.

25. McPherson, *Battle Cry of Freedom,* 644–645. Only the Battle of Antietam on September 17, 1862, stuck out as a blemish on Lee's otherwise illustrious record, and many Southern printers portrayed that misadventure as yet another notch in Lee's belt. Charles Barnwell Rhett's anti-Davis *Charleston Mercury* scored Antietam a non-failure when he reported in late 1862: "General Lee knows his business and that army [the Army of Northern Virginia] has yet known no such word as fail." Cowardin's pro-Davis *Dispatch* claimed as late as July 6, 1863, that Antietam "was anything but indecisive." Union general George B. McClellan was "beaten with immense slaughter." *Charleston Mercury,* December 15, 1862; *Daily Dispatch* (Richmond), July 6, 1863.

26. Quoted in Brooks, *Washington in Lincoln's Time,* 58.

27. McPherson, *Battle Cry of Freedom,* 645.

28. *Richmond Enquirer,* May 8, 1863.

29. For more on Jackson and what he meant to the Confederacy, see Robertson, *Stonewall Jackson.*

30. Guelzo, *Gettysburg,* 62.

31. *Chattanooga Daily Rebel,* June 18, 1863. The *Rebel* proved Chattanooga's sole news provider and one of the last Confederate papers still operating in Tennessee when Lee launched his second invasion of the North. About one month after Gettysburg, however, Union general William Rosecrans uprooted the *Rebel* from its namesake city, forcing the paper on the tour that earned it the nickname "Rebel on Wheels."

32. *Daily Dispatch* (Richmond), June 18, 1863.

33. *Memphis Daily Appeal,* June 22, 1863.

34. *Richmond Enquirer,* June 26, 1863.

35. *Daily Dispatch* (Richmond), July 2, 1863.

36. Andrews, *The South Reports the Civil War,* 319.

37. *Richmond Enquirer,* May 8, 1863.

38. *Richmond Enquirer,* June 30, 1863.

39. *Richmond Enquirer,* July 3, 1863.

40. *Tri-Weekly Telegraph* (Houston), July 20, 1863. For a compilation of *Telegraph* stories published in the crucial war year of 1863, see "[Houston] Tri-Weekly Telegraph, 1863," Scholar Works at UT Tyler, https://scholarworks.uttyler.edu/cw_newstitles/55.

41. *Daily Dispatch* (Richmond), June 12, 1863.

42. Ibid.

43. *Daily Dispatch* (Richmond), July 6, 1863.

44. *Daily Dispatch* (Richmond), June 12, 1863.

45. *Daily Dispatch* (Richmond), July 6, 1863.

46. *Chattanooga Daily Rebel*, July 8, 1863.

47. *Fayetteville (N.C.) Observer*, July 9, 1863.

48. *Daily Dispatch* (Richmond), July 9, 1863.

49. *Richmond Enquirer*, July 24, 1863. This comes from *Enquirer* correspondent Jonathan W. Albertson.

50. *Sentinel* (Richmond), July 20, 1863. This comes from the one and only *Sentinel* correspondent with Lee's army at Gettysburg, a reporter who used the alias "Gwen."

51. *Richmond Enquirer*, July 24, 1863. This comes from *Enquirer* correspondent Jonathan W. Albertson.

52. *Sentinel* (Richmond), July 20, 1863. This comes from *Sentinel* correspondent "Gwen."

53. *Daily Dispatch* (Richmond), July 13, 1863.

54. *Abingdon Virginian*, July 24, 1863. For more on the Confederate town of Abingdon, see Shaffer, *Washington County, Virginia, in the Civil War*.

55. Bridges, "The Memphis Daily Appeal's 'Dixie,'" 378; *Memphis Daily Appeal*, July 20, 1863.

56. *Chattanooga Daily Rebel*, July 14, 1863. This widely recycled line originated in the Richmond *Dispatch* on July 10 and is attributed to a wounded officer from General Ambrose Ransom Wright's brigade, of A. P. Hill's corps, who arrived in the Confederate capital on the evening of July 9. See *Daily Dispatch* (Richmond), July 10, 1863.

57. G. Gallagher, *Two Witnesses at Gettysburg*, 21, 50.

58. *Daily Dispatch* (Richmond), July 10, 1863.

59. Freeman, *Lee's Lieutenants*, vol. 3, 195–196.

60. Gaillard, "Letter from Franklin Gaillard to Maria," July 17, 1863, Gaillard Papers, Southern Historical Collection, University of North Carolina, Chapel Hill.

61. *Abingdon Virginian*, July 24, 1863.

62. *Sentinel* (Richmond), July 27, 1863.

63. *Sentinel* (Richmond), July 20, 1863.

64. *Chattanooga Daily Rebel*, July 14, 1863. This also came from the widely recycled account of the wounded officer from Wright's brigade. *Daily Dispatch* (Richmond), July 10, 1863; and reprinted in the *Staunton (Va.) Spectator*, July 28, 1863.

65. *Richmond Enquirer*, July 21, 1863.

66. *Richmond Enquirer*, July 21, 1863. At least one officer agreed with X's overall point. "Col. Bradley T. Johnson, who commanded a brigade at Gettysburg, [maintained], on the first day we carried everything before us . . . the error was in not following up the attack with all our forces immediately." Jones, *A Rebel War Clerk's Diary*, vol. 1, 385.

67. *Richmond Enquirer*, July 21, 1863.

68. Emery and Emery, *The Press and America*, 138.

69. Reardon, *Pickett's Charge in History and Memory*, 40.

70. *Richmond Enquirer*, July 23, 1863. Also cited in Emery and Emery, *The Press and America*, 138.

71. *Sentinel* (Richmond), July 20, 1863.

72. *Staunton (Va.) Spectator*, July 28, 1863.

73. Reardon, *Pickett's Charge in History and Memory*, 3

74. *Daily Dispatch* (Richmond), July 13, 1863.

75. *Richmond Enquirer*, July 23, 1863. Albertson also indicted Confederate artillerists for exhausting their ammunition and thereby failing to support Pickett's assault.

76. Reprinted in the *Richmond Enquirer*, July 28, 1863. See also *Raleigh Register*, July 25 and July 26, 1863.

77. *Richmond Enquirer*, July 28, 1863. The *Enquirer* loosely drew on Peter W. Alexander's report to justify maintaining its original position. Although Alexander never cited a scapegoat, he asserted that "a want of proper support" and "the movement of the enemy upon his [Pickett's] exposed and bleeding flanks" compelled the Virginians to retreat. Quoted in Reardon, *Pickett's Charge in History and Memory*, 47.

78. Jones, *A Rebel War Clerk's Diary*, vol. 1, 391. For more on the Virginia–North Carolina press feud, see Tucker, *Zebulon Vance*, 266–272.

79. Reardon, *Pickett's Charge in History and Memory*, 61.

80. Due to injuries suffered on July 1 and 2, command of Heth's and Pender's divisions fell, respectively, to Pettigrew and Major General Isaac Trimble. Pickett, Pettigrew, and Trimble, then, led the rebel attack. Albeit less concise than "Pickett's Charge," a rebrand to the "Pickett-Pettigrew-Trimble Charge" would not only better reflect the attack itself but also destabilize the Virginia-centered narrative established immediately afterward.

81. Jones, *A Rebel War Clerk's Diary*, vol. 1, 391.

82. Jones, *A Rebel War Clerk's Diary*, vol. 2, 3, 42.

83. *Daily Dispatch* (Richmond), July 10, 1863.

84. *Memphis Daily Appeal*, July 20, 1863.

85. In a late July letter to Davis, Lee unofficially estimated his losses at no less than twenty thousand. See "Letter from Robert E. Lee to Jefferson Davis," July 29, 1863, in Lee, *The Wartime Papers of R. E. Lee*, 563.

86. McNeely, Van Tuyll, and Schulte, *Knights of the Quill*.

87. *Richmond Enquirer*, July 21, 1863.

88. *Richmond Enquirer*, July 23, 1863.

89. *Daily Dispatch* (Richmond), July 22, 1863.

90. *Sentinel* (Richmond), July 24, 1863. To protect their commands from scrutiny, commanders often submitted formal battle reports months later that underestimated their own losses and overestimated the enemy's. Lee's official Gettysburg report, submitted January 1864, claimed his army captured "nearly 7,000 prisoners," over two thousand more than the best estimates. Lee, "General Robert E. Lee's Report of the Gettysburg Campaign," January 20, 1864, in *The War of the Rebellion*, series 1, vol. 27, pt. 2, 328.

91. *Abingdon Virginian*, July 24, 1863; *Staunton (Va.) Spectator*, July 14, 1863.

92. *Tri-Weekly Telegraph* (Houston), July 31, 1863.

93. *Daily Dispatch* (Richmond), June 12, 1863.

94. *Daily Dispatch* (Richmond), July 22, 1863.

95. *Sentinel* (Richmond), July 11, 1863.

96. "Letter from Robert E. Lee to Jefferson Davis," July 14, 1863, in Lee, *The Wartime Papers of R. E. Lee*, 550.

97. *Daily Dispatch* (Richmond), July 22, 1863.

98. Quoted in G. Gallagher, *Lee and His Army in Confederate History*, 89.

99. *Daily Dispatch* (Richmond), July 18, 1863.

100. Reprinted in the *Chattanooga Daily Rebel*, July 18, 1863.

101. *Sentinel* (Richmond), July 22, 1863.

102. Reprinted in the *Chattanooga Daily Rebel*, July 18, 1863; *Chattanooga Daily Rebel*, July 23, 1863.

103. Holmes and Edmondston quoted in G. Gallagher, *Lee and His Army in Confederate History*, 88. For the original quote, see Edmonston, *Journal of a Secesh Lady*, 440. For more on how the press shaped women's perspectives of the Gettysburg campaign, see Rable, *Civil Wars*, 211.

104. *Sentinel* (Richmond), July 24, 1863.

105. *Richmond Enquirer*, June 27, 1863, and July 15, 1863. After calling Gettysburg a victory, the *Southern Field and Fireside*—a Georgia magazine that proudly published women-authored columns throughout the war—rationalized the mismatch between the campaign's results and its expectations. "There is . . . no substantial ground for our people being dissatisfied. The fact of the matter is, we expected Gen. Lee to perform impossibilities, and because our extraordinary expectations have not been realized, we are not satisfied with the result." *Southern Field and Fireside*, July 25, 1863.

106. *Memphis Daily Appeal*, July 18, 1863.

107. Quoted in G. Gallagher, *Lee and His Army in Confederate History*, 86; *Daily Dispatch* (Richmond), July 18, 1863.

108. *Daily Dispatch* (Richmond), July 18, 1863. At least one Copperhead agreed with this assessment of the campaign. The *New York Daily News* conceded, "The incursion of Gen. Lee into the North [yielded his men] an abundance of provisions, enough to last them till the next year's crops." *New York Daily News*, July 17, 1863. For more on this, see R. Brown, *The Retreat from Gettysburg*, 389.

109. *Daily Dispatch* (Richmond), July 28, 1863.

110. *Richmond Enquirer*, July 15, 1863.

111. Andrews, *The South Reports the Civil War*, 319.

112. *Richmond Enquirer*, July 23, 1863.

113. *Daily Dispatch* (Richmond), July 20, 1863.

114. *Fayetteville (N.C.) Observer*, July 13, 1863.

115. *Daily Intelligencer* (Atlanta), October 7, 1863.

116. *Charleston (S.C.) Daily Courier*, July 14, 1863.

117. *Tri-Weekly Telegraph* (Houston), July 20, 1863.

118. *Tri-Weekly Telegraph* (Houston), July 21, 1863.

119. Chesnut, *A Diary from Dixie*, 219.

120. Jones, *A Rebel War Clerk's Diary*, vol. 1, 375.

121. *Daily Dispatch* (Richmond), June 16, 1863.

122. *Daily Dispatch* (Richmond), June 30, 1863. The assurances kept coming. On June 18 the *Chattanooga Daily Rebel* steeled the public, "We are not in a panic about Vicksburg.

There is no occasion to fear." And on June 20, in an attempt to dispel rumors to the contrary, the *Memphis Daily Appeal* swore, "The garrisons of Port Hudson and Vicksburg are both . . . in fine spirits" with "abundant supplies."

123. *Mississippian* (Jackson), June 16, 1863.

124. *Mississippian* (Jackson), July 3, 1863.

125. See Andrews, "The Confederate Press and Public Morale," 453–454. The *Chicago Tribune* captured the effect of hyping expectations never realized when it quipped "Hope deferred makes the heart sick." *Chicago Tribune*, July 15, 1861.

126. *Sentinel* (Richmond), July 9, 1863.

127. *Staunton (Va.) Spectator*, July 21, 1863.

128. *Chattanooga Daily Rebel*, July 14, 1863.

129. *Fayetteville (N.C.) Observer*, July 13, 1863. Similar sentiments pervaded the pro-Davis press. The *Sentinel* described the Union capture of Vicksburg as "a barren acquisition" because the rebels could now attack Yankee vessels from "every bluff" along the Mississippi. The paper added, "Nothing can navigate it in safety but iron clads." *Sentinel* (Richmond), July 10, 1863.

130. *Daily Dispatch* (Richmond), July 10, 1863; *Fayetteville (N.C.) Observer*, July 13, 1863; *Tri-Weekly Telegraph* (Houston), July 24, 1863.

131. *Memphis Daily Appeal*, July 13, 1863.

132. *Sentinel* (Richmond), July 13, 1863.

133. "Letter from Jefferson Davis to Robert E. Lee," July 28, 1863, in Jefferson Davis, *Jefferson Davis, Constitutionalist*, vol. 5, 579.

134. *Chattanooga Daily Rebel*, July 8, 1863.

135. *Tri-Weekly Telegraph* (Houston), July 24, 1863.

136. The *Sentinel* ran Gettysburg casualty reports into early August. See *Sentinel*, August 1, 1863.

137. *Memphis Daily Appeal*, July 15, 1863.

138. Andrews, "The Confederate Press and Public Morale," 453.

139. *Daily Dispatch* (Richmond), July 18, 1863; *Chattanooga Daily Rebel*, July 22, 1863.

140. *Charleston (S.C.) Daily Courier*, July 14, 1863.

141. *Fayetteville (N.C.) Observer*, July 13, 1863.

142. McPherson, *This Mighty Scourge*, 162.

143. *Tri-Weekly Telegraph* (Houston), July 24, 1863.

Chapter Five. "Waterloo Eclipsed"

1. Quoted in Andrews, "The Press Reports the Battle of Gettysburg," 194.

2. Quoted in Starr, *Bohemian Brigade*, 217. For the abbreviated Byington story, see *New-York Tribune*, July 7, 1863.

3. Quoted in Starr, *Bohemian Brigade*, 6.

4. Raasch, *Imperfect Union*, 121.

5. Quoted in Starr, *Bohemian Brigade*, 217, 218.

6. Ibid.

7. Welles, *Diary of Gideon Welles*, vol. 1, 357.

8. Starr, *Bohemian Brigade*, 218.

9. Welles, *Diary of Gideon Welles*, vol. 1, 357.

10. Andrews, *The North Reports the Civil War*, 428. For the Byington story, see also *Official Program of the Centennial of Incorporation of the Borough of Hanover Pennsylvania*, 37–38.

11. *Philadelphia Inquirer*, July 6, 1863.

12. *Evening Telegraph* (Harrisburg), July 6, 1863.

13. Strong, *The Diary of George Templeton Strong*, vol. 3, 330, 328. Strong remained distrustful. "If we can believe what we hear, Lee is smitten hip and thigh, and his invincible 'army of Northern Virginia' shattered and destroyed," he wrote. "But I am skeptical, especially as to news of victory, and expect to find large deductions from our alleged success in tomorrow morning's newspapers." Large deductions followed over the next few days.

14. Andrews, *The North Reports the Civil War*, 430–431.

15. On July 6 the *Tribune* announced "The Rebel General Longstreet Killed" and reported the capture of "20,000 Rebels," the enemy's "Remains driven into the Mountains," and the seizure of 118 of Lee's estimated 270 guns. This was not the first time the *Tribune* reported Longstreet's death. A day after Antietam—on September 18, 1862—the *Tribune* celebrated "Longstreet killed," only to correct itself later.

16. *Millennial Harbinger* 5, no. 1 (January 1834), 3.

17. *New-York Tribune*, July 4, 1863.

18. Andrews, "The Press Reports the Battle of Gettysburg," 177. For more on Raymond, see Maverick, *Henry J. Raymond and the New York Press for Thirty Years*.

19. Holzer and Symonds, *The New York Times Complete Civil War*, 247. Crounse only admitted to "confusion" when the Eleventh Corps was "retiring" through the town.

20. Ibid. One *Tribune* correspondent placed the rebels' strength at "over 60,000 men" on July 1. *New-York Tribune*, July 6, 1863.

21. McPherson, *Battle Cry of Freedom*, 654.

22. *New-York Tribune*, July 4, 1863; *New York Times*, July 4, 1863.

23. *New-York Tribune*, July 6, 1863. Many Northern printers did not detail the Wednesday and Thursday battles after July 6. By then, news of the Friday victory overshadowed any need to revisit the less encouraging days that preceded it.

24. Holzer and Symonds, *The New York Times Complete Civil War*, 249.

25. *New-York Tribune*, July 6, 1863, and July 14, 1863.

26. *Sun* (New York), July 6, 1863.

27. New-*York Evening Post*, July 7, 1863. For more on this important New York City paper, see Nevins, *The Evening Post*.

28. *Evening Telegraph* (Harrisburg), July 6, 1863.

29. *Philadelphia Inquirer*, July 6, 1863.

30. *Press* (Philadelphia), July 7, 1863.

31. *Philadelphia Inquirer*, July 6, 1863.

32. *Press* (Philadelphia), July 7, 1863.

33. Hessler, *Sickles at Gettysburg*, 244.

34. Keneally, *American Scoundrel*, 291.

35. Rusling, *Men and Things I Saw in Civil War Days*, 14.

36. Quoted in ibid. Meade purportedly said, "If Dan had not lost his leg at Gettysburg, he would have been court-martialed." Keneally, *American Scoundrel*, 297.

37. *New York Times*, July 6, 1863.
38. Quoted in Hessler, *Sickles at Gettysburg*, 279.
39. Ibid., 245.
40. *Philadelphia Inquirer*, July 9, 1863.
41. *Press* (Philadelphia), July 7, 1863.
42. *Press* (Philadelphia), July 8, 1863.
43. *Press* (Philadelphia), July 7, 1863.
44. McPherson, *This Mighty Scourge*, 161.
45. *Press* (Philadelphia), July 11, 1863.
46. *Press* (Philadelphia), July 7, 1863.
47. *Chicago Tribune*, July 4, 1863.
48. *Chicago Tribune*, July 6, 1863.
49. *Chicago Tribune*, July 6 and July 8, 1863.
50. *Chicago Tribune*, July 6, 1863.
51. *Chicago Tribune*, July 6 and July 7, 1863. Meade marched about 88,000 men to Gettysburg. This translated to nearly three-fourths of the 120,000 troops mustered in the Army of the Potomac four months earlier.
52. F. Kennedy, *The Civil War Battlefield Guide*, 120.
53. *New-York Tribune*, September 20, 1862.
54. *New-York Tribune*, July 15, 1863. Greeley made this revealing comment in reaction to the different Vicksburg numbers submitted by the Union and Confederate armies. He noted, "The Rebel officers and soldiers will report their losses as small as possible, while on the other hand there is a predisposition to exaggerate even this really great achievement of our arms."
55. *Chicago Tribune*, July 6, 1863.
56. *Boston Daily Journal*, July 7, 1863.
57. *Cleveland Morning Leader*, July 6, 1863.
58. *Daily National Republican*, July 3, 1863. Although the face of the operation, Murtagh copublished the *National Republican* with Louis Clephane, Martin Buell, and William Blanchard. The four launched the paper on November 26, 1860, to support Lincoln's presidency as the sole Republican paper in the Union capital.
59. *Cleveland Morning Leader*, July 6, 1863.
60. *Boston Daily Journal*, July 7, 1863.
61. *Daily National Republican*, July 6, 1863.
62. *Boston Daily Journal*, July 7, 1863.
63. *Daily National Republican*, July 6, 1863.
64. *Baltimore Clipper*, July 8, 1863; *Daily National Republican*, July 8, 1863. For more on Whiteley, see R. Miller, *States at War*, vol. 4, 488.
65. *Baltimore Clipper*, July 6, 1863. Whiteley revised Confederate casualties over the next several days. On July 8 he only slightly overestimated rebel losses at "thirty thousand." But on July 11 he backtracked, concluding that Lee lost "not less than 35,000 to 40,000."
66. *St. Cloud Democrat*, July 9, 1863. In June 1863, just as the Gettysburg campaign heated up, Mitchell purchased the *St. Cloud Democrat* from his aunt, Jane Grey Swisshelm—an outspoken abolitionist and women's rights activist. For more on this distinctive and influential newspaperwoman, see Hoffert, *Jane Grey Swisshelm*.

67. *Cleveland Morning Leader*, July 6, 1863. Cowles at least had the humility to admit the figure might need revising later.

68. Strong, *The Diary of George Templeton Strong*, vol. 3, 330.

69. *Press* (Philadelphia), July 7, 1863.

70. *New-York Evening Post*, July 6, 1863.

71. *New York Times*, July 7, 1863.

72. *Baltimore Clipper*, July 5, 1863.

73. *Baltimore Clipper*, July 6, 1863.

74. *Evening Telegraph* (Harrisburg), July 7, 1863.

75. *Baltimore Clipper*, July 3, 1863.

76. *Press* (Philadelphia), July 7, 1863.

77. *Press* (Philadelphia), June 30, 1863.

78. *Press* (Philadelphia), July 1, 1863.

79. *Press* (Philadelphia), July 7, 1863.

80. Ibid.

81. Quoted in Emery and Emery, *The Press and America*, 137.

82. Holzer and Symonds, *The New York Times Complete Civil War*, 251.

83. *New York Times*, July 6, 1863.

84. Quoted in Reardon, *Pickett's Charge in History and Memory*, 49. See also Gallagher, *Two Witnesses at Gettysburg*, 76.

85. *Boston Daily Journal*, July 7, 1863. For more from Coffin on this and other war reporting, see Coffin, *Marching to Victory*.

86. Pollard, *The Presidents and the Press*, 313.

87. Holzer, *Lincoln and the Power of the Press*, 434.

88. Lincoln, "The Gettysburg Address."

89. *Philadelphia Inquirer*, July 9, 1863.

90. Holzer and Symonds, *The New York Times Complete Civil War*, 255.

91. *Press* (Philadelphia), July 10, 1863.

92. *Harrisburg Evening Telegraph*, July 7, 1863.

93. *Cleveland Morning Leader*, July 6, 1863.

94. *Baltimore Clipper*, July 9, 1863. Although less common, others shared the *Clipper*'s atypical view toward Vicksburg. The New York *Sun* maintained on July 8, "The capture of Vicksburg is the most staggering blow that has yet been dealt to the Confederacy, and reflects the highest credit on the skill and energy of Gen. Grant."

95. *New-York Tribune*, July 6, 1863.

96. *Press* (Philadelphia), July 7, 1863.

97. *Press* (Philadelphia), July 8, 1863.

98. *Cleveland Morning Leader*, July 6, 1863; *Chicago Tribune*, July 6, 7, 1863.

99. *New-York Evening Post*, July 6, 1863; *Baltimore Clipper*, July 6, 1863.

100. *Sun* (New York), July 7, 1863.

101. Quoted in Guelzo, "General Meade's Mixed Legacy," 41.

102. Quoted in Andrews, *The North Reports*, 427.

103. *Cleveland Morning Leader*, July 7, 1863.

104. *Daily National Republican*, July 8, 1863; *Press* (Philadelphia), July 8, 1863.

105. *New-York Tribune*, July 10, 1863.

106. *Wisconsin State Journal*, July 7, 1863.

107. Burmeister, "George C. Burmeister Diary, 1863," July 14, 1863.

108. Quotes in McPherson, *Battle Cry of Freedom*, 666, 667.

109. *Press* (Philadelphia), July 8, 1863.

110. Burlingame, *Abraham Lincoln*, vol. 2, 514.

111. Lincoln, "Letter from President Abraham Lincoln to George G. Meade," July 14, 1863. Albeit unsent, Lincoln's letter conveyed his true feelings. Robert Lincoln recalled his father sobbing like an infant alone in his room, "head bowed upon his arms resting on the table at which he sat." After Robert inquired as to what happened, the president replied heavily, "I have just learned that at a Council of War, of Meade and his Generals, it had been determined not to pursue Lee, and now the opportune chance of ending this bitter conflict is lost." Quoted in Thatcher, "Lincoln and Meade after Gettysburg," 282.

112. Quoted in Hassler, "George G. Meade and His Role in the Gettysburg Campaign," 402. Meade also wrote his wife, "It is hard after working as hard as I have done and accomplishing as much to be found fault with for not doing impossibilities." Quoted in Bruce Catton, *Never Call Retreat*, 212.

113. For more on this and related topics, see Huntington, *Searching for George Gordon Meade*.

114. *Philadelphia Inquirer*, July 16, 1863.

115. *New-York Tribune*, July 16, 1863. Some pro-Lincoln printers offered excuses to avoid impugning the man credited with saving the Union. Greeley added on July 16, "[Lee was] able still to resist terrible onslaughts [and thus] it would have been madness [for] a commanding general to have pushed the advance guard of his army, not knowing the position and disposition of the enemy."

116. *Baltimore Clipper*, July 16, 1863.

117. Quoted in Smith, *Command Conflicts in Grant's Overland Campaign*, 99. No Civil War general proved impervious to press criticism. Immediately after costly battles, when emotions ran rawest, commanders often turned woeful in the face of what they considered unfair journalistic treatment. After Shiloh in April 1862, Grant himself wizened under the weight of press scrutiny. "I should like to go to New Mexico, or some other remote place, and have a small command out of the reach of the newspapers," he confided to one newsman. Ultimately, Grant weathered the criticism and stayed on the main stage of the war until he ended it at Appomattox three Aprils later. Quoted in Chernow, *Grant*, 212.

118. Hessler, *Sickles at Gettysburg*, 262, 287; Coddington, "The Strange Reputation of General Meade," 157–158.

119. Lincoln, "Letter from President Abraham Lincoln to George G. Meade," July 14, 1863.

120. Burmeister, "George C. Burmeister Diary, 1863," July 30, 1863.

121. Quoted in Pollard, *The Presidents and the Press*, 365.

122. Greeley proved the primary culprit. Under the headline "The Nation's War-Cry," he shouted, "Forward to Richmond! Forward to Richmond!" "The Nation's War-Cry," as he dubbed it, first appeared in the *New-York Tribune* on June 26, 1861. It remained in each subsequent issue for a week.

123. Quoted in Pollard, *The Presidents and the Press*, 365.

124. *Chattanooga Daily Rebel*, July 14, 1863.

125. *Cleveland Morning Leader,* July 17, 1863. For a concise look into the war's turning point, the summer of 1863, see B. Reid, "1863."

126. *Press* (Philadelphia), July 8, 1863.

127. *Press* (Philadelphia), July 18, 1863.

128. *Chicago Tribune,* July 13, 1863.

129. Dawson, *A Confederate Girl's Diary,* 396.

130. G. Gallagher, *Lee and His Army in Confederate History,* 83.

131. *Chicago Tribune,* July 15, 1863.

132. Tocqueville, *Democracy in America,* 254.

133. *New-York Tribune,* July 15, 1863.

134. *Chicago Tribune,* July 15, 1863.

135. Cook, *The Armies of the Streets,* 87.

136. Holzer and Symonds, *The New York Times Complete Civil War,* 261.

137. *Liberator,* July 17, 1863.

138. *Douglass' Monthly,* August 1863.

139. *Christian Recorder,* July 18, 1863.

140. *Chicago Tribune,* July 16, 1863.

141. G. Gallagher, *Two Witnesses at Gettysburg,* 68; Guelzo, *Gettysburg,* 465.

142. *Philadelphia Inquirer,* July 6, 1863.

Chapter Six. Ronin of the South

1. *Savannah Republican,* July 25, 1863.

2. Quoted in Andrews, *The South Reports the Civil War,* 50.

3. *Savannah Republican,* July 25, 1863.

4. Ibid.; *Savannah Republican,* August 11, 1863. Born in 1836 (the exact day and month remain elusive), Captain Virgil Adam Stewart Parks would have been either twenty-six or twenty-seven years old when he fell at Gettysburg. For more on Parks and his life before the war, see *Savannah Republican,* August 7, 1863.

5. Quoted in Andrews, *The South Reports the Civil War,* 50.

6. *Savannah Republican,* July 25, 1863.

7. Ibid.

8. Ibid.

9. Ibid., July 12, 1863.

10. Gallagher, *Lee and His Army in Confederate History,* 86.

11. *Savannah Republican,* June 13, 1863; *Richmond Enquirer,* June 16, 1863. Of course, this unflattering press provoked the vain Stuart to redeem his image with a headline-grabbing raid through Maryland and Pennsylvania, the consequences of which proved seismic.

12. Guelzo, *Gettysburg,* 62.

13. *Southern Confederacy,* June 30, 1863.

14. Trexler, "The Davis Administration and the Richmond Press," 190.

15. *Richmond Whig,* June 18, 1863.

16. Quoted in Raper, "William W. Holden and the Peace Movement," 493.

17. Ibid., 494.

18. *Sentinel* (Richmond), July 25, 1863.

19. The South's other great anti-administration and antiwar printer, William Gannaway Brownlow, ran *Brownlow's Knoxville Whig* in East Tennessee. Brownlow's unfiltered antiwar rhetoric made him an early and rare victim of government censorship in the South. In 1861, Confederate authorities shut the *Whig* down, charged Brownlow with high treason, and then dealt him Clement Vallandigham's sentence in reverse, banishing Brownlow to Yankeedom. When federal forces took Knoxville on September 1, 1863, however, Brownlow triumphantly returned to his home and rebooted his paper. Unfortunately, the *Whig* remained out of print during the Gettysburg campaign. For more on the Brownlow story, see Humphrey, *That D—d Brownlow*.

20. *North Carolina Standard,* June 19, 1863.

21. *Southern Confederacy,* June 30, 1863.

22. *Southern Confederacy,* June 29, 1863.

23. *Southern Confederacy,* June 28, 1863.

24. *North Carolina Standard,* June 23, 1863.

25. For more on Antietam supplying the impetus for Lincoln's preliminary Emancipation Proclamation, see Whitman, *Antietam 1862*.

26. *North Carolina Standard,* June 23, 1863.

27. Lee, "General Order No. 72," June 21, 1863, *War of the Rebellion,* series 1, vol. 27. pt. 3, 912–914.

28. McPherson, *Battle Cry of Freedom,* 649.

29. Daniel's *Richmond Examiner* epitomized Southern press opposition to Davis. Houston's pro-Davis *Tri-Weekly Telegraph* once complained, "The *Examiner* has always been opposed to the administration, and has been the mouthpiece of every discontented whim in the Confederacy." *Tri-Weekly Telegraph* (Houston), July 31, 1863.

30. Daniel, *The Richmond Examiner During the War,* 94.

31. Written from Chambersburg on June 28, 1863, and published in the *Savannah Republican,* July 25, 1863. For more on how Lee's men conducted themselves, see Coddington, "The Confederate Plunder of Pennsylvania," chapter 7 in *The Gettysburg Campaign*.

32. Daniel, *The Richmond Examiner During the War,* 93. Ironically, the satisfied few included the chronically dissatisfied Robert Barnwell Rhett. The *Charleston Mercury* claimed Lee's policy "acted like a charm" because it inclined Pennsylvanians to exchange their property for Confederate currency. This not only showered Lee with much-needed supplies, argued the paper, but also made depreciated Confederate currency more competitive with the Northern greenback. *Charleston Mercury,* July 8, 1863.

33. *Richmond Enquirer,* July 3, 1863.

34. *Richmond Enquirer,* July 17, 1863.

35. Edmondston, *Journal of a Secesh Lady,* 416. Edmondston specifically directed her ire at General Ulysses S. Grant and the way his subordinates roughly handled the citizens of Jackson, Mississippi, during the Vicksburg campaign.

36. Stone, *Brokenburn,* 227.

37. Edmondston, *Journal of a Secesh Lady,* 416. Curiously, Edmondston first learned of Lee's restraint on Northern soil through Northern reports of the unfolding campaign. For more on the Civil War's hard turn, see Grimsley, *The Hard Hand of War*.

38. Tocqueville, *Democracy in America,* 211.

39. *North Carolina Standard,* June 26, 1863.

40. *Richmond Whig*, July 6, 1863.

41. Ibid.

42. *Richmond Whig*, July 7, 1863.

43. *Savannah Republican*, July 7, 1863. Smitten by the alleged victory, Sneed and Sims added, "Such an achievement has no parallel in history, whether as regards the brilliancy of the fight, the number of prisoners taken, or the probable results of the victory. . . . In Lee, Napoleon, Wellington, [and] Eugene have found their peer, if not a star of still greater magnitude, before the splendor of whose rays the world shall bow in admiration and awe."

44. *Richmond Whig*, July 9, 1863.

45. *Richmond Whig*, July 14, 1863.

46. *Savannah Republican*, July 25, 1863.

47. Ibid.

48. Daniel, *The Richmond Examiner During the War*, 97.

49. *North Carolina Standard*, July 14, 1863.

50. *Richmond Whig*, July 14, 1863. This comes from the report furnished by the *Whig*'s lone correspondent.

51. Daniel, *The Richmond Examiner During the War*, 97.

52. For X's account, see *Richmond Enquirer*, July 21, 1863.

53. *Savannah Republican*, July 25, 1863.

54. Ibid.

55. This count includes Gwen of the Richmond *Sentinel*, X and A of the *Richmond Enquirer*, Tout-le-Monde of the *Savannah Republican*, and Georgian of the *Southern Confederacy*.

56. Quoted in Andrews, *The North Reports the Civil War*, 359.

57. *Charleston Mercury*, May 13, 1863. The cult-like press worship of Lee began after Lee hurled the Army of the Potomac back from Richmond's doorstep in the Seven Days' Battles in July 1862.

58. Alfriend, *The Life of Jefferson Davis*, 407.

59. Since X wrote for the pro-Davis *Richmond Enquirer* and Tout-le-Monde for the anti-Davis *Savannah Republican*, anonymity, rather than newspaper partisanship, proved a better predictor of a correspondent's willingness to criticize Lee.

60. Quoted in Starr, *Bohemian Brigade*, 195.

61. For more on this, see Borchard, *The Sage Encyclopedia of Journalism*, 265–266.

62. Starr, *Bohemian Brigade*, 195.

63. Quoted in Andrews, *The South Reports the Civil War*, 50.

64. *Savannah Republican*, July 25, 1863.

65. Ibid.

66. Andrews, "The Press Reports the Battle of Gettysburg," 197; Reardon, *Pickett's Charge in History and Memory*, 57.

67. Emery and Emery, *The Press and America*, 138; Reardon, *Pickett's Charge in History and Memory*, 40.

68. Andrews, "The Confederate Press and Public Morale," 451.

69. *Daily Dispatch* (Richmond), June 18, 1863.

70. *Memphis Daily Appeal*, July 21, 1863.

71. Daniel, *The Richmond Examiner During the War*, 95.

72. *Savannah Republican,* July 25, 1863, written by Tout-le-Monde on July 13 while with Lee's army at Hagerstown, Maryland.

73. *Raleigh Standard,* July 17, 1863.

74. *Savannah Republican,* July 25, 1863. The *Richmond Whig,* July 14, 1863, also recognized the precarious situation at Williamsport. "The enemy destroyed our pontoon bridge at Falling Waters, five miles below Williamsport. . . . The heavy rains continue to-day, and the Potomac has swollen several feet, rendering fording impossible."

75. *Southern Confederacy,* July 20, 1863.

76. *Raleigh Standard,* July 14, 1863.

77. *Richmond Whig,* July 14, 1863.

78. Daniel, *The Richmond Examiner During the War,* 99.

79. *Savannah Republican,* July 25, 1863.

80. Daniel, *The Richmond Examiner During the War,* 99. Like Alexander and X, however, Daniel pulled his punches when it came to Lee. He added, "Many persons now blame General Lee for attacking the enemy there; but we shall be slow to criticise an officer of his service until the facts are better known."

81. *Richmond Whig,* July 29, 1863.

82. *Southern Confederacy,* July 20, 1863.

83. G. Gallagher and Waugh, *The American War,* 120.

84. *Raleigh Standard,* July 17, 1863.

85. Mendoza, *Confederate Struggle for Command,* 33.

86. *Raleigh Standard,* October 2, 1863 (Holden's first issue after the incident).

87. Mendoza, *Confederate Struggle for Command,* 33.

88. *Charleston Mercury,* July 18, 1863.

89. *Charleston Mercury,* July 30, 1863.

90. *Southern Confederacy,* June 27, 1863.

91. Catton, *Grant Moves South,* 479.

92. *Savannah Republican,* July 9, 1863.

93. *Southern Confederacy,* July 9, 1863. McDonald told his readers, "The fall of Vicksburg and Port Hudson, while the moral influence may be considerable, [fails to] advance the enemy one step in the work of opening up the Mississippi." *Richmond Whig,* July 16, 1863.

94. *North Carolina Standard,* July 14, 1863.

95. Daniel, *The Richmond Examiner During the War,* 98.

96. *North Carolina Standard,* July 17, 1863.

97. *Charleston Mercury,* July 22, 1863.

98. "Letter from Robert E. Lee to Jefferson Davis," July 31, 1863, in Lee, *The Wartime Papers of R. E. Lee,* 564.

99. "Letter from Robert E. Lee to Jefferson Davis," August 8, 1863, in Lee, *The Wartime Papers of R.E. Lee,* 586.

100. "Letter from Jefferson Davis to Robert E. Lee," August 11, 1863, in Davis, *Jefferson Davis, Constitutionalist,* vol. 5, 589.

101. *Richmond Whig,* July 17, 1863.

102. *Richmond Whig,* August 2, 1863.

103. *Savannah Republican,* July 25, 1863.

104. Daniel, *The Richmond Examiner During the War,* 104–105.

105. *Richmond Whig,* July 20, 1863.
106. Reardon, *Pickett's Charge in History and Memory,* 61.
107. G. Gallagher, *Lee and His Army in Confederate History,* 86.

Chapter Seven. Divided Opposition

1. Starr, *Bohemian Brigade,* 210.
2. *New York Herald,* July 4, 1863. For Hosmer's full account, see Hosmer, *The Battle of Gettysburg.*
3. *New York Herald,* July 4, 1863.
4. *New York Herald,* July 6, 1863.
5. Ibid. Emphasis in source.
6. *New York Herald,* July 9, 1863. For more on Knox's war reporting, see Knox, *Camp-fire and Cotton-field.*
7. Starr, *Bohemian Brigade,* 203.
8. *New York Herald,* July 6, 1863.
9. Starr, *Bohemian Brigade,* 30
10. Quoted in Crouthamel, "The Newspaper Revolution in New York," 96.
11. *New York Herald,* July 9, 1863; *Evening Star* (Washington, D.C.), July 6, 1863.
12. *Crisis* (Columbus, Ohio), July 8, 1863.
13. *New York Daily News,* July 8, 1863.
14. *Millennial Harbinger* 5, no. 1 (January 1834), 3.
15. Andrews, "The Press Reports the Battle of Gettysburg," 177; *New York Herald,* July 3, 1863.
16. Reprinted in *Herald* (Carlisle, Pa.), July 17, 1863.
17. *Brooklyn Daily Eagle,* July 6, 1863.
18. Ibid.
19. *New York Herald,* July 3, 1863.
20. *New York Herald,* July 7, 1863.
21. Reprinted in *Herald* (Carlisle, Pa.), July 17, 1863; *Brooklyn Daily Eagle,* July 6, 1863.
22. *Brooklyn Daily Eagle,* July 6, 1863.
23. *New York Herald,* July 4, 1863.
24. *New York Herald,* July 6, 1863.
25. Mott, *American Journalism, a History,* 339–340.
26. In July 1861, the *World* absorbed the *Courier and Enquirer* to become one of New York City's leading publications just as the war began. The *World* "had the fifth[-largest] circulation among New York papers—less than that of the *Times,* more than that of the *Evening Post.*" Mott, *American Journalism, a History,* 351.
27. *New York Herald,* July 4, 1863.
28. Reprinted in the *New Albany (Ind.) Daily Ledger,* July 11, 1863.
29. *New York Herald,* July 7, 1863.
30. *New York Herald,* July 9, 1863.
31. *New York Herald,* July 7, 1863.
32. *New York Herald,* July 8, 1863.
33. Andrews, *The North Reports the Civil War,* 431.

34. Quoted in ibid.

35. *Evening Star* (Washington, D.C.), July 3, 1863.

36. *Plain Dealer* (Cleveland), July 6, 1863. Stephenson took over the *Plain Dealer* in 1862 after its founder and longtime printer, James W. Gray, passed away. As Gray's estate administrator and someone unschooled in journalism, Stephenson gradually steered the *Plain Dealer* away from Gray's more business-sound, moderate views and toward his own radical Copperheadism. While the paper still reflected Gray's vision during the Gettysburg campaign, by early 1865 Stephenson's Copperheadism had driven the tract so deep into the ground that public and private pressures pushed him from the paper. For the *Plain Dealer*'s history, see Shaw, *The Plain Dealer*.

37. *Plain Dealer* (Cleveland), July 6, 1863.

38. *Plain Dealer* (Cleveland), July 6, 1863; *Evening Star* (Washington, D.C.), July 6, 1863.

39. Barcousky, *Civil War Pittsburgh*, 67, 79; Andrews, "The Pennsylvania Press During the Civil War," 24.

40. *Pittsburgh Post*, July 6 and July 8, 1863.

41. Applegate, "The Detroit Free Press During the Civil War," 3–4. Henry N. Walker became the *Free Press*'s proprietor in June 1861 after purchasing the paper from Wilbur F. Storey (who then left Detroit for Chicago to take up his mantle at the *Times*). But as managing editor and, in 1863, partial owner, Quinby rather than Walker proved the *Free Press*'s heart and soul.

42. *Detroit Free Press*, July 6, 1863.

43. *Plain Dealer* (Cleveland), July 6, 1863.

44. *Detroit Free Press*, July 6, 1863.

45. *New York Herald*, July 7, 1863.

46. *Detroit Free Press*, July 6, 1863.

47. *Pittsburgh Post*, July 6, 1863.

48. *Detroit Free Press*, July 9, 1863.

49. *Plain Dealer* (Cleveland), July 6, 1863.

50. Ibid.

51. *Pittsburgh Post*, July 8, 1863.

52. *Plain Dealer* (Cleveland), July 6, 1863. Emphasis in original.

53. *New York Herald*, July 6, 1863. Although most moderate printers expected Meade to finish Lee before he escaped, some toed a less optimistic line. Marble's New York *World* remarked, "We would not be at all surprised if he [Lee] got [away] with what was left of his army across the Virginia shore.—To speculate on the loss of Lee's army is decidedly premature." Reprinted in the *Daily Patriot and Union* (Harrisburg), July 8, 1863.

54. *Daily Patriot and Union* (Harrisburg), July 7, 1863.

55. *Evening Star* (Washington, D.C.), July 8, 1863.

56. *Plain Dealer* (Cleveland), July 7, 1863.

57. *Detroit Free Press*, July 11, 1863.

58. *New York Herald*, July 6, 1863.

59. *Brooklyn Daily Eagle*, July 15, 1863.

60. *New York Herald*, July 4 and July 15, 1863.

61. *New York Herald*, July 15, 1863. While the *Herald* initially rushed to Meade's defense, it later pulled back. On July 18, for example, the newspaper argued that "Meade lost a grand and golden opportunity" by not attacking Lee at Williamsport.

62. Stanton, "Edwin M. Stanton to Alexander K. McClure," July 22, 1863, Edwin M. Stanton Papers, Library of Congress.

63. Huntington, *Searching for George Gordon Meade*, 197.

64. *Report of the Joint Committee on the Conduct of the War*, vol. 4, lxxv.

65. Hessler, *Sickles at Gettysburg*, 304.

66. Pollard, *The Presidents and the Press*, 365.

67. *Plain Dealer* (Cleveland), July 17, 1863.

68. *New York Herald*, July 18, 1863.

69. *Plain Dealer* (Cleveland), July 16, 1863.

70. *Pittsburgh Post*, July 17, 1863.

71. Ibid.

72. *Janesville (Wis.) Daily Gazette*, July 18, 1863; *Evening Telegraph* (Harrisburg), July 14, 1863.

73. *Detroit Free Press*, July 18, 1863; *New York Daily News*, July 16, 1863.

74. *New York Daily News*, July 15, 1863.

75. *Plain Dealer* (Cleveland), July 18, 1863.

76. *State Sentinel* (Indianapolis), July 8, 1863.

77. *Democratic Banner* (Clearfield, Pa.), July 15, 1863.

78. *New York Daily News*, July 4, 1863.

79. Holzer, *Lincoln and the Power of the Press*, 350.

80. *New York Daily News*, July 8, 1863.

81. *Crisis* (Columbus, Ohio), July 8, 1863.

82. *Crisis* (Columbus, Ohio), July 29, 1863.

83. *Democratic Banner* (Clearfield, Pa.), July 15, 1863.

84. Rhodes, *History of the United States*, vol. 4, 253.

85. Reprinted in the *Weekly Democrat* (Plymouth, Ind.), July 9, 1863.

86. Quoted in Rhodes, *History of the United States*, vol. 4, 253.

87. Ibid., 254.

88. Sachsman, Rushing, and Van Tuyll, *The Civil War and the Press*, 293.

89. Sanger, "The *Chicago Times* and the Civil War," 568.

90. Quoted in Williamson, *The 47th Indiana Volunteer Infantry*, 107.

91. *New York Daily News*, July 7, 1863.

92. *Democratic Banner* (Clearfield, Pa.), July 15, 1863.

93. *Crisis* (Columbus, Ohio), July 15, 1863.

94. *State Sentinel* (Indianapolis), July 7, 1863.

95. *New York Daily News*, July 7, 1863.

96. *New York Times*, July 4, 1863.

97. Reprinted in the *Weekly Democrat* (Plymouth, Ind.), July 9, 1863.

98. *New York Times*, July 4, 1863. For Meade's perspective on the battle and broader campaign, see Meade, *The Life and Letters of George Gordon Meade*, vol. 2, 1–135.

99. *Crisis* (Columbus, Ohio), July 15, 1863.

100. *State Sentinel* (Indianapolis), July 7, 1863.

101. Reprinted in the *Weekly Democrat* (Plymouth, Ind.), July 9, 1863.

102. Ibid.

103. *New York Daily News,* July 10, 1863.

104. *New York Daily News,* July 15, 1863.

105. *Democratic Banner* (Clearfield, Pa.), July 22, 1863.

106. *Crisis* (Columbus, Ohio), July 22, 1863.

107. *State Sentinel* (Indianapolis), July 17, 1863.

108. *Crisis* (Columbus, Ohio), July 22, 1863.

109. Reprinted in *New Albany (Ind.) Daily Ledger,* July 11, 1863; and *Carlisle (Pa.) Herald,* July 17, 1863.

110. *Pittsburgh Post,* July 3, 4, 6, 1863.

111. *Crisis* (Columbus, Ohio), July 8, 1863.

112. *New York Daily News,* July 8, 1863.

113. *New York Herald,* July 6, 1863.

114. Reprinted in the *Carlisle (Pa.) Herald,* July 17, 1863.

115. Reprinted in the *New Albany (Ind.) Daily Ledger,* July 11, 1863.

116. Andrews, "The Press Reports the Battle of Gettysburg," 197.

117. *Crisis* (Ohio), July 15, 1863.

118. *New York Daily News,* July 8, 1863.

119. *Democratic Watchman* (Bellefonte, Pa.), July 24, 1863.

120. Ibid.

121. *New York Herald,* July 8, 1863.

122. *Brooklyn Daily Eagle,* July 8, 1863.

123. *Evening Star* (Washington, D.C.), July 7, 1863.

124. *Pittsburgh Post,* July 8, 1863.

125. *Detroit Free Press,* July 8, 1863.

126. *Plain Dealer* (Cleveland), July 8, 1863.

127. *State Sentinel* (Indianapolis), July 16, 1863.

128. *Chicago Tribune,* July 15, 1863.

129. *New-York Evening Post,* May 20, 1863.

130. Quoted in Douglas, *The Golden Age of the Newspaper,* 62.

Chapter Eight. The Press and Gettysburg

1. Gorgas, *The Civil War Diary of General Josiah Gorgas,* 55.

2. *Richmond Whig,* July 8, 1863. According to the *Whig,* parents swarmed its Richmond office with comments like these after every battle.

3. Ibid.

4. Ibid.

5. Douglas, *The Golden Age of the Newspaper,* 56.

6. Tocqueville, *Democracy in America,* 210.

7. Sachsman, *A Press Divided,* xiii.

8. For more on the Lost Cause, see Gallagher and Nolan, *The Myth of the Lost Cause and Civil War History;* and Wilson, *Baptized in Blood.*

9. Connelly, *The Marble Man,* 90–91.

10. Ibid., 25, 38.

11. *Fayetteville (N.C.) Observer*, July 13, 1863; *Charleston Daily Courier*, July 14, 1863.

12. For still more on the Lost Cause and on the postwar evolution of the cult of Lee, see Blight, *Race and Reunion*.

13. *Press* (Philadelphia), July 8, 1863.

14. Quoted in G. Gallagher, *Lee and His Army in Confederate History*, 87.

15. In a July 11 report, the Copperhead *New York Daily News* dubbed the contradictory accounts of the Northern and Southern presses "the two versions of the Battle of Gettysburg." The paper explained, "At the North [Gettysburg] was claimed as a glorious victory, resulting in the . . . 'annihilation' of the great invading Army of Virginia . . . [whereas] the Richmond journals . . . not only represent that we achieved no victory, but that we suffered a severe defeat." The *Daily News* decided, "One story is good until another is told, and this proves to be remarkably applicable to the reports of the late battle of Gettysburg." *New York Daily News*, July 11, 1863.

16. This point reinforces one Reardon makes: "In later years, the Northern press's celebration of a great victory and the Southern search for a scapegoat . . . would prove irresistible to chroniclers of the event. These sentiments would help win for Gettysburg . . . the special designation of the turning point of the rebellion." Reardon, *Pickett's Charge in History and Memory*, 61.

17. Andrews, *The South Reports the Civil War*, 319.

18. *Philadelphia Inquirer*, July 6, 1863; *Tri-Weekly Telegraph* (Houston), July 24, 1863.

19. *New York Daily News*, July 11, 1863.

20. *Southern Confederacy*, July 6, 1863.

21. *New York Daily News*, July 14, 1864.

22. *Cleveland Morning Leader*, July 6, 1863.

23. Andrews, "The Press Reports the Battle of Gettysburg," 194.

24. *New York Herald*, July 9, 1863.

25. "Midwest" here includes all Northern states west of Pennsylvania and north of the Ohio and Missouri Rivers, while "New England and the Mid-Atlantic" includes all Union states east of Ohio.

26. *Tri-Weekly Telegraph* (Houston), July 21, 1863; *Detroit Free Press*, July 6, 1863.

27. *Daily Dispatch* (Richmond), June 24, 1863; *Memphis Daily Appeal*, August 5, 1863.

28. *Press* (Philadelphia), July 8, 1863.

29. For a brief but incisive take on the Gettysburg Address, see LaFantasie, "Lincoln and the Gettysburg Awakening," 73–89. For a tour de force, see Wills, *Lincoln at Gettysburg*.

30. Reardon, *Pickett's Charge in History and Memory*; *New York Times*, August 19, 1858.

31. *Fayetteville (N.C.) Observer*, July 9, 1863.

32. *Fayetteville (N.C.) Observer*, July 13, 1863; Daniel, *The Richmond Examiner During the War*, 97.

33. Ballard, *Vicksburg*, 430. Ballard goes on to write, "The loss of Vicksburg and the Mississippi in effect shrank the Western Confederacy from Texas to the Alabama-Georgia border. The ordnance lost when Pemberton surrendered could not be replaced. The impact of the surrender on Southern morale was considerably greater than that of Lee's withdrawal from Pennsylvania. In fact it is one of the unfortunate paradoxes of the Civil War that Vicksburg mattered more and is remembered less than many campaigns and battles of distinctly smaller consequence."

34. *Mobile Daily Advertiser and Register*, July 14, 1863.

35. G. Gallagher, *Lee and His Army in Confederate History*, 83.

36. Schudson, *Discovering the News*, 4.

37. See Reardon's *Pickett's Charge in History and Memory* for how interpretations of Gettysburg, particularly Pickett's Charge, developed over time.

38. Webb, *An Address Delivered at Gettysburg*, 11.

Epilogue

1. Apparently, the temperature kept pleasant enough for veterans twenty years past their prime to play a scratch game of football that afternoon. See the *Star and Sentinel* (Gettysburg), August 29, 1883.

2. *Star and Sentinel* (Gettysburg), August 29, 1883.

3. Webb, *An Address Delivered at Gettysburg*, 13, 17.

4. Ibid., 4, 11.

5. Gross, *The Battle-Field of Gettysburg*, 18–19.

6. *Press* (Philadelphia), July 4, 1865. George Templeton Strong shared the same sentiments at almost exactly the same time. "We begin now to be able to look at the Union war as a whole," wrote Strong on June 30, 1865. "Of course, we shall have a better view of it as we get further off, but from our present position, July 4th, 1863, stands out as the critical day that determined its result. Gettysburg seems to have been the turning point of the four years' struggle." Strong, *The Diary of George Templeton Strong*, vol. 4, 14.

7. Quoted in Guelzo, *Gettysburg*, 465.

Bibliography

Newspapers

Abingdon Virginian
Baltimore Clipper
Boston Daily Journal
Brooklyn Daily Eagle
Brownslow's Knoxville Whig
Carlisle (Pa.) Herald
Charleston (S.C.) Daily Courier
Charleston (S.C.) Mercury
Chattanooga Daily Rebel
Chicago Times
Chicago Tribune
Christian Recorder
Cincinnati Daily Gazette
Cleveland Morning Leader
Columbus (Ga.) Enquirer
Courier and Enquirer (New York City)
Crisis (Columbus, Ohio)
Daily Citizen (Vicksburg)
Daily Dispatch (Richmond)
Daily Intelligencer (Atlanta)
Daily National Republican (Washington, D.C.)
Daily Patriot and Union (Harrisburg, Pa.)
Daily Register (Knoxville)
Daily Standard (Raleigh, N.C.)
Democratic Banner (Clearfield, Pa.)
Democratic Watchman (Bellefonte, Pa.)
Detroit Free Press
Evening Star (Washington, D.C.)
Evening Telegraph (Harrisburg, Pa.)
Fayetteville (N.C.) Observer
Frederick Douglass' Paper (Rochester, N.Y.)
Galveston Weekly News
Janesville (Wis.) Daily Gazette
Liberator
Memphis Daily Appeal
Mississippian (Jackson)
Mobile (Ala.) Daily Advertiser and Register
National Republican (Washington, D.C.)
New Albany (Ind.) Daily Ledger
New Orleans Bulletin
New York Daily News
New York Herald
New York Times
New-York Evening Post
New-York Morning Post
New-York Tribune
North Carolina Standard (Raleigh)
Philadelphia Inquirer
Pittsburgh Post
Plain Dealer (Cleveland)
Press (Philadelphia)
Raleigh (N.C.) Register
Richmond Enquirer
Richmond Whig
Sacramento Daily Union
St. Cloud (Minn.) Democrat
San Antonio Herald
Savannah Republican
Sentinel (Richmond)
Southern Confederacy (Atlanta)
Southern Field and Fireside (Augusta, Ga.)
Star and Sentinel (Gettysburg, Pa.)
State Sentinel (Indianapolis)
Staunton (Va.) Spectator
Sun (New York City)
Tri-Weekly Telegraph (Houston)
Weekly Democrat (Plymouth, Ind.)
Wisconsin State Journal
World (New York City)

Works Cited

Adams, John Quincy. *John Quincy Adams Diary*. October 3, 1816. Adams Family Archives, Massachusetts Historical Society, Boston.

Alfriend, Frank H. *The Life of Jefferson Davis*. Cincinnati: Caxton, 1868.

Alleman, Matilda "Tillie" Pierce. *At Gettysburg, or, What a Girl Saw and Heard of the Battle*. New York: W. Lake Borland, 1889.

Andrews, J. Cutler. "The Confederate Press and Public Morale." *Journal of Southern History* 32, no. 4 (November 1966): 451–455.

———. *The North Reports the Civil War*. Pittsburgh: University of Pittsburgh Press, 1955.

———. "The Pennsylvania Press During the Civil War." *Pennsylvania History* 9, no. 1 (January 1942): 24–30.

———. "The Press Reports the Battle of Gettysburg." *Pennsylvania History* 31, no. 2 (April 1964): 177–197.

———. "The Southern Telegraph Company, 1861–1865: A Chapter in the History of Wartime Communication." *Journal of Southern History* 30, no. 3 (August 1964): 319.

———. *The South Reports the Civil War*. Pittsburgh: University of Pittsburgh Press, 1985.

Applegate, Margaret J. "The Detroit Free Press During the Civil War." Master's thesis, Wayne State University, 1938.

Baker, Thomas H. "Refugee Newspaper: The Memphis *Daily Appeal*, 1862–1865." *Journal of Southern History* 29, no. 3 (August 1963): 326–334.

Ballard, Michael B. *Vicksburg: The Campaign That Opened the Mississippi*. Chapel Hill: University of North Carolina Press, 2005.

Barcousky, Len. *Civil War Pittsburgh: Forge of the Union*. Charleston, S.C.: The History Press, 2013.

Belford, Barbara. *Brilliant Bylines: A Biographical Anthology of Notable Newspaperwomen in America*. New York: Columbia University Press, 1986.

Binder, John J. "The Transportation Revolution and Antebellum Sectional Disagreement." *Social Science History* 35, no. 1 (Spring 2011): 20.

Blight, David W. *Race and Reunion: The Civil War in American Memory*. Cambridge, Mass.: Harvard University Press, 2001.

Boorstin, Daniel J. *The Americans: The National Experience*. New York: Random House, 1965.

Borchard, Gregory A., ed. *The Sage Encyclopedia of Journalism*. Los Angeles: Sage Publications, 2002.

Boylan, Anne M. *Sunday School: The Formation of an American Institution, 1790–1880*. New Haven, Conn.: Yale University Press, 1988.

Bridges, Lamar W. "The Memphis Daily Appeal's 'Dixie': Civil War Capital Correspondent." *Tennessee Historical Quarterly* 28, no. 4 (Winter 1969): 378.

Broadwater, Robert P., ed. *Gettysburg as the Generals Remembered It: Postwar Perspectives of Ten Commanders*. Jefferson, N.C.: McFarlan, 2010.

Brooks, Noah. *Washington in Lincoln's Time*. New York: Century, 1895.

Brown, Kent Masterson. *Meade at Gettysburg: A Study in Command*. Chapel Hill: University of North Carolina Press, 2021.

———. *The Retreat from Gettysburg: Lee, Logistics, and the Pennsylvania Campaign*. Chapel Hill: University of North Carolina Press, 2005.

Brown, Richard D. *The Strength of a People: The Idea of an Informed Citizenry, 1650–1870.* Chapel Hill: University of North Carolina Press, 1996.

Bulla, David W., and Gregory A. Borchard. *Journalism in the Civil War Era.* 2nd ed. New York: Peter Lang, 2023.

Bullard, F. Lauriston. *Famous War Correspondents.* Boston: Little, Brown, 1914.

Burlingame, Michael. *Abraham Lincoln: A Life,* vol. 2. Baltimore: Johns Hopkins University Press, 2008.

Burmeister, George C. "George C. Burmeister Diary, 1863." Civil War Diaries and Letters, Special Collections, University of Iowa Libraries, Iowa City.

Cadwallader, Sylvanus. *Three Years with Grant as Recalled by War Correspondent Sylvanus Cadwallader.* New York: Alfred A. Knopf, 1955.

Campanella, Richard. *Lincoln in New Orleans: The 1828–1831 Flatboat Voyages and Their Place in History.* Lafayette: University of Louisiana at Lafayette Press, 2011.

Campion, Susan. "Wallpaper Newspapers of the American Civil War." *Journal of the American Institute for Conservation* 34, no. 2 (Summer 1995): 132–133.

Carrol, Thomas F. "Freedom of Speech and of the Press during the Civil War." *Virginia Law Review* 9, no. 7 (May 1923): 516–551.

Casdorph, Paul D. *Confederate General R. S. Ewell: Robert E. Lee's Hesitant Commander.* Lexington: University Press of Kentucky, 2004.

Catton, Bruce. *The Civil War.* New York: Mariner Books, 2004.

———. *The Coming Fury.* Garden City, N.Y.: Doubleday, 1961.

———. *Grant Moves South.* Boston: Little, Brown, 1960.

———. *Never Call Retreat.* London: Phoenix Press, 2001.

———. *Terrible Swift Sword.* New York: Doubleday, 1967.

Chernow, Ron. *Grant.* New York: Penguin Books, 2018.

Chesnut, Mary Boykin. *A Diary from Dixie.* New York: D. Appleton, 1905.

Coddington, Edwin B. *The Gettysburg Campaign: A Study in Command.* New York: Touchstone, 1997. First published in 1968.

———. "The Strange Reputation of General Meade: A Lesson in Historiography." *The Historian* 23, no. 2 (February 1961): 157–158.

Coffin, Charles Carleton. *Marching to Victory: The Second Period of the Rebellion Including the Year 1863.* New York: Harper & Brothers, 1888.

Confederate States of America, Post Office Department. *Instructions to Post Masters.* Richmond, Va.: Ritchie and Dunnavant, 1861.

Connelly, Thomas L. *The Marble Man: Robert E. Lee and His Image in American Society.* Baton Rouge: Louisiana State University Press, 1977.

Cook, Adrian. *The Armies of the Streets: The New York City Draft Riots of 1863.* Lexington: University Press of Kentucky, 1974.

Crouthamel, James L. *Bennett's New York Herald and the Rise of the Popular Press.* Syracuse, N.Y.: Syracuse University Press, 1989.

———. "The Newspaper Revolution in New York, 1830–1860." *New York History* 45, no. 2 (April 1964): 96–101.

Crozier, Emmet. *Yankee Reporters, 1861–1865.* New York: Oxford University Press, 1956.

Daniel, John M. *The Richmond Examiner During the War, or The Writings of John M. Daniel.* New York: Printed for the author, 1868.

Davis, Jefferson. *Jefferson Davis, Constitutionalist: His Letters, Papers and Speeches*, vol. 5. New York: J. J. Little & Ives, 1923.

Dawson, Sarah Morgan. *A Confederate Girl's Diary*. Boston: Houghton Mifflin, 1913.

De Bow, James D. B. "The South and the Union," *De Bow's Review* 10 (February 1851): 152.

De Fontaine, Felix Gregory. "The First Day of Real War." *Southern Bivouac* 2 (July 1886): 77.

———. *Marginalia, or Gleanings from an Army Notebook*. Columbia, S.C.: Steam Power Press of F. G. De Fontaine & Co., 1864.

Dicken-Garcia, Hazel. *Journalistic Standards in Nineteenth-Century America*. Madison: University of Wisconsin Press, 1989.

Dill, William A. "Growth of Newspapers in the United States." Master's thesis, University of Kansas, 1928.

Douglas, George H. *The Golden Age of the Newspaper*. Westport, Conn.: Greenwood Press, 1999.

Douglass, Frederick. *Narrative of the Life of Frederick Douglass: An American Slave, Written by Himself*. 2nd ed. Boston: Bedford/St. Martin's, 2003. First published in 1845.

DuBoff, Richard B. "The Telegraph in Nineteenth-Century America: Technology and Monopoly." *Comparative Studies in Society and History* 26, no. 4 (October 1984): 573.

Duncan, Bingham. *Whitelaw Reid: Journalist, Politician, Diplomat*. Athens: University of Georgia Press, 1975.

Edmonston, Catherine Ann Devereaux. *Journal of a Secesh Lady: The Diary of Catherine Ann Devereux Edmondston, 1860–66*. Edited by Beth Gilbert Crabtree and James W. Patton. Raleigh: North Carolina Division of Archives and History, 1979.

Emery, Michael, and Edwin Emery. *The Press and America: An Interpretive History of the Mass Media*. 8th ed. Needham Heights, Mass.: Allyn and Bacon, 1996.

Endres, Kathleen L. "The Women's Press in the Civil War: A Portrait of Patriotism, Propaganda, and Prodding." *Civil War History* 30, no. 1 (March 1984): 31–53.

Fishlow, Albert. *American Railroads and the Transformation of the Antebellum Economy*. Cambridge, Mass.: Harvard University Press, 1965.

Foote, Shelby. *The Civil War, a Narrative: Fredericksburg to Meridian*. New York: Random House, 1963.

Fox, Louis H. "New York City Newspapers, 1820–1850: A Bibliography." *Papers of the Bibliographical Society of America* 21, nos. 1–2 (1927): 122–133.

Freeman, Douglas Southall. *Lee's Lieutenants: A Study in Command, Gettysburg to Appomattox*, vol. 3. New York: Charles Scribner's Sons, 1946.

Fremantle, Arthur James Lyon. *The Fremantle Diary: A Journal of the Confederacy*. Edited by Walter Lord. Ithaca, N.Y.: Burford Books, 2001. First published 1954.

Friedman, Lillian, and Belle Becker Sideman, eds. *Europe Looks at the Civil War*. New York: Orion Press, 1960.

Fuller, J. F. C. *The Generalship of Ulysses S. Grant*. New York: Dodd, Mead, 1929.

Gaillard, Franklin. "Letter from Franklin Gaillard to Maria." July 17, 1863. Gaillard Papers, Southern Historical Collection, Wilson Library, University of North Carolina, Chapel Hill.

Gallagher, Gary W. *Lee and His Army in Confederate History*. Chapel Hill: University of North Carolina Press, 2001.

———, ed. *The Second Day at Gettysburg: Essays on Confederate and Union Leadership*. Kent, Ohio: Kent State University Press, 1993.

———, ed. *Two Witnesses at Gettysburg: The Personal Accounts of Whitelaw Reid and A. J. L. Fremantle*. 2nd ed. Chichester, U.K.: Wiley-Blackwell, 2009.

Gallagher, Gary W., and Alan T. Nolan, eds. *The Myth of the Lost Cause and Civil War History*. Bloomington: Indiana University Press, 2000.

Gallagher, Gary W., and Joan Waugh. *The American War: A History of the Civil War Era*. State College, Pa.: Flip Learning, 2015.

Gallagher, Winifred. *How the Post Office Created America*. New York: Penguin Random House, 2006.

Glatthar, Joseph. *General Lee's Army: From Victory to Collapse*. New York: Free Press, 2008.

Gordon, John Steele. *An Empire of Wealth: The Epic History of American Economic Power*. New York: Harper Perennial, 2005.

Gorgas, Josiah. *The Civil War Diary of General Josiah Gorgas*. Edited by Frank E. Vandiver. Tuscaloosa: University of Alabama Press, 1947.

Grimsley, Mark. *The Hard Hand of War: Union Military Policy Toward Southern Civilians, 1861–65*. Cambridge, U.K.: Cambridge University Press, 1995.

Gross, George J. *The Battle-Field of Gettysburg*. Philadelphia: Collins, 1866.

Guelzo, Allen. "General Meade's Mixed Legacy: The General Won at Gettysburg in Spite of Himself." *Civil War Times*, June 2013, 41.

———. *Gettysburg: The Last Invasion*. New York: Alfred A. Knopf, 2013.

Hacker, David. "A Census-Based Count of the Civil War Dead." *Civil War History* 57, no. 4 (2011): 307–348.

Hamilton, Thomas. *Men and Manners in America*, vol. 2. Edinburgh: William Blackwood, 1833.

Harris, Brayton. *War News: Blue and Gray in Black and White: Newspapers in the Civil War*. Scotts Valley, Calif.: CreateSpace, 2010.

Hassler, Warren W., Jr. "George G. Meade and His Role in the Gettysburg Campaign." *Pennsylvania History* 32, no. 4 (October 1965): 402–404.

Henkin, David M. *The Postal Age: The Emergence of Modern Communications in Nineteenth-Century America*. Chicago: University of Chicago Press, 2006.

Hessler, James A. *Sickles at Gettysburg: The Controversial Civil War General Who Committed Murder, Abandoned Little Round Top, and Declared Himself the Hero of Gettysburg*. New York: Savas Beatie, 2009.

Hochfelder, Richard. *The Telegraph in America, 1832–1920*. Baltimore: Johns Hopkins University Press, 2012.

Hoffert, Sylvia D. *Jane Grey Swisshelm: An Unconventional Life, 1815–1884*. Chapel Hill: University of North Carolina Press, 2004.

Holmes, Oliver Wendell. "Bread and the Newspaper." In *The Oxford Book of American Essays, Chosen by Brander Matthews*, 114–127. New York: Oxford University Press, 1914.

Holt, Michael F. *The Political Crisis of the 1850s*. New York: W. W. Norton, 1983.

Holzer, Harold. *Lincoln and the Power of the Press: The War for Public Opinion*. New York: Simon & Schuster, 2014.

Holzer, Harold, and Craig Symonds, eds. *The New York Times Complete Civil War 1861–1865*. New York: Black Dog and Leventhal, 2010.

Hosmer, George Washington. *The Battle of Gettysburg*. New York: Press Publishing, 1913.

Houghton, W. R., and M. B. Houghton. *Two Boys in the Civil War and After*. Montgomery, Ala.: Paragon Press, 1912.

Howe, Daniel Walker. *What Hath God Wrought: The Transformation of America, 1815–1848*. Oxford: Oxford University Press, 2007.

Humphrey, Steve. *That D—d Brownlow: Being a Saucy and Malicious Description of Fighting Parson William Gannaway Brownlow*. Boone, N.C.: Appalachian State University, 1978.

Huntington, Tom. *Searching for George Gordon Meade: The Forgotten Victor of Gettysburg*. Mechanicsburg, Pa.: Stackpole Books, 2013.

Hutton, Frankie. *The Early Black Press in America, 1827–1860*. Westport, Conn.: Greenwood Press, 1993.

Isbell, Timothy T. *Shiloh and Corinth: Sentinels of Stone*. Jackson: University Press of Mississippi, 2007

John, Richard R. *Spreading the News: The American Postal System from Franklin to Morse*. Cambridge, Mass.: Harvard University Press, 1998.

———. "Taking Sabbatarianism Seriously: The Postal System, the Sabbath, and the Transformation of American Political Culture." *Journal of the Early Republic* 10, no. 4 (Winter 1990): 519.

Jones, J. B. *A Rebel War Clerk's Diary at the Confederate States Capital*. 2 volumes. Philadelphia, Pa.: J. B. Lippincott, 1866.

Kaestle, Carl F. *Pillars of the Republic: Common Schools and American Society, 1780–1860*. New York: Hill and Wang, 1983.

Karuka, Manu. *Empire's Tracks: Indigenous Nations, Chinese Workers, and the Transcontinental Railroad*. Oakland: University of California Press, 2019.

Keilbowicz, Richard B. *News in the Mail: The Press, Post Office, and Public Information, 1700–1860s*. New York: Greenwood Press, 1989.

Kelley, Mary. *Learning to Stand and Speak: Women, Education, and Public Life in America's Republic*. Chapel Hill: University of North Carolina Press, 2006.

Keneally, Thomas. *American Scoundrel: The Life of the Notorious Civil War General Dan Sickles*. New York: Anchor Books, 2003.

Kennedy, Frances H. *The Civil War Battlefield Guide*. 2nd ed. New York: Houghton Mifflin, 1998.

Kennedy, J. C. G. *Catalogue of the Newspapers and Periodicals Published in the United States: Showing the Town and Country in Which the Same Are Published, How Often Issued, Their Character, and Circulation*. New York: John Livingston, 1852.

Kinsley, Philip. *The Chicago Tribune: Its First Hundred Years*, vol. 1, *1847–1865*. New York: A. A. Knopf, 1943.

Knox, Thomas Wallace. *Camp-fire and Cotton-field: Southern Adventure in Time of War: Life with the Union Armies and Residence on a Louisiana Plantation*. New York: Bleblock, 1865.

Krick, Robert K. *Conquering the Valley: Stonewall Jackson at Port Republic*. Baton Rouge: Louisiana State University Press, 2002.

LaFantasie, Glenn. "Lincoln and the Gettysburg Awakening." *Journal of the Abraham Lincoln Association* 16, no. 1 (Winter 1995): 73–89.

Lee, Robert E. *The Wartime Papers of R. E. Lee*. Boston: Little, Brown, 1967.

Lee Family Digital Archive, Stratford Hall Historic Preserve, https://leefamilyarchive.org/.
Leon, Louis. *The Diary of a Tar Heel Confederate Soldier*. Charlotte, N.C.: Stone Publishing, 1913.
Lincoln, Abraham. "The Gettysburg Address." Alexander Bliss copy. Abraham Lincoln Online, https://www.abrahamlincolnonline.org/lincoln/speeches/gettysburg.htm.
———. *Speeches and Letters of Abraham Lincoln*. New York: E. P. Dutton, 1894.
Linderman, Gerald. *Embattled Courage: The Experience of Combat in the American Civil War*. New York: Free Press, 1989.
Longstreet, James. "James Longstreet's Account of the Campaign and Battle of Gettysburg." *Southern Historical Society Papers*, vol. 5 (January–June 1878): 60–65.
Lutz, Earl. "Soldier Newspapers of the Civil War." *Papers of the Bibliographical Society of America* 46, no. 4 (1952): 381.
MacKay, Winnifred K. "Philadelphia During the Civil War, 1861–1865." *Pennsylvania Magazine of History and Biography* 70, no 1 (January 1946): 4.
Malone, Henry T. "Atlanta Journalism During the Confederacy." *Georgia Historical Quarterly* 37, no. 3 (September 1953): 210–219.
Mathews, Joseph J. *Reporting the Wars*. Minneapolis: University of Minnesota Press, 1957.
Maverick, Augustus. *Henry J. Raymond and the New York Press for Thirty Years*. Hartford, Conn.: A. S. Hale, 1870.
McCardell, John. *The Idea of a Southern Nation: Southern Nationalists and Southern Nationalism, 1830–1860*. New York: W. W. Norton, 1979.
McNeely, Patricia G, Debra Reddin Van Tuyll, and Henry H. Schulte. *Knights of the Quill: Confederate Correspondents and Their Civil War Reporting*. West Lafayette, Ind.: Purdue University Press, 2010.
McPherson, James. *Battle Cry of Freedom: The Civil War Era*. New York: Oxford University Press, 1988.
———. *This Mighty Scourge: Perspectives on the Civil War*. Oxford, U.K.: Oxford University Press, 2007.
———. *The War That Forged a Nation: Why the Civil War Still Matters*. New York: Oxford University Press, 2017.
Meade, George. *The Life and Letters of George Gordon Meade, Major-General United States Army*, vol. 2. New York: Charles Scribner's Sons, 1913.
Mendoza, Alexander. *Confederate Struggle for Command: General James Longstreet and the First Corps in the West*. College Station: Texas A&M University Press.
Miller, Nathan. *The Enterprise of a Free People: Aspects of Economic Development in New York State During the Canal Period, 1792–1838*. Ithaca, N.Y.: Cornell University Press, 1962.
Miller, Richard F., ed. *States at War*, vol. 4, *A Reference Guide for Delaware, Maryland, and New Jersey in the Civil War*. Lebanon, N.H.: University Press of New England, 2015.
Mingus, Scott L., and Eric J. Wittenberg. *The Second Battle of Winchester: The Confederate Victory That Opened the Door to Gettysburg*. El Dorado Hills, Calif.: Savas Beatie, 2016.
Mott, Frank Luther. *American Journalism, a History: 1690–1960*. 3rd ed. New York: MacMillan, 1962.
Neiderheiser, Cloudaugh. "Some Civil War: Wallpaper Newspapers." *Minnesota History* 33, no. 5 (Spring 1953): 211–213.

Nevins, Allan. *The Evening Post: A Century of Journalism*. New York: Boni and Liveright, 1922.

Norton, Oliver Willcox. *Army Letters: 1861–1865*. Chicago: O. L. Deming, 1903.

Official Program of the Centennial of Incorporation of the Borough of Hanover, Pennsylvania. Hanover, Pa.: Anthony Printing, 1915.

Perry, Carolyn, and Louise Weaks, eds. *The History of Southern Women's Literature*. Baton Rouge: Louisiana State University Press, 2002.

Perry, James A. *A Bohemian Brigade: The Civil War Correspondents, Mostly Rough, Sometimes Ready*. New York: John Wiley & Sons, 2000.

Piston, William Garrett. *Lee's Tarnished Lieutenant: James Longstreet and His Place in Southern History*. Athens: University of Georgia Press, 1987.

Pollard, James E. *The Presidents and the Press*. New York: Macmillan, 1947.

Pred, Allen. *Urban Growth and the Circulation of Information*. Cambridge, Mass.: Harvard University Press, 1973.

Quinn, Katrina J., and David B. Sachsman, eds. *The Civil War Soldier and the Press*. New York: Routledge, 2023.

Raasch, Chuck. *Imperfect Union: A Father's Search for His Son in the Aftermath of the Battle of Gettysburg*. Lanham, Md.: Stackpole Books, 2016.

Rable, George C. *Civil Wars: Women and the Crisis of Southern Nationalism*. Urbana: University of Illinois Press, 1989.

Randall, Garfield James. "The Newspaper Problem in Its Bearing upon Military Secrecy during the Civil War." *American Historical Review* 23 (January 1918): 303–323.

Raper, Horace W. "William W. Holden and the Peace Movement in North Carolina." *North Carolina Historical Review* 31, no. 4 (October 1954): 493.

Reardon, Carol. *Pickett's Charge in History and Memory*. Chapel Hill: University of North Carolina Press, 1997.

Reid, Brian Holden. "1863: Military Turning Points, Gettysburg, Vicksburg, Tullahoma." *OAH Magazine of History* 27, no. 2 (April 2013): 23–27.

Reid, Whitelaw. *A Radical View: The "Agate" Dispatches of Whitelaw Reid, 1861–65*. Edited by James G. Smart. 2 volumes. Memphis: Memphis State University, 1976.

———. *A Southern Tour: May 1, 1865, to May 1, 1866*. Cincinnati: Moore, Wilstach, & Baldwin, 1866.

Report of the Joint Committee on the Conduct of the War at the Second Session, Thirty-Eighth Congress. 4 volumes. Washington, D.C.: Government Printing Office, 1865.

Rhodes, James Ford. "The Battle of Gettysburg." *American Historical Review* 4, no. 4 (July 1899): 672.

———. *History of the United States: From the Compromise of 1850 to the Restoration of Home Rule at the South in 1877*, vol. 4, *1862–1864*. New York: Macmillan, 1910.

Risley, Ford. *Civil War Journalism*. Westport, Conn.: Praeger, 2012.

Robertson, James I. *Stonewall Jackson: The Man, the Soldier, the Legend*. New York: MacMillan, 1997.

Robinson, Elwyn Burns. "The Public Press of Philadelphia During the Civil War." Ph.D. diss. Cleveland: Western Reserve University, 1936.

Rusling, James F. *Men and Things I Saw in Civil War Days*. New York: Eaton & Mains, 1899.

Sachsman, David. ed. *A Press Divided: Newspaper Coverage of the Civil War*. New York: Taylor & Francis, 2014.

Sachsman, David, and Gregory A. Borchard, eds. *The Antebellum Press: Setting the Stage for Civil War*. New York: Routledge, 2019.

Sachsman, David, S. Kittrell Rushing, and Debra Reddin Van Tuyll, eds. *The Civil War and the Press*. New Brunswick, N.J.: Transaction Publishers, 2000.

Sanger, Donald Bridgman. "The *Chicago Times* and the Civil War." *Mississippi Valley Historical Review* 17, no. 4 (March 1931): 568.

Scarborough, William K. "Propagandists for Secession: Edmund Ruffin of Virginia and Robert Barnwell Rhett of South Carolina." *South Carolina Historical Magazine* 112, nos. 3–4 (July–October 2011): 137–138.

Scharf, J. Thomas, and Thompson Wescott. *History of Philadelphia, 1609–1884*, vol. 3. Philadelphia, Pa.: L. H. Everts, 1884.

Schudson, Michael. *Discovering the News: A Social History of American Newspapers*. New York: Basic Books, 1978.

Shaara, Michael. *The Killer Angels*. New York: Ballantine Books, 2003.

Shaffer, Michael K. *Washington County, Virginia, in the Civil War*. Charleston, S.C.: History Press, 2012.

Shaw, Archer H. *The Plain Dealer, One Hundred Years in Cleveland*. New York: A. A. Knopf, 1942.

Smith, Diane Monroe. *Command Conflicts in Grant's Overland Campaign: Ambition and Animosity in the Army of the Potomac*. Jefferson, N.C.: McFarland, 2013.

Span, Christopher M. "Learning in Spite of Opposition: African Americans and Their History of Educational Exclusion in Antebellum America." *Counterpoints* 131 (2005): 26–53.

Starr, Louis M. *Bohemian Brigade: Civil War Newsmen in Action*. Madison: University of Wisconsin Press, 1987.

Sternhell, Yael A. "Communicating War: The Culture of Information in Richmond during the American Civil War." *Past and Present Society*, no. 202 (February 2009): 179–196.

Stone, Kate. *Brokenburn: The Journal of Kate Stone, 1861–1868*. Baton Rouge: Louisiana State University Press, 2012.

Strong, George Templeton. *The Diary of George Templeton Strong*, vol. 4, *Post-War Years, 1865–1875*. New York: MacMillan, 1952.

———. *The Diary of George Templeton Strong*, vol. 3, *The Civil War, 1860–1865*. New York: Macmillan, 1952.

Styple, William B., ed. *Writing and Fighting the Civil War: Soldier Correspondence to the New York Sunday Mercury*. Kearny, N.J.: Belle Grove, 2000.

Taylor, George R. *The Transportation Revolution, 1815–1860*. New York: Rinehart, 1951.

Thatcher, George H. "Lincoln and Meade after Gettysburg." *American Historical Review* 32, no. 2 (January 1927): 282.

Thompson, William Fletcher. *The Image of War: The Pictorial Reporting of the American Civil War*. New York: Thomas Yoseloff, 1960.

Tocqueville, Alexis de. *Democracy in America*. State College: Pennsylvania State University, 2002. First published in 1835.

Trexler, Harrison A. "The Davis Administration and the Richmond Press, 1861–65." *Journal of Southern History* 16, no. 2 (May 1950): 184–190.

Trudeau, Noah Andre. *Robert E. Lee*. New York: Palgrave Macmillan, 2010.

Tucker, Glenn. *Zebulon Vance: Champion of Personal Freedom.* Indianapolis: Bobbs-Merrill, 1965.

Tunnell, Ted. "Newspapers in Virginia During the Civil War, Confederate." *Encyclopedia Virginia* (July 2010), accessed September 11, 2025, https://encyclopediavirginia.org/entries/newspapers-in-virginia-during-the-civil-war-confederate.

The War of the Rebellion: A Compilation of the Official Records of the Union and Confederate Armies, series 1, vol. 27, pts. 1–2. Washington, D.C.: Government Printing Office, 1889.

Watson, Harry. *Liberty and Power: The Politics of Jacksonian America.* New York: Hill and Wang, 1990.

Waugh, John. *Reelecting Lincoln: The Battle for the 1864 Presidency.* Cambridge, Mass.: Da Capo Press, 2001.

Webb, Alexander Stewart. *An Address Delivered at Gettysburg: August 27, 1883.* Philadelphia: Porter & Coates, 1883.

Weisberger, Bernard A. *Reporters for the Union.* Boston: Little, Brown, 1953.

Welles, Gideon. *Diary of Gideon Welles, Secretary of the Navy Under Lincoln and Johnson,* vol. 1. Boston: Houghton Mifflin, 1911.

Wells, Jonathan Daniel. *Women Writers and Journalists in the Nineteenth-Century South.* New York: Cambridge University Press, 2011.

Whitman, T. Stephen. *Antietam 1862: Gateway to Emancipation.* New York: Bloomsbury, 2012.

Wiley, Bell Irvin. "Camp Newspapers of the Confederacy." *North Carolina Historical Review* 20, no. 4 (October 1943): 327–335.

Williamson, David. *The 47th Indiana Volunteer Infantry: A Civil War History.* Jefferson, N.C.: McFarland, 2012.

Wills, Garry. *Lincoln at Gettysburg: The Words That Remade America.* New York: Simon and Schuster, 1992.

Wilson, Charles Reagan. *Baptized in Blood: The Religion of the Lost Cause.* Athens: University of Georgia Press, 1980.

Wood, Gordon S. *Empire of Liberty: A History of the Early Republic, 1789–1815.* New York: Oxford University Press, 2009.

Zboray, Ronald J. "The Transportation Revolution and Antebellum Book Distribution Reconsidered." *American Quarterly* 38, no. 1 (Spring 1986): 63.

Index

www.ingramcontent.com/pod-product-compliance
Lightning Source LLC
LaVergne TN
LVHW101333180926
848251LV00033B/188
* 9 7 8 0 8 2 0 3 7 7 5 4 4 *